AF601862

MY ACRE OF LAND

MY ACRE OF LAND

ANGIE CASTILLO

Copyright © 2026 by Angie Castillo

All rights reserved. No part of this publication may be reproduced, distributed, or transmitted in any form or by any means, including photocopying, recording, or other electronic or mechanical methods, without the prior written permission of the copyright owner and the publisher, except in the case of brief quotations embodied in critical reviews and certain other noncommercial uses permitted by copyright law. For permission requests,write to the publisher, addressed "Attention: Permissions Coordinator," at the address below.

CITIOFBOOKS, INC.
3736 Eubank NE Suite A1
Albuquerque, NM 87111-3579
www.citiofbooks.com
Hotline:1 (877) 389-2759
Fax:1 (505) 930-7244

Ordering Information:
Quantity sales. Special discounts are available on quantity purchases by corporations, associations, and others. For details, contact the publisher at the address above.

Printed in the United States of America.

ISBN-13:	Paperback	979-8-90124-440-1
	eBook	979-8-90124-441-8

Library of Congress Control Number: 2026910808

TABLE OF CONTENTS

TRAVIS AND MARIE

At one hundred eighty pounds, six foot five, hazel green eyes, auburn hair and at 20 years of age, Travis Bennett and his friend Matt Williams were the most eligible bachelors in town. Any girl would gladly have dated either one, but Travis and Matt had not found the one girl they wanted to marry, settle down, and have a family. At this time in their lives, they were to busy to date. Both were attending the local university and had no time for girls.

One day Travis and his friend Matt went to the Pelican Lighthouse after their classes were over as they had heard it had been renovated and was under new management. They wanted to see if the food was better now than before. On this drizzly and humid evening, Marie was extremely busy as she kept up with the orders the members of the Local Fireman's Committee were ordering. Having taken care of the firefighters, Marie went to take Travis and Matt's order. She greeted them, as she would other customers, but for Travis it was different. He could not take his eyes off that beautiful smile, and the girl it belonged to. Marie had long red hair, green eyes, freckles, was about his height, slender and as beautiful as any girl could be, not to mention her sexy walk. Now what was she doing waiting on tables, when she could be a model walking down a runway in a sexy low cut dress. When Travis was asked what he wanted to order, he had Matt order, as he needed a few minutes to catch his breath. Matt ordered the fried soft shell crab platter, with the special sauce, and extra lemons on the side. Travis ordered the fried jumbo shrimp platter with sautéed onions, and both ordered a frosted mug of beer. After Marie took their order to the cook, she returned with a complimentary plate of sweet hush puppies, and their beer. As Marie walked away, Travis could not take his eyes off the server. Seeing how Travis looked at the waitress, Matt joked that he wasn't going to be able to eat if she was in the room. Not aware of his behavior, Travis replied that Marie was a very friendly waitress and that was all.

"Besides, I already have a girlfriend."

"Sissy is not your girlfriend; she is your next-door neighbor."

"Yeah, but if I asked her, she could be," Travis said.

When Marie returned with their food, Matt asked her if she was new to the neighborhood. Marie replied, "She graduated from high school a couple of years ago, and came to work at the Pelican Restaurant to supplement her income for college. She was majoring in business and since her classes didn't start until August, that gave her a few months to earn extra money to go with her scholarship. Once her classes started, she would probably be working fewer hours as she didn't know how much time her classes would take."

On that special day, Travis could not remember eating anything they ordered. All he could think of was Marie with no last name. From that day forward, Travis made it a point to eat at the Pelican Restaurant at least twice a month if not more, so he could get to know Marie. Every morning Travis would stop to get a cup of coffee to go, hoping Marie was working the morning shift. When she was not working, Travis would order his coffee and would be on his way. Hoping Marie would be working the evening shift Travis would again go to the restaurant. By this time, the other servers now knew Travis and his friend, and they would tell him whether Marie was working, or not.

Not expecting Marie to be at the restaurant, Matt went in wanting to order his cup of coffee but instead, he saw the girl of his dreams and decided to ask her to join him. Marie was about to go home when she saw Travis come in. Accepting his invitation, they sat at a table in the corner where they could be alone. This was exactly what Travis had been waiting for and this was the chance to get to talk to Marie. He already knew she was going to start classes in the fall and he told her he could help her with her homework. He would do anything just to spend the extra time with the girl he never wanted to let go. With a smile that lit up the room, Marie told Travis her last name was Thompson, and in turn, she asked him what his last name was and he replied it was Bennett. Having had their cup of coffee and exchanged their surnames and other information, they wanted to know, they left the restaurant.

Those who knew Travis and Marie soon started to wonder when they were going to get married. Marie would laugh and tell their friends they were still dating. Marriage will come later if that's what is in our future. Before the year was over, Travis went to Marie's work with one thing on his mind. Happy to see him but unaware of what he was going to do, Marie went to take his order. When she asked him what he wanted to order, he got on one knee and proposed. Shocked, but madly in love with Travis, Marie accepted his proposal. With a round of applause from the customers and the staff, Travis placed the engagement ring on her finger. Had it not been that he had a class debate, Travis would have taken Marie away to a movie, and later out to dinner, but today, that was not to be. Instead, Marie returned to work and Travis went to his class. The other girls who worked with Marie knew what he was going to do, but they were sworn to secrecy. When Travis left, the girls could not stop admiring her diamond ring. It wasn't the biggest diamond, but Marie loved it and that was all that mattered. Two years later on a cold wintery weekend, they eloped.

Months passed, and everything was perfect, as Travis was nearing the end of his education when Marie told him she was expecting. What a joyful time that was as they planned for the baby. Now more than ever they knew they had to save for the birth of their child, and things were getting harder. When they were told their baby was a girl, Travis and Marie decorated the baby's room.

One day Marie was at work, when she started to feel bad. Thinking the baby was on her way, she was rushed to the hospital. After the doctor examined her, he told her she had to stay off her feet as much as possible. That meant she would have to quit her job, but she could continue her schooling, as that didn't require her staying on her feet for long periods at a time. When Marie told her friends, they were sad to see her leave, but they knew the baby was at risk. For as much as Marie hated to quit her job, she did as the doctor told her to do, but that did not stop her from visiting her friends.

Travis was taking his final exam when he was told his wife was having the baby. Not knowing what to do, he explained the situation to his professor. Travis asked if he could finish taking the test the following day.

"I'll have to give you a different test," the professor told him.

Agreeing to that, Travis turned his paper in, ran out of the room and rushed to the hospital. Minutes after he got to the hospital, their baby girl was born. Marcella was a beautiful baby with auburn hair, a few freckles on her face, deep blue eyes, and rosy cheeks. The minute Travis saw his daughter; he could not stop admiring her and was anxious to take his family home.

Everyday Marcella grew, and to her parents she was the perfect child. Soon, she started to recognize her parents, and knew whose attention she could get if she wanted to get out of her crib. Of course, Travis was the first to go get his little girl, who by this time had him tied, around her little finger. Before long, Marcella was teething, and when Travis put his finger in her mouth, she bit him. After that incident, he knew better than to examine her mouth. Marcella grew day by day, and Travis and Marie were now dealing with their baby getting the chickenpox, measles, earaches, and everything children get.

Everything was fine until Caleb was born. Caleb was a small baby and needed more attention than Marcella did. Caleb had his father's looks, and the bluest eyes anyone had ever seen. When Marcella saw her brother, she became unruly, and neither Travis nor Marie knew what to do. However, that changed when Marie spanked her daughter. After that episode, Marcella knew she couldn't continue throwing her tantrums, and pinching the baby.

Now that the family was growing, Travis knew the apartment they lived in was too small for the family, and he started looking for a bigger apartment. A month or so later, he found a three bedroom redbrick apartment with a small front and back yard. Fortunately, for Travis, it was only five miles away from his job, and the rent was not much more than the one they were in now. While Travis moved their belongings to their new apartment, Marie took care of the children. Marie was happy with their new living arrangements as they now had enough space for the entire family. Once again, Travis and Marie knew they would have to cut back on the things they did, but they also knew once things got better, they would be fine.

Marcella and Caleb were typical children who played, and fought with each other. Yet, each in their own way demanded their parent's attention. Marie and Travis had their hands full as their children went through the sickly childhood phases. When Caleb turned two, he started to bite and pinch Marcella. At first, Marie did not know why Marcella was crying, but after she saw what Caleb was doing to his sister, Marie spanked him. The first time Caleb was spanked, it did not bother him, but he learned the second time.

For Travis and Marie, it seemed that they blinked a couple of times, and Marcella, now four-years-old, was thinking like a ten-year-old. Caleb, a toddler of two, acted as a two year old, but the kids managed to get along.

Years passed, and Marie and Travis could not believe how quickly the years had come and gone as Marcella was now in school. Everything was good for the family except for Marcella. From the first day she went to school, some of the other girls bullied her. They made fun of her freckles, took her toys from her, and made her cry, as they laughed at her. Marcella was not one to fight back, and was constantly going to her teacher crying the other girls were hitting her and being mean. No matter how many times the teacher disciplined the other girls it did Marcella no good. Actually, it seemed as if the bulling got worse. It did not matter if Marcella and her friends were out in the playground, or playing in their neighborhood, she was the attention of the bulling. Marie talked to the mother's, but that did not seem to matter as they only told her, "Kids are kids, they will outgrow it." However, that did not happen. Marcella continued to be bullied, but Caleb had no problem with the kids in the neighborhood.

One day, Marcella asked her parents if she could shorten her name to Marci. Travis looked at this daughter and asked her, "Why?

"Maybe if I do this, the girls will stop teasing me," she said.

Travis and Marie looked at each other, and said they did not see anything wrong with that and Marcella no longer existed.

After Travis earned his degree in Special Education, Travis sent applications to every state looking for teachers whose degree was in special education. Travis did not have to look too far as he was offered a part time job with the Virginia Beach City Public Schools. Travis accepted the position, but he knew he could not support his family working so few hours and had to get another job to make ends meet. Marie offered to get a job, but Travis thought it best if she stayed home and took care of the children.

As the years passed, Travis and Marie continued to save money to build their dream house. Both wanted to move out of the apartment they were living in. The kids were growing up and Travis and Marie wanted to have their own house where they could entertain and the kids could invite their friends. After the kids were in bed, Marie and Travis talked about their dream house. Both knew they wanted to leave Virginia, but they were not sure where they wanted to move to.

Once again, Travis started to read the want ads for teaching positions in other states. One day during his lunch break, he was reading the Virginia Beach Chronical, when he saw a job posting for a full-time Special Education teacher in New Mexico. His salary would increase, and best of all he would have his own classroom and fewer students. Travis made a copy of the posting, and when he got home, he showed it to Marie. Both agreed he should apply, as it wouldn't hurt to try. The next week, Travis sent his application along with the required information. Now all he had to do was to wait for a call from New Mexico telling him he was one of the applicants selected to be interviewed. He knew it would take time before he was notified, so all he could do was wait. Having waited six weeks, Travis got the call he was waiting for, and within a couple of days was on his way to New Mexico to interview for the position he was hoping would be his.

The children were missing their father, and would ask Marie when Daddy was coming home. She told her children, "Daddy went to a meeting, and would be home in a couple of days." Suddenly, Marci and Caleb stopped obeying their mother and cried for Travis. They wanted their father, and no matter what Marie did, or told them, they were not happy. When Travis called that he was in New Mexico, he talked to his children, and that seemed to help them. They were happy, and Marie was able to go about her household chores.

While in New Mexico, Travis toured the town he would move to if he did get the job. He had a chance to taste the local food, experience the heat during the day and the drop in temperature in the evening. After the second interview, and being away from home for a week, Travis returned to Virginia. When he got home, he told Marie what he had seen, and told her if he got the job; he knew where they would build their house. He had seen a piece of land, and after he made some inquiries, he knew they could afford to build their house, with some left over. He also told Marie he felt so at home. It was as if he had been there before, but that was impossible because he had never been out of Virginia. Now all he could do was to continue working and wait for a call or a letter from New Mexico letting him know if the job was his.

One day Marie was in the kitchen enjoying a glass of Mint-Iced Tea, when her ten-year-old daughter slammed her schoolbooks on the kitchen counter. Not bothering to pick the books that fell to the floor, Marci went to the refrigerator and got a coke.

As she sat across the kitchen table from her mother, she said, "Mom, I hate school. I hate it, hate it, hate it," and she wiped the tears from her eyes. Everything happened so fast Marie was stunned at her daughter's actions. Getting up from her chair, Marie went to comfort Marci as she put her arms around her, she asked, "Honey, what's wrong?" Before Marci could tell her mother what was going on, Marci's cat came running into the kitchen, and jumped on her lap. Arching her back, Marci's calico cat, Cleopatra started to purr as she expected to have her back scratched. Upset as she was, Marci put the cat down. However, Cleopatra was persistent, and again jumped on Marci's lap. This time Marci started to scratch the cat's back and in a few minutes, Marci and Marie heard Cleopatra purring. Annoyed by Cleopatra's comforting purr as she normally did, Marci asked, "Mom, why does Cleopatra have to purr so loud?" Seeing, but not knowing why her daughter was angry, Marie told her daughter, "Cleopatra was happy she was home." That seemed to satisfy Marci, and she continued to scratch the cat's back. "Marci, what has you so upset," her mother asked.

"Mom, I hate school. Sandy, Virginia, and Maryann are up to their old tricks. Today, a new girl came into our class, and she is hateful, and mean like Sandy. Her father is very rich, and she is hanging around with Sandy's crowd. For some reason, they started poking fun at me. They started to call me names, and threw my books out of my locker as I was getting them for my next class. Sandy even embarrassed me in front of a cute boy who asked me to help him with his math." "Do you want me to talk to the principal, and your teacher?" Marie asked.

"No, Mom that will only make matters worse. I'm the one who has to put up with them not you."

"Well honey, I know it is hard, but you will have to try to avoid them until we can figure something out."

"I know Mom, but why does Sandy have to be so hateful? Other than Vanessa and my friends, I hate this school. We only have a few more months of school, so why does she have to be so mean? Sometimes I wish we didn't live here," she continued.

By this time, Marci was a little calmer, and she remembered Caleb telling her something earlier while they were in school. Mom, this afternoon as Caleb was going to play basketball with his friends, he told me we are moving. "I asked him to tell me what he was talking about," but as he ran into the gym, he said, 'Ask mom.' "So what is he talking about that I don't know?"

"Oh honey, you know your brother; he's as bad as a journalist with a hot tip. Caleb cannot keep anything to himself if his life depends on it. He has to spread the news as fast as he can, and this afternoon was no different. Your father wanted to break the news to you and Caleb, but your brother overheard our conversation. We asked him not to say anything, but Caleb just doesn't know how to keep a secret."

"Yes mom, but what does Caleb know that you haven't told me?"

Going back to her chair, Marie took a drink of her Mint-Iced Tea, and thought this was the right time to tell her daughter what Caleb overheard. "Well sweetheart, before I tell you, I would like to ask you a few questions."

Marci looked at her mother with a puzzled look, and said, "Okay, but why do I have to answer your questions, why can't you just answer mine?"

"Marci, you are right. Well what we wanted to surprise you, and Caleb with, is that your father and I decided to build us a house in the country. I don't want to keep you guessing, but the best thing about it, is that we will be moving into our new house very soon. Marci, you are going to love this house. It is not like this one where you can only invite one friend at a time. In our new house, you will be able to invite as many friends as you want. I cannot tell you anymore, but when your father gets home, he will tell you where we are moving to and why we decided to build our house where we did. What your dad does not know is that today while he was at work, and you kids were at school, the landlord came, and wanted to know if we were going to renew our lease. I told him we are building a house and it will be ready in a few months. Happy that we were building us a house in the country, he told me we have to be out when our lease is up even if our house is not ready. He was going to call the couple who wants to rent the house, and tell them they could lease it. The landlord also told me they want to get out of their apartment and move into a bigger place that is closer to his job. Seems they want to move in as soon as we move out. The couple has a daughter your age, and a two-month-old baby. You see Marci, no matter how bad you think things are; something is always happening to make things better. Soon you will have nothing to worry about, and Sandy and her friends will not bother you anymore. Your wish to move is about to come true."

Eyes big as saucers, Marci told her mother she had to call Vanessa so she could tell her the great news. She didn't want to tell her over the phone because she wanted to see her reaction. "I know she is going to be as excited as I am," Marci told her mother. "It's okay, right Mom?" Marci asked. As she said this, she pushed the chair away from the table, and Cleopatra woke up from her nap to find herself on the floor. For Marci this news could not wait until tomorrow, and like Caleb, she had to spread the fantastic news. Rushing into the living room to call Vanessa, Marie told Marci, she had not told her everything she needed to know. Don't worry, Mom, you can tell me later, right now have to tell Vanessa. Marci was so excited she did not let her mother finish telling her where they were moving to.

"Hi, Vanessa, this is Marci, you have to meet me at the park. I have some great news, and I cannot tell you over the phone. Don't ask me any questions because mom just told me something wonderful, and I want to share it with my friends." Soon as Marci finished talking with Vanessa, she got on her bike, and peddled to the park as fast as she could. By the time Marci arrived, Vanessa was waiting for her.

"Marci, what took you so long? I can't wait to hear your exciting news. Is your mother going to have a baby?" Vanessa asked.

"Oh Vanessa, don't be gross! Besides, it's better than a baby. Anyway, I'm so excited because my mom and dad are building us a house out in the country, and we will be moving when school lets out." As soon as Marci told Vanessa her news they jumped around, made somersaults, and held on to each other as they jumped some more. Just then, Anne, Cecilia, and Magdalene raced down the sidewalk wanting to hear what Marci had to tell them. Vanessa was so excited she told the girls about Marci's new house before Marci had a chance to say anything. Had anyone been driving by the park, it would have seemed the girls were cheerleaders practicing their routine. Once the girls stopped jumping, they sat on the grass talking about their visit to Marci's new house in the country.

"Mom and I have so much cleaning and packing to do," Marci told her friends. Magdalene, the true friend that she was, immediately volunteered the group to help Marci move into her new house. Marci thanked her friends, and the girls decided they would start packing her belongings on Saturday. Now that they had a plan on how they would help Marci, the girls got on their bikes and left. Rounding the corner, Marci saw her father and brother were also coming home. When the family was together, Marie told Travis the kids knew about the move.

Honey, the only thing they don't know is where we built our house. "Well", Travis said, "This calls for a family meeting because we have a lot to talk about, and this is a good time to do it." As the family gathered around the kitchen table, Travis told his children he accepted a job out in the country, and that was why they were moving. Before Travis could say anything else, Marie decided to prepare dinner, and said, "They could continue the conversation while they ate." Anxious to hear what her father had to say, Marci helped her mother. As they were eating, Travis had his daughter's undivided attention, but as he went on, she stopped listening. Her father's voice faded into the distance as he was telling, Marci, and Caleb about the job he accepted. All Marci could think about was how she and her friends would spend the weekends together. Where they were moving to did not matter because she knew it wasn't going to be far from the city, and her friends. Not to mention she would be leaving the school bullies behind. Marci thought, *Friday and Saturday my friends and I will camp outdoors in my country house. Sunday after church, we will go to the mall to watch a movie, and after dinner, Dad and I will take my friends home.* Marci was so deep in thought she almost failed to hear her father say this would be their last year in Virginia. Snapping out of her daydream, Marci heard her father say, "Okay kids, your mother, and I have told you everything except, where we built our house. Well I am happy to tell you we are moving to New Mexico. My job will still be teaching children who are in special education, but now it will be in a different state. Your mother and I are very excited about the move, and we know you will be just as happy."

"Dad, what do you mean we are moving to Mexico?" Marc asked.

"Little one, it's not Mexico," Travis replied as Marci started to cry.

"Mom, I thought you were talking about the outskirts of Virginia. How could you and Dad possibly let another family move into our beautiful house?"

"Marci, I tried to tell you this afternoon when you got home from school, but you didn't give me a chance. You wanted to call Vanessa because you were so excited and left the house." Marci could not believe she was leaving her beloved state, and that her brother was excited. But, what did she expect? Caleb didn't care where he lived so long as he had a place to play basketball, sleep, eat, and play cowboys and Indians. In reality, Caleb was a three-year-old boy in an eight-year-old body, who did not know any better. Yet, at ten- years of age, Marci knew she was level headed, and grown-up, but thought her parents did not give her enough credit. Not willing to listen where the family was moving to, Marci ran into her bedroom. As she threw herself on the bed, she thought it was the end of her world. Marci could not imagine moving away from her friends. How was she going to tell her friends she would not be seeing them anymore? The most unbearable thought of all was that Marci was leaving, and they were going to forget her. Marci knew she could not leave the only place she called home. Marie followed her daughter, and tried to comfort her, but Marci did not want to listen to what she had to say about the move.

"Mom," Marcie sobbed, "My friends are here in Virginia, so why are you and Dad taking me away from them? I cannot leave my friends. How can you do this to me?"

"Honey, how can you say that? Earlier this afternoon you told me, you wished you could move from here. Well your wish is coming true."

"Mom, I was angry, and I just wanted to release my frustration."

"You know how angry Sandy makes me."

Marie tried to tell her daughter they were not punishing her. This was something they had planned for a long time, and wanted to surprise her and Caleb. Marci wasn't ready to listen, so Marie left her daughter alone until she stopped crying, and coped with the fact the family was leaving Virginia. Now that the kids knew everything about the move, Travis and Marie decided to go to bed, but before they did, they went into their daughter's bedroom. Once again, they tried to comfort her, and Travis told his daughter she would like living in the country.

"Little one, your mother, and I did this for you and your brother. I know it is going to be hard for you to leave your friends, but you will like the desert as much as I do," he said.

"You don't understand how I feel," Marci told her father."

Again, Marie tried to comfort her daughter by telling her it was an exciting time in their lives. Trying to see the bright side of the move, Marie told Marci, "One day we are going to look back on this and have a good laugh." How could her mother think it would be funny later on? It was not funny now, and Marci knew it would not be funny in the future. Marci did not want to hear her mother say her father knew what he was doing. All she wanted was for her mother to tell her they were staying, and her father would be coming home on weekends, but that did not happen. When her parents left her bedroom, Marci knew she had to come up with a plan to stop the family from moving out of state. Now that she was forced to move, all Marci could do was cry until she had no more tears to shed.

A week after Marci was told they were moving, the family started to make plans on how they would furnish their new home. Marie tried to get her daughter involved in decorating her bedroom, but Marci was still in a state of denial. She was hoping, and praying it was all a bad dream, but for Marci it was a nightmare. One that she was not going to wake up from, for it was real—they were moving.

Not only was the family going to move out of state, but they would also be living in a foreign country, and Marci had never been so scared. Marci knew moving to Mexico was going to be the worst time in her life, but there was nothing she could do to change things. She started to think how she would no longer go to the beach with her friends, wouldn't go to the movies, to the mall, nor would she go to Carvel's Ice Cream Parlor. There would also be no more monthly meetings, and she would never see her friend Beth Perine. Beth was a petite woman with short blond hair who resembled Doris Day, and was like their second mother. Beth owned the Mom and Pop place for kids to hangout after school, or on the weekends. If there was anything Beth enjoyed, it was seeing the kids having a good time while they enjoyed the novelties she prepared for them. Marci also knew she would have to tell her teachers she would never see them because she was moving to a Third World Country. Angry, Marci looked around her room and visualized the ten-year-old girl putting her things all over her room and that did not help. To think this girl was going to make them forget her made Marci furious. In her anger, Marci imagined Cecilia say, "Vanessa, what was the name of the girl who used to live here?" Anne would add, "Never mind, it doesn't matter," and they would go with the new girl. "How dare she make my friends forget me!"

That night as the rain cascaded down the window, so too did the tears run down Marci's face. The more she thought of her friends, the harder she pressed her face into her pillow. Marci finally fell asleep, but she tossed and turned as she dreamt of the day her family would move out of their house, and move to the house in a foreign country.

The next day being Saturday, Marci woke up exhausted, and was angry the sun was shining, and the birds were chirping. *Now what do they have to be so happy about,* she thought. Getting out of bed, Marci went into the kitchen where her mother was washing the breakfast dishes, while her father was outside cleaning the yard.

"Morning Marci, do you want me to fix you something to eat?"

"Mom, how can you think of food? I can't eat. I have to call Vanessa and tell her the bad news."

"Okay, but you might feel like eating after you get dressed," Marie told her daughter. Marci must not have heard her mother because she walked around the house in her pajamas moping about like someone who lost her most prized possession. Instead of doing what her mother suggested, she said, "Mom, how am I going to tell my friends we are moving out of state? I thought you and Dad built the house here in Virginia. Instead, I'm leaving the country." "Marci, you are not leaving the country. You are moving to another state."

"What difference does it make, Mexico, old or new, it's all the same."

"Well, Vanessa called while you were sleeping. If you don't want to eat, you could ride your bike to her house. You know Vanessa can always make you feel better."

Not wanting to return Vanessa's call, Marci walked into her bedroom, got dressed, and rode her bike to her friend's house. Dreading the thought of telling her friends, she was moving out of state, Marci took her time. However, it did not matter how slow she peddled, Marci got to Vanessa's house sooner than she expected.

"Hey Marci, didn't your mother tell you to call me?"

Not waiting for an answer, Vanessa told Marci she went to the store, and bought her something for her new house. Now there was no way Marci could hold back the tears.

"Marci, what's the matter, did I say something wrong?"

Between sobs, Marci told Vanessa she had better sit down because she had some bad news to tell her. Marci sat down next to her best friend and told her that her parents did not build their house in Virginia. Instead, she told Vanessa they were moving out of state, and she would no longer live close to her because last night, her father told her and Caleb they were moving to Mexico.

Jumping up from where she was sitting, Vanessa exclaimed, "What!" Marci, Mexico is a Third World Country and you don't know anything about it. What are you going to do?" Between sobs, Marci told Vanessa she was right, and that she was so scared because she didn't know what was going to happen. Vanessa and Marci started to cry as they comforted one another because they did not know when they would see each other. When Vanessa's mother heard the girls crying, she came running to see what was going on. Vanessa told her mother Marci was moving out of state, and she told Marci she was sorry, and left the girls alone. Vanessa was so absorbed in Marci's dilemma she failed to hear her mother tell her breakfast was ready. The girls were still crying, and hugging each other when once again Vanessa's mother called her to go in for breakfast. Vanessa invited Marci to join her, but Marci could not eat. Instead, she got on her bike and went home.

When Marci got home, she put her bike in the garage, and went into her bedroom. As she was about to take a nap, Vanessa called her friend to remind her of their weekly meeting at Carvel's. Forgetting what day it was, Marci told Vanessa she would be there as soon as she washed her face. By the time Marci got to Carvel's, her friends were waiting for her.

Marci was the perfectionist and the tallest of the girls. Cecilia was the jokester, and always kept the girls laughing. Anne, the listener, always thought things over before she expressed her opinion. As for Magdalene, she was the one who volunteered the group to help anyone who needed help. Vanessa was always watching her weight because she wanted to be a model—not to mention her obsession with her hair.

On any other day, Marci would have been happy to see Beth behind the counter, but today was not that day. As the girls entered the ice cream parlor, they went to the counter to place their order. When Beth looked at Marci, she knew something was wrong. Then it was Marci's turn to place her order, and Beth asked if she was okay because it looked as if she had been crying. The only thing Marci could do was to shake her head. Beth had known these girls far too long for her not to know when one of them had a problem.

"Well I hope it isn't anything serious," Beth said. Marci managed to smile and placed her order, but Beth knew better and she decided to brighten the girl's day. When she brought their order there was an extra helping of whipped cream and cherries on their banana splits. The girls were delighted, and for a few minutes, Marci forgot about the move, and thanked Beth for her kindness. As the girls were about to finish their banana splits, Vanessa told them Marci had something to tell them, but she would not say anything until they finished eating. Vanessa should never have told the girls Marci had something to say because they immediately put their spoons down. Anne said, "Come on Marci, what's your news? You know the rules; you cannot keep us in suspense. Tell us or we will bug you until you do."

Vanessa jumped in and said, "No! We have to finish our banana splits, or Marci won't tell you."

Feeling a bit calmer, Marci took her time eating, as she wanted to delay telling her friends her horrible news. However, the girls were looking at Marci, and there was no way she could look them in the eye. Not able to control her emotions she lowered her head because this was going to be harder than she imagined.

With her head bowed, Marci said, "You know the house my dad built for us in the country, well it's in Mexico.

When she told her friends her news, she lifted her head, and all she could see was the shocked look on their faces. Marci thought she was done crying, but she cried along with her friends when they told her she couldn't leave them.

Beth heard the girls crying, and had an employee take care of the customers. Going to the booth where they were seated, she asked what was going on, and, if she could help. When Marci's friends told her Marci was moving to Mexico, Beth now knew why the girls looked so sad, and was relieved it wasn't something serious.

"Marci, what an experience this is going to be," Beth told her. "Sometimes we have to do things we do not want to do, but we do them anyway. Just think of it as a vacation, and imagine all the pictures you will be able to send your friends and me."

Having said that, Beth reached over and hugged Marci, and said she would miss her. If Marci thought it was painful to leave her friends; leaving Beth was just as hard. How Marci wished she had waited for her mother to tell her where they were going to live. Then she would have been spared the heartbreak she was now experiencing.

Whether they were at home, or at school, Marci and her friends walked around like zombies unaware of anyone else around them. No matter how hard they tried to look happy, nothing worked because their friend was going to live in a Third World Country. Even Cecilia who always made Marci laugh was unable to do that. Their teachers tried to help the girls, but some gave up because there was nothing they could do.

However, Ms. Andersen, Marci's geography teacher bought a videotape titled, New Mexico and its Desert Insects, as she was determined to help Marci through this traumatic time in her life. As part of her geography lesson, Ms. Andersen wanted Marci's classmates to see where she was going to live. Popping the video into the VCR,

Ms. Andersen told her students to take notes as they were going to be quizzed on what they saw, and heard.

““Don’t worry about the test as you will be able to use your notes. This will be good exercise for you as you advance to higher grades,” she said. When the students took their binders out, Ms. Andersen turned the VCR on, and the governor of New Mexico, then welcomed them to The Land of Enchantment. He told them about New Mexico’s culture, the food, scenery, and the stories the older generation tell their children as they share information about their beloved state. After the governor finished, talking, the narrator took over.

Marci’s notes included, New Mexico was admitted to statehood on January 6, 1912; the state capital is Santa Fe; the state song is, *O Fair New Mexico*; the state bird is the *Roadrunner* and the state tree is the *Piñon tree*, but no matter how many notes she took, they were of no interest to her. For some reason Marci wrote the name of the governor, as she was sure this was going to be on the quiz. The students learned there are four states whose borders meet, and are known as the four corner states, New Mexico being one. The last bit of information Marci wrote, was how a small brown bear was rescued from a forest fire, when his mother was killed. The class had all heard about *Smokey Bear* but they did not know how he got his name. It was sad to learn this bear cub was found shaking, and holding on to a branch at the top of a partially burnt tree. By this time, Marci had taken plenty of notes, but *Smokey Bear* was what she remembered most. Marci also learned someone wrote a song about him, but she did not remember who wrote it.

When the narrator said the Rio Grande is New Mexico’s longest river, and runs the entire length of the state, Marci realized how much she loved Virginia with its beaches. As she put her pencil down she thought, *There is no way I am going to go swimming in a polluted river that has factories dumping their debris into it.* The narrator wanted to give the students information on not only the historical, but on the landscape, animals, and insects that live out in the desert. Focusing his camera on a beautiful cactus blooming out in the desert, everything started to look better. Marci was starting to think the move might not be so bad. As the narrator moved the camera from one cactus to the next, a coyote came into the scene. Marci loved animals and this got her attention when another coyote walked toward his friend to join him in the pool of water. To their surprise, what they thought was water were actually heat waves. The students had never heard of heat waves, and today they learned how they are a product of the hot sun creating a mirage as if there is water in the distance. Seeing the coyotes run off into the desert until they were no longer in view, the narrator pointed his camera on the parched desert ground.

At one point, the narrator kicked a piece of the dry ground and a scorpion came out from where he was sleeping. Since they hunt at night, and seek shelter during the day in the cool underground holes, or under rocks, the scorpion came out to see who had disturbed his sleep. With his tail raised high, he crawled toward the intruder. "Scorpions have bitten some people as they sleep, and because some are poisonous, they have to go to the hospital." The narrator then walked a few feet as he saw a tarantula, dragging a centipede, and said, "Along with the scorpions, tarantulas, and centipedes, these are but a few of the insects that survive in the desert. However, they can also be found inside people's homes. Many residents have also found these insects in their clothing, so be sure to check them before you get dressed." At this time, not even Ms. Andersen knew what to say as she glanced over to where Marci was sitting. Not only did Marci think she was going to die, but when Ms. Andersen closed her eyes, her false eyelashes reminded Marci of the centipede's legs. Marci, also thought Ms. Andersen was thinking, *you poor child, I am so sorry for you.*

School was over, and Sandy and her friends walked behind Marci asking her if she was going to make friends with the scorpions. Marci told the girls to be quiet and they laughed as they walked away. Marci took her time getting home because she knew every day brought her closer to the unknown. Going home, she kicked every rock that was in her way, and stopped to see who was washing their clothes at the

Laundromat. When she got home, Marci saw Caleb, and her parents going over the blueprints to their new house. Trying to sneak past them, she heard her father tell Caleb his room was going to be upstairs on the west side of the house. He also pointed to the area where the basketball court would be, and where he and his friends would play.

When Marie saw her daughter, she tried to include her in their conversation, but Marci wanted no part of their discussion. As she ran into her room, Marie saw the tears on her daughters face. She knew Marci was having a difficult time accepting the fact they were moving. Once Marci was in her bedroom, she locked the door. In the ten years she called this house her home, she had never locked it. This afternoon she felt she needed to let her parents know she did not approve of the move. As soon as she was in her bedroom, Marci started to cry and spoke as if she were talking to them. *Is this what you want for my brother and me? Do you want me to find a scorpion in my clothing, so it can sting me, or do you even care? You and daddy did not see the dry, hot, and ugly desert as I did. None of you saw how not even the insects can tolerate the heat, so how are we going to survive?*

Behind closed doors, Marci sat at her desk, and started to plan how she would stay in Virginia, and not move to the Mexican desert. Taking her diary from her desk drawer, Marci wrote how she would ask her best friend, Vanessa Alvarado to let her move in with her. Vanessa came from a family of four, but she would help Marci if she could. She knew there was no way Vanessa's parents could afford to take care of another child, but Marci would help. Even though she was ten years of age, she was confident she could get a job. Her grades were above average, she was respectful of her elders, and she knew how to clean her room. Marci continued to write how she was willing to do her part of the housework and help in any way she could. Besides, Vanessa's mother would never think of sending her daughter to live in a Third World Country.

If that did not work, Marci would ask Beth if she would adopt her. Beth was like her second mother, and she loved these girls and they loved her. Marci knew Beth could give her a job at her Ice Cream

Shoppe, and she would pay for her share of the expenses. It's not like Marci didn't know how to make a banana split. How could Beth not take her in? Once Beth adopted Marci, she would show her how much help she could be, and would repay her for her kindness.

Then Marci thought, *what do I care, I am not going to move, especially after I saw the video on the Mexican desert.* Now that Marci had a plan, she felt better, and everything was going to be just fine. She continued to jot her thoughts in her diary, and the last thing she wrote was if she couldn't move in with her friend, Vanessa Alvarado, or with Beth, she would run away. Once her parents and Caleb discovered she was gone, they would stay. As Marci placed her pen on her desk, she started to visualize how her family would grieve for her. With no one to talk to, Marci felt betrayed—and so alone. It did not bother her that she was going to bring grief to her family even if she was feeling sorry for herself. It's not like she was the one who suggested the family move to a foreign country!

Having solved the problem of her leaving, Marci joined her parents who were still going over the blueprints to their new house. Caleb had gone to his friend's house to play, and her parents were alone. Sitting next to her father, Marci asked him to show her where her room was going to be. Wanting to fool them into thinking she had changed her mind Marci asked if her room was going to be upstairs. Excited Marci was showing interest in their new house, Travis flipped the sheets of the blueprints to show his daughter her room was downstairs. Immediately, Marci felt her face getting hot when her father told her Caleb's bedroom was upstairs. Knowing she dare not say anything, she thought, *how dare they put Caleb's bedroom where he cannot see the scorpions crawling all over the desert. Yet, when I open the drapes in my bedroom, I will see millions of scorpions trying to escape the heat, and crawling up my window.* Marci kept a straight face as she continued to smile, and let her father continue to show her the blueprints to their new house.

Once Travis finished showing Marci where her bedroom was going to be, she went outside and sat on the grass where she could be by herself. Marci did not care if her bedroom was where she could see the scorpions, spiders and the coyotes hiding from the sun. It did not matter because she already knew she was not moving. In her mind that was all there was to this nonsense. The one thing she did know was that she had to continue pretending everything was all right, and was excited for the big move. Now there was no going back on her plans to stay in Virginia. No one was the wiser as to what was going on in Marci's mind as she continued to hide her true feelings. Most of her friends thought Marci was happy because she did not let anyone know how she was feeling—except for Vanessa. She knew exactly how Marci felt, but Vanessa was sworn to secrecy, and she could not tell Marci's parents. So far, she had managed to fool her parents, and most of her friends. Everyone was excited Marci had accepted the fact she was moving to New Mexico. Even Ms. Andersen thought Marci had gotten over the shock she was moving to what she thought was a Third World Country.

When Marci came home from school, she saw her mother packing their belongings for the movers. Marci helped her mother pack, and she continued to pretend she was happy. Now all Marci had were her spelling bee trophies, but she needed bigger boxes to put them in. She was not about to have them damaged as she had studied so hard to get them. Besides, Marci knew Vanessa's house did not have the space for them. She thought, *when my mom and dad put the trophies on the mantel it will remind them of the daughter they left behind.*

In the meantime, neighbors, and friends came to see what her parents were selling. Not only did Travis sell the family car, but most of the furniture. Once they were in their new house, Travis would buy another car, and Marie would buy furniture to complement their new home.

To Marci's surprise, school was over before she knew it, and the family was now ready to move to New Mexico. In the end, Marci had no say in whether she was staying or moving. Marci was so busy pretending everything was all right she even fooled herself. The day finally came when Marci, along with her friends, Anne, Vanessa, Magdalene, and

Cecilia went to tell Beth good-bye. The girls cried, and swore they would write long letters as they hugged each other. They also promised they would never forget what they shared both as friends and at school.

Marie also had her share of tears, but at twenty-eight-years-of-age, she was an adult, and Marci knew it was not as painful for her mother as it was for her. Marie was not leaving her best friends and school buddies behind. Now it was too late and they were on their way to New Mexico, The Land of Enchantment—but for whom? For Marci, everything was about to change, and this would be the beginning of a new chapter in her life.

New Mexico

When the airplane taxied off the runway, Marci looked out the window as the tears ran down her face. She did not want Caleb to see her crying, and embarrass her in front of these strangers. Marci was not sure why she was concerned about Caleb because he was too busy talking to the boy sitting across the aisle. As the tears rolled down Marci's cheeks, she could hear her parents talking about their new house. How Marci wished she could share their excitement, but that was not to be. The only thing Marci could think about was how much she was missing her friends, Beth, her teacher, Ms. Andersen, and her school. Not wanting to hear her parent's conversation, she covered her ears, but this only made her stop, and think of what she left behind. To Marci even this made the flight to Mexico emotionally exhausting.

Two hours later, Marci and her family landed at the airport in Dallas, Texas where they had a short layover. While they waited for the next airplane to take them to Albuquerque, New Mexico, they went to get something to eat. Marci was extremely hungry, and the food served in the airplane was not what she was used to eating. Once the family finished eating, they walked around the terminal like the other passengers. Having seen everything there was to see; the family sat down, and waited to board the airplane. When Marci saw friends hugging each other, she had to look the other way because it reminded her of the friends she left behind.

When the family boarded the airplane that was going to take them to their destination, Marci choose to sit by the window. Family and friends were waving goodbye to their loved ones, and again Marci thought of her friends. This made her wonder if her friends were still crying for her as she was for them. She also wondered if they had gone to Carvel's Ice Cream Parlor, or had they gone to the mall because they missed her. As the plane slowly taxied off the runway, she watched the airport disappear from her view as she did in Virginia. Marci must have dozed off for a while because she was startled when the pilot's voice came over the intercom. As she heard the pilot welcome the passengers to New Mexico, she looked around to see if anyone saw her jump out of her seat. He told the passengers they would be landing in twenty-five minutes, and thanked them for choosing Southwest Airlines. When the pilot announced they were in New Mexico, Marci was scared, and thought, *oh no, now that I'm here, what am I going to do without my friends?*

For the passengers who were sitting next to a window, the pilot told them to look to the left to see the Sandia Mountains. "These mountains rise 10,678 feet above sea level, and as the sun sets, they take on a reddish color. For those of you who do not know, Sandia is also the Spanish word for watermelon."

When the pilot told the passengers the Sandia Mountains are the most visited mountains in New Mexico, Marci's curiosity took over. Tears were once again running down her face, and all she could see was the silhouette of a mountain. To the passengers seated to the right side of the airplane, the pilot told them to look down and they could see the Rio Grande. This was the longest river that runs the entire length of the state. Remembering she learned this in Ms. Andersen's geography class, Marci looked down. As she did, she thought it was silly for the pilot to tell them to look at mountains, and rivers she could not see. All she wanted was to ask her parents to take her back home, but she had a lump in her throat that did not allow her to say what she was thinking.

Given permission to land, the pilot was now taxing the airplane down the runway. When it came to a complete stop, all Marci wanted was to stay behind and go back to Virginia, but she knew that was not going to happen. After Marie and Marci departed from the airplane, they waited for Cleopatra and their luggage, while Travis and Caleb went to get the keys to the rental car. Having loaded the luggage, Cleopatra, and the family in the car, they went in search of a restaurant. Luckily for them, they did not have to drive very far as they found a place to eat down the street. The restaurant was small, and the rich aroma of the food made Marci hungry. At eight o'clock in the evening the restaurant was empty other than a young couple sitting in the booth, four men eating at a table, a group of women took up two tables, and two police officers were drinking coffee at the counter.

When Travis and his family entered the restaurant, a sign was posted letting the customers know they could sit wherever they wanted. Choosing a booth to sit on, a polite and friendly waitress came to take their order. To Marci's surprise, the waitress actually spoke English. Not wanting to eat something she might not like, Marci ordered a hamburger. Marie, Travis, and Caleb wanted to try the local food, and asked for the special of the day. Having taken their order the waitress went to the table across from them. This time she spoke to the young couple in Spanish, and Marci was totally convinced they were in Mexico.

While the family waited for their dinner, Marci listened to the customers sitting at the other tables. She thought it strange to hear some of the customers speak English while others spoke other languages. Marci was also amazed at the fact that not only were they speaking English, but they also spoke it so fluently. Then it dawned on her, they were tourist. When she was satisfied why some were speaking different languages she sat back, and drank her lemonade. A few minutes later, a brown-skinned waitress placed the food on the table, and Marci said, "Can I ask you a question?"

" Of course, you can," replied the woman. Not sure what Marci was up to, her parents looked at her with a puzzled look on their faces. This was Marci's chance to find out if they were in Mexico.

Not knowing any better, Marci asked, "How come you speak both English and Spanish if we are in Mexico? Aren't you supposed to only speak Spanish?"

Marie was shocked and told her daughter to apologize. She did, but Marci wasn't sure why, because she just asked a simple question. The server assured Marci's mother it was okay.

She then asked Marci, "Where do you come from because you obviously are not familiar with New Mexico."

"We are moving here from Virginia," Marci replied.

"Oh, well, to answer your question, I speak both English and Spanish because that is what I was taught and learned as I was growing up. Let me assure you and your family, you are not in Mexico. You are in New Mexico, and we are part of the United States. Like you and your family, we are born in America, and that makes us American citizens. Our president is the same here in New Mexico as in Virginia.

The server also told Marci she wasn't trying to be rude, and said, I know Virginia is part of the United States; it is one of the thirteen colonies, and Richmond is the capital of Virginia. I also know Virginia was named after Queen Elizabeth I—the 'Virgin Queen'. Unlike you, we had to do our homework and find interesting facts about the different states. Now when you write to your friends in Virginia please let them know what you just learned. So let me be the first to welcome you to New Mexico, and I hope you enjoy living here as much as I do."

"Well I know Jerry Apodaca is the governor, and that Smoky Bear is New Mexico's mascot," Marci replied.

As the waitress smiled, she turned to Travis and said, "I'm sorry, but this isn't the first time I am asked if this is Mexico. I get tired of people asking me this question. However, your daughter was kind enough not to ask if we take siestas."

Marci's parents were embarrassed and did not know what to do. Travis apologized, but the server was very kind and told him, "Not to worry about it." She then left to escort other customers to their booth and take their order.

When the server was out of hearing range, Marci's mother asked her daughter how could she be so rude. While her mother was scolding her, Caleb was agreeing with his mother, and said, "Yeah Marci, you should watch what you say, you dummy." Marci ate her hamburger in silence while her father said, "Little one, I'm sorry you were scolded. We know you were just asking a question, but you should have asked me. I could have answered it for you. You have to be careful what you say when you meet people for the first time. Of course, I also learned something, as I had forgotten Virginia was named after a virgin queen. Do not worry little one, we are not angry with you," and having said that, he ate his dinner.

Marci was feeling depressed, that was, until she lifted her head, and saw Caleb's face and his expression. Now it was her turn to laugh at her brother. Caleb had just had a taste of the green chili and his face was extremely red. The foolish boy did not realize the food he ordered was extremely spicy, and after he drank his water, he asked the server for another glass of water. When he drank it, he asked Marci if he could drink her water, but she told him she was thirsty, and drank it very slowly. She even let some drip down her mouth.

By this time Caleb was actually crying, and rubbing his huge ears because they were ringing—or so he said. And, for Travis and his family, this was the introduction to New Mexico's red or green chili. When they finished eating, Travis left the server a ten-dollar tip for educating his family, and being so kind.

On their way to the hotel, Caleb continued to tease his sister as he stuck his tongue out at her, and shook his finger in her face. All the while, he was doing this he was laughing. Then he wanted to know if she had any more questions. Marci would gladly have beaten him up, but she would have been the one to get in trouble. Glad she was holding Cleopatra, Marci put her face on her cat's fur, and let the tears fall. As she did this, Marci heard Cleopatra's comforting purr and as tired as she was, Marci wiped her eyes and fell asleep before they arrived at the hotel. The next thing she knew, her mother was waking her up. Thinking she was home, Marci told her mother she would get up in a few minutes. Realizing she was not in Virginia, she rubbed the sleep from her eyes and saw the drapes were closed, yet, she could see the light filtering in. Curious as to what awaited them, Marci opened the drapes, and the sunshine flooded the room. Once her eyes adjusted to the blinding sunlight, she saw buildings here and there. Suddenly she thought of the scorpions that might have crawled into the room at night, and backed away from the window as she shook her clothes and checked her shoes before she got dressed. After the family was dressed, the luggage, and Cleopatra in the car they went to Denny's restaurant. This time when the server came around, Marci kept quiet so that she would not get in trouble. Marci was so hungry she ordered two eggs over medium, hash browns, bacon, wheat toast, a glass of orange juice, and a waffle as a side order.

When the server brought their breakfast, Caleb said, "Hey sis, you going to eat everything you ordered?"

He knew Marci was still angry with him, but today she ignored him because she was famished. Besides, Marci was going to give Cleopatra her bacon. With that, Marci ate what she thought was the most delicious breakfast she had eaten in a long time. When Marie and Travis saw their daughter had eaten all she ordered, they were surprised. Not to mention Marci also ate the bacon she was going to give her cat. Once the family finished eating, they got into the car, and Travis was now going to drive them to what would now be their new home.

While Travis drove his family to their new home, Marci saw the landscape go by and thought of the airline pilot. Looking at the

Sandia Mountains, she now knew why he wanted the passengers to take advantage of the view. Although tears clouded her eyes while she was aboard the airplane, she knew these mountains were extremely high. When the sun peaked over the horizon, Marci thought the sun was affecting her vision, as the Sandia Mountains seemed to change color from a blue to an almost purple. The sight of the sun changing the color of this huge mountain reminded her of the line, *For Purple Mountains, Majesty*, from *America the Beautiful.*

Now no matter how many turns in the road Travis took, or how far he drove, Marci was amazed, as she had never seen so many mountains in her life.

Afraid the next town her father drove into would be her future home, Marci lowered her face into Cleopatra's fur. As they drove past the Indian Reservation, Marci's heart raced as she clung to her cat, and slid down the seat. Caleb looked all over, but did not see any Indians. Yet, he told Marci he saw a few that were coming down from the hill on their horses. Once Marci felt safe, she sat up and looked out the window to make sure they were not being followed. Driving more than thirty miles, Travis passed the first gas station in the village they were going to call home. As soon as he told his family they were a block, or so from their new home, Marci had a queasy feeling come over her. She closed her eyes because she did not want to see the house she knew she would never call home. Slowing the car and driving into the driveway, Travis proudly announced, "We're home!"

Marci still had her face buried in Cleopatra's fur because she was not sure she wanted to see the house. Lifting her head, Marci saw their new house, and thought it was the ugliest house she had ever seen. Brown had always been Marci's favorite color, but this time she thought it was drab and ugly. Everything she saw when she lifted her head as her father drove his family to their new home was brown. There was no color to this place, or the house as it almost blended in with the ground. She hated what she saw, and all Marci wanted was to go back home where everything was nice and green. Home was now thousands of miles away and once again, the tears ran down her cheeks. *So was this the house her parents expected her to hang her friend's pictures on the wall, and where supposedly she would display her trophies?* On the other hand, Caleb found no fault with his new house, and could not wait to get down. Until her brother opened the car door, the family did not realize how hot it was outside. They had been in an air-conditioned vehicle, and Marci now felt a burst of heat like nothing she had ever felt before. Although she knew not to say things she did not mean, Marci thought her parents moved her and Caleb just outside the gates of hell because it was so hot!

Then she thought of Sister Ruby, the nun who told her catechism students hell was the hottest place anywhere, and wondered if this was what she meant. Bolting out of the car, Caleb ran to the backyard to see if the contractor had truly built him the basketball court he wanted. No sooner had Marci seen her brother jump out of the car and run around the house, when she heard him scream at the top of his lungs. Marci thought Caleb had seen a nest of scorpions, and she too bolted out of the car, and ran to see what was going on. Never had she heard her brother scream like that and when she got to the backyard, Marci saw Caleb jumping up and down.

"Caleb, what's wrong," Marci yelled as she looked for the nest of scorpions.

"Marci, look at my basketball court, and all the space I have to play," Caleb replied. "Isn't it great?"

What was wrong with this child, could he not see the ugliness of this place? Was he blind, and only she could see it? By this time, Travis came to join his children in the backyard, and by his son's reaction, he knew Caleb was happy. Before Marci could say anything, Caleb asked his father if he could go into the neighborhood, and invite the boys to play basketball. Of course, Travis told his son no because he had to help take the luggage indoors.

"You will have to wait until we get everything down, or better yet, wait until tomorrow. There will be plenty of time for you to meet the neighbors, and they can come over anytime they want," Travis replied.

Caleb then went inside and Marci now had a chance to look around. When she ran to the backyard, her only concern was to rescue her brother from the nest of scorpions. At no time was she thinking what the backyard might look like. Thoroughly surprised, she saw flowers alongside the fence, and a huge oak tree with a tire swing on one of its branches. Then there were the rosebushes that were in full bloom along the fence and on the side of the house. Still holding on to her cat, Travis asked his daughter if she was ready to go inside and see her new house.

"Dad, I need a few minutes," Marci replied, "is that all right with you?"

"Sure, little one, take your time, I will be here until you are ready to go inside," Travis told his daughter.

For the time Marci stood out in the heat, she could not get over what a pretty backyard they had. As much as she wanted to stay admiring the backyard she was also curious to see what this house looked like inside. Other than the color of the house, Marci was starting to like what she was seeing. Caleb had already seen his room, and as he ran from room to room, everyone could hear him screaming throughout the house. Yet, Marci had not made her entrance. Marie was hoping her daughter would like her new house and was ready for her to go indoors. Marie knew her daughter was unhappy, and wanted to make it easier for her if she truly did not like it. Of course, she did not know what she could do to change what had to be done. When Marie was in the dining room she saw Travis coming up the porch, and Marci was lagging behind holding Cleopatra. As she walked through the front door, Marci was looking down, and holding on to her cat. She felt she needed to hold on to something she knew belonged to her. Yet, all it took was one-step into this house, and suddenly Marci felt like she belonged. It was as if someone or something was gently guiding her into what she thought was an ugly house. Suddenly, Marci felt herself smile, but she could not let her mother know she liked what she was seeing. When Marci saw her mother standing in the dining room watching her, she pretended she was crying. Marci did not want her to see her smiling, so she continued to look down, and put Cleopatra up to her face.

"Everything will be okay Marci," Marie said, as she put her arm around her daughter, and led her into her bedroom.

Secretly, Marci was ready to see what her bedroom looked like, and what a surprise awaited this ten-year-old. Her bedroom was carpeted, and spacious. The view outside her bedroom window was nothing to what Marci thought it would be. The windows that faced the backyard had lilac swag curtains with white inserts that matched her bedspread and pillow shams. In one corner of the room was an oak rollup top desk, and on the other side was a white vanity dresser with a tri fold mirror. On the dresser was a gold plated brush and comb set so she could brush her hair, or comb Cleopatra if she wanted. Never in her wildest dreams did she think she would be living where she could see beyond the neighbor's yard. She could actually see for miles, and for a few minutes, Marci did not think of what might be crawling outside her window. In their old house, all they had was a small yard with enough room for Caleb's portable basketball goal, a small barbeque pit, and nothing else. Here, it was like there was no end to their backyard. Truly, it did not matter because the beauty of her backyard was breathtaking. Marci now knew she could not let her parents know she liked what she saw—not until she was ready.

The first night in her new house, Marci found it hard to sleep, so she got up and wrote her first letter to Vanessa from New Mexico. Marci was not sure how to start, but once she did, she could not stop. In her letter, she asked Vanessa to read it to the rest of her friends. She told her friends about her experience with the waitress, the mountains and how amazed she was at how much unoccupied land there is in New Mexico. Yet, most of her letter was how beautiful her house was, how her room was three times the size of her old one, and how she wished, her friends were able to visit her.

The next day Caleb went up and down the neighborhood asking the boys to come to his house to play basketball. First, there were a couple, then there were six, and before Marie knew it, the backyard was full of boys. Caleb could not believe there could be so many boys in one neighborhood.

As for Marci, she did not intend to go looking for other girls she could play with. She stayed in her bedroom, and continued to ask her mother when they were moving back to Virginia. Several weeks passed, and Caleb was making friends wherever he went. It was different with Marci; she stayed indoors as much as she could, and when she went out it was but for a few minutes.

Doctor Ralph Brewer

On a hot and humid June afternoon, Marci's mother was passing by her bedroom and heard her crying. Entering Marci's bedroom, Marie asked her daughter, "What's wrong?" Marci replied, "I don't know I just fell so miserable."

When Marie left her daughter's bedroom, she called the first doctor listed in the phonebook, and scheduled an appointment for her. That day, and for the rest of the week Marci stayed in her room, and things did not get any better. She picked at her food, cried and slept most of the day. She also lost weight, and not even Caleb's childish ways bothered her. All Marci thought about were the friends she left behind.

That week Marie took Marci to see the doctor and he asked Marci many questions. When she answered them, he wrote her answers on the chart. Once the doctor stopped asking Marci his questions, he looked at Marie, and told her there was nothing medically wrong with her daughter. "The only thing wrong with your child is that she is spoiled. I suggest you take her home and have her do some chores to keep her mind occupied," he said.

The minute Marie heard this, she was furious. Marie knew he was right. Her daughter was spoiled, but she also knew that was not what was wrong. Taking Marci by the hand, she rushed her out of the examining room.

Travis was furious when his wife told him what the doctor said. However, that did not solve Marci's problem, and Marie continued to look for a doctor who could help their daughter. By this time, Marie had gotten to know some of her neighbors, so she asked them if they knew of a family doctor, they could recommend. Her neighbor Emily Montoya gave her the name and number of a family doctor she went to. With her neighbor's recommendation, Marie went home and scheduled another appointment for her daughter. This time, Travis insisted he was going to go with them, and together they hoped this doctor would help Marci. On the day, Marci had her appointment Caleb decided to stay with a friend; why should he tell his sister, "I told you so, when the doctor told her she was crazy."

Doctor Ralph Brewer was sixty years old, husky, wore glasses, and had a great smile. This time, when Marci walked into Doctor Brewer's office, she had a good feeling about him. She did not want to get her hopes up, but she thought he was going to be better than the other one. He too asked her questions, and as he did, he took a good look at her reaction to both the questions and her answers. When he finished writing, he looked at Marci, smiled, and put his arm around her shoulder. Doctor Brewer sat next to Marci, faced her parents, and told them their daughter was indeed sick.

"But doctor, I don't feel sick, I just feel sad most of the time," Marci replied.

"Well Marci, in a sense you are sick"." You see, there are many ways a person can be sick, and not know it. Even though you don't feel sick, you are going through a phase in your life where you do need to see a doctor."

Doctor Brewer told Travis and Marie their daughter was experiencing severe depression. He could put her on medication, but he wanted to try something different. In extreme cases, he had to prescribe pills, but that could be addictive, and very expensive. In my years of practice, I have seen many children, and adults who move to New Mexico go through the same thing you are experiencing. What I'm going to suggest won't cost your parents anything, but for you, Marci, it could be a lifesaver.

As he went to get his prescription pad, Doctor Brewer continued, "I have prescribed this form of therapy to many of my patients both young, and old, and I am always surprised at the results."

"So Marci, do you want to know what I have in mind for you?"

Looking at her parents, Marci replied, "Yes."

"What I am prescribing for you, is that you go home and write everything you have been going through. It does not matter if what you write happened last week, when you moved to New Mexico or if it happened today. If it makes no sense to you, that too, is all right. Once you have written everything that is bothering you, put your spiral where you can get to it. By the next visit, we can talk about it. Are you up to doing that?"

"Yes, but how is that going to help me?"

"I think by the time you come back, you will be able to answer that question better than anyone else can," Doctor Brewer replied.

Doctor Brewer turned to Marci's parents and said, "Your daughter reminds me of my son when he was her age. When I moved my family from Washington to New Mexico, my son also went through severe depression, but we were not able to help him. It has taken my wife and me a long time to accept our son's untimely departure. So we have devoted our lives to helping anyone who is depressed—especially the young. As parents, we never want another child, or parent to go through what we did with our son. If what I prescribed for your daughter does not work, then I will put her on medication."

By this time, Marci was willing to try anything, and she told Doctor Brewer she was tired of crying, and moping about the house. She also did not want to see her mother and father worrying about her, and agreed to do what he suggested. Now all she wanted was to go home and rest. Marci didn't really know how she was feeling, but she knew it was good. As Doctor Brewer helped Marci down from the examining table, he gave her a gentle hug that made her feel this doctor truly cared.

In the month that followed, Marci wrote everything down, and by the time she went to her next appointment, not only was she feeling better; she had two spirals full of things she had written that she wanted to discuss with her doctor. The minute Doctor Brewer saw Marci; he saw a big change in her. This time Marci asked her parents if she could go in by herself. When they hesitated, Doctor Brewer told them she would be fine. Marci saw her parents' worried look, but she also saw the doctor smile and wink his eye at them.

"So Marci, how are you doing?"

"Doctor Brewer, I still cry for no reason, but it's not as bad, and I can see my mom and dad are not as worried about me. I think I'm happy, and I am starting to make friends."

"I can see you are happy, and that is what I want for you," Doctor Brewer replied.

As she smiled, Marci told Doctor Brewer, I'm still asking Daddy if he will take me back to Virginia because I don't like the heat, but I think I'm getting used to it."

Doctor Brewer and Marci talked for almost an hour, and by the time Marci left his office, she managed to laugh aloud, which made her feel like her old self. When the doctor walked her to the lobby, he told her parents, Marci was going to be fine. She thanked him, and hungry as she was, she asked her parents if they could get something to eat.

Thanks to Doctor Brewer, Marci got better, and eventually stopped seeing him. Marci got over the fact she was angry, and made friends with the neighborhood kids. She didn't know how she broke the ice; all she knew was that she now had as many friends as she did in Virginia, or possibly more. Until now, Marci had not realized how silly she had been, and she could not blame the kids in the neighborhood who still thought she was a snobbish city girl. However, she was determined to prove them wrong, no matter how long it took. When she finally realized the move was not all bad, she and her new friends made plans to spend time together.

Just as their parents did, Caleb and Marci would sit and talk about what happened to them during the day. Back in Virginia they had very little in common, but here, they shared things about themselves they thought would be of interest to the other.

The first time Travis took his family out to explore the desert, Marci was scared she was going to see the scorpions and tarantulas seeking shelter. However, Marie saw it as a huge garden of fragrant wild flowers she could place throughout the house. She had vases of the butterfly weeds in the den, desert marigolds in the dining room, and placed sunflowers in Marci's bedroom. When Marci saw the flowers her mother picked, she thought they looked as pretty as any that were in the flower shops. Having visited The New Mexico Extension Office, Marie had a brochure of the wild flowers, and the vegetation that grows in New Mexico. The receptionist would tell her what wildflowers she could pick, and the ones she should stay away from because she could be allergic to them. Marie was such a frequent visitor the employees soon got to know her.

The receptionist told her, "When the monsoon season comes you will see the desert transform into a landscape of wild flowers. That's when you want to pick as many flowers as you can." She also gave Marie spearmint and peppermint seeds to plant in her flowerbed. When the plants grow, you can brew some fresh tea that leaves a nice lingering aroma in your house.

"Thank you. I will do just that. I have always enjoyed sitting outdoors with a good cup of tea. Come over anytime, and while we enjoy each other's company, we can also watch the humming birds drink from the feeders I have hanging in the porch," Marie replied.

Now anytime the family traveled to a different location, Marie had the information she needed. She also learned how quickly the weather changes, and always reminded her family to carry a light sweater or jacket should they stay out after dusk.

Marci was not sure what she was going to do, as she did not feel like calling any of her friends. Looking around her bedroom, she decided to rearrange the furniture. When she was dusting her bookshelf she saw her spelling bee trophies, and realized other than gathering dust, they no longer meant much to her. Going into the garage, she looked for space, where she could store her trophies. Then, she had an idea so she went to ask her father for his opinion. Knowing her father was working on a special project for his students once school started, and asked not to be disturbed, she still knocked on the door and went in.

"Hi dad, I know you are busy, but can we talk?"

"Sure little one, but can you wait until I finish?"

"Umm, I know you have a lot to do, but this is important."

"Okay honey, but can I continue my project while you talk?"

"Dad, what would you think if I was to give the trophies I have in my room to the children, you will be teaching. There is no reason why they should be collecting dust when your kids can have them for their special events. I think they would help the parents who cannot afford to buy one. All you have to do is to remove the piece of tin that has my name on it, and add the name of the kids who win in their Special Olympics."

Not believing what he was hearing, Travis put his pencil down, and removed his glasses. Getting up from his chair, he went into Marci's bedroom. Marci followed her father, as she was not sure what he was going to do.

"Little one, you worked so hard to earn your trophies, are you sure you want to give them away?" Travis asked.

Marci told her father she would be happy to get them out of her room because she could use the space. Taking one of the trophies down, he told Marci he would remove the tin, and have them framed as a reminder of what she accomplished. Once that was done, she could hang them on the wall, or store them wherever she wanted.

Patting his daughter on the head, Travis told her, "Yes, little one, I will be very happy to tell the parents they won't have to buy trophies this year."

With her father's permission, Marci put her trophies in the garage, and started to clean her room. As she was taking her trophies down, Cleopatra climbed up on her bed. Marci then decided to put the cat out in the front yard. She knew she was not going to get anything accomplished if she stopped to play with her. When she looked out her window, Marci saw Cleopatra relaxing out on the grass. Marci knew she did not have to worry because Cleopatra would not go anywhere without her. Happy to be outdoors, Cleopatra could run around; catch grasshoppers, and chase lizards. Turning the radio up, Marci started to sing along with the music deejay Carlos Garcia was playing.

Marci was enjoying herself as she sang along, but when the song ended, Caleb told his sister she sounded like a dead frog. Caleb, "You are so dumb, dead frogs can't sing." "Yeah, I know, and neither can you," Caleb replied as he laughed, and went upstairs.

By this time, Marci had her room nice and clean, and as she was putting the vacuum away, she heard someone or something let out a painfully, sharp, and piercing scream. Unaware of what happened she continued to put things away. A few minutes later, the doorbell rang followed by a couple of loud and urgent knocks on the door. As her mother opened the door Marci came out of her bedroom, and Travis ran out of his office as he too heard the commotion. The neighbor, Sal Duran, was white as a sheet as he held Cleopatra in his arms, and told Marie the cat was hurt. "I was cutting the grass when I heard something scream, and I saw Marci's cat under the mower. The only thing I could do was to pick her up and bring her to you," he said.

Cleopatra

Hearing something happened to Cleopatra, Marci ran to the door. When she saw her precious cat wrapped in a dirty, oily rag soaked in blood, Marci thought her cat was going to die. Marie called the veterinarian who lived five miles from their house while Sal held Cleopatra in the blood soaked rag. When the veterinarian heard what happened to the cat, he told her to bring it in immediately. While Marie was calling the vet, Travis wasted no time taking the car out of the garage so they could take Cleopatra. Holding on to Cleopatra, Marci got into the car and Travis drove as fast as he could without getting a speeding ticket. For Marci it seemed as if her father was taking his sweet time. Arriving at the pet hospital, Travis drove up to the emergency entrance where the doctor was waiting for them.

Cleopatra was in so much pain, she tried to bite the doctor as he gave her a shot to calm her down. Then he gently lifted her from Marci's bloody arms. Marci and Travis were right on the doctor's heels as he told them it did not look good. Rushing Cleopatra into the operating room, he closed the door behind him. Travis and Marci went to sit in the waiting room while the doctor tried to save Marci's cat. When the doctor took Cleopatra, Travis asked the receptionist for some paper towels so he could wipe the blood off his daughters' hands. The receptionist told Marci she could go into the employee's restroom and wash her hands.

After Marci came out of the restroom, and as they waited for the doctor, she closed her eyes and asked God to save her precious Cleopatra. She reminded God what a good cat Cleopatra was, how they were inseparable, and not to forget how Cleopatra was always at her side. While she was asking God to spare her cat, Marci thought of her seventh birthday, when Vanessa came to her party with a tiny calico kitten. At that time, Marci wondered what she was going to do with a kitten that was weaned from her mother a few weeks earlier. Cleopatra was a cute and loveable kitten who always managed to get out of whatever mischief she got into. However, as this kitten grew, she got Marci into more trouble than Marci could imagine.

Hours went by and the doctor finally came out of the operating room, and Marci closed her eyes, and covered her ears, as she did not want to hear what he had to say. That did not help as she heard, "I'm sorry…" thinking the doctor was going to say Cleopatra was dead; Marci turned to her father, and started to cry. The doctor sat next to Marci, and told her "Cleopatra was alive, but he had to amputate her leg. There was no way he could save it because the leg was mangled beyond repair. To make sure Cleopatra was healing properly, she had to stay with him for a couple of days. He wanted to make sure the stump was not infected before he released his patient." To Marci, all that mattered was that her precious cat was going to live, and she hugged the doctor who saved her.

Every day as soon as Marci got up, and before she ate breakfast, she called the doctor to ask how her precious cat was doing. Now all she wanted was to bring Cleopatra home so she could nurture her back to health. She wanted to make sure Cleopatra was healing as the doctor said she would. When the doctor told Marci, Cleopatra was coming home; she and Caleb prepared a bed for her. Caleb even brought her an old pillow he no longer wanted. Soon everything was ready for Marci and Travis to bring the family cat home. Marci was overjoyed when she saw Cleopatra, and how well she looked. Before she could take Cleopatra home, the veterinarian gave Marci strict instructions. He told her she was to take the cat back immediately if her leg started to bleed. Marci was not to give her milk, as the medication and milk would make her throw up. She also had to make sure the cat did not try to bite the stitches off the stump of her leg. The doctor then sedated Cleopatra so she would not wake up for another couple of hours.

Travis drove slowly as Marci held Cleopatra in the cushioned box. He didn't want her to feel the bumps in the road, but she slept through it. When they arrived, Marie and Caleb were waiting at the front door to welcome Cleopatra home. Best of all, Caleb was being very kind as he opened the door so Marci could get out of the car. Marci then took Cleopatra and placed her in the bed she and Caleb prepared. Cleopatra was alive and back home, and Marci, and the family would now nurse her back to health. When Cleopatra woke up, and in her excitement to have Cleopatra home, Marci forgot what the doctor told her and she started to warm a dish of milk, but her father stopped her. Marci, don't you remember what the doctor told you about giving Cleopatra milk?

After that Marci made sure she followed the doctor's orders, and the weeks of loving and tender care helped Cleopatra heal. One evening as the family was watching TV, Marci took Cleopatra into the den so her family could see how well she was doing. However, Cleopatra did not move until Marci coaxed her to get up. Then slowly, and ever so slowly, the family watched Cleopatra get up when Marci called her. Determined to show her family what she could do, Cleopatra took a few steps. Seeing how difficult it was for her to walk, and how hard she was trying, the family clapped and cheered her on, as she managed to take a few more steps. This time Travis brought her a bowl of ice cream as a reward for her efforts.

Late one evening while Marci was reading, Cleopatra started to meow to get her attention. Putting her book down, Marci got up to see what she wanted. Her cat looked all right so Marci started to scratch her head. Then she surprised Marci by climbing out of her box. Marci watched her cat hobble around the room, and the closer she got to her bed the louder Cleopatra meowed. Now that Marci knew what her cat wanted, she helped her get up on the bed. Cleopatra was walking and Marci now knew she had done a good job in nursing her back to health. While Marci was talking to Cleopatra, Caleb came into her bedroom. Smiling, Marci thought Caleb wanted to tell Cleopatra good night. Instead, all Caleb wanted to do was imitate how Cleopatra learned to walk. As he got on his hands and knees, Caleb proceeded to crawl around the room with one leg stretched out to his side. As he fell down, he wanted to see if he could make Marci cry, as he knew how sensitive she was. However, this time Marci got so angry, she kicked him on the butt. Now who was the one crying, and hobbling around the room, not Cleopatra! The following day, Cleopatra was allowed to go outdoors, but Marci made sure her cat never went to the neighbor's yard.

The hot summer days lingered, and Marci and her father spent more time outdoors than indoors. On weekends, Travis searched for arrowheads, while Marci took pictures of the sunrise and the sunset. She wanted her friends in Virginia to see what she woke up to in the mornings, and what she saw before she went to bed. Marci was not used to so much sun, and no matter how much lotion she rubbed on her body, it was absorbed like a sponge. Then a horrible thing happened, Marci's skin started to dry and flake off as she rubbed her hands across her arms and legs. Not only did her skin itch from the dryness, her lips were also cracked, and dry which reminded her of the desert.

Early one morning while Marci and her father were watching the sunrise he remarked, "Little one, see how God displays his artwork for all to see, but so few take advantage of it." Her father's words were so profound they made her look at the beautiful sunrise. She had never thought about the things she saw in that way.

Anytime Marci wrote to her friends in Virginia, she told them everything she did, but never told them how her soft skin took on the characteristics of a snake or an Iguana. How it was dry, scaly, and peeled when she rubbed her hands across her arms or legs. She also did not write that she was turning into a desert creature, and expected to start crawling at any moment. If lucky enough to have a boyfriend, and he decided to kiss her, she would probably leave a piece of her dried lips on his. Even worse, she could use her hands to file her nails. Once she got over the shock of seeing her skin peel off, Marci realized she loved the feel of the sun. Not even the sun with its burning rays was going to move her away from the place she was getting to know, and love. Yet, she was not the only one whose skin tone changed. The entire family was now sporting a nice tan. Caleb's was a bit darker than the rest of the family because he was outdoors most of the time. However, that wasn't going to stop her from going out to the desert with her father.

When Marci got to know her acre of land, she thought back to the video she saw in Ms. Andersen's classroom. Sure, the ground would dry up, but with some water and work, the land became fertile. Marci now wondered what part of New Mexico the narrator was referring to because she was yet to see the ground so dry and cracked. She was still waiting to see the nest of scorpions that were looking for a place to hide. Marci also wondered why they didn't show the ranches with alfalfa, wheat, corn and chili that is abundant in New Mexico. If it was in the video, she must not have been paying attention because at that time she was scared, and feeling sorry for herself. Out of curiosity, Marci dug up the video Ms. Andersen gave her. Then, and only then, did she see the label on the cover, and the video were different. The cover was titled, *New Mexico, the Land of Enchantment,* while the video was titled, *Mexico's Desert Crawlers.*

Marci laughed as she thought of what Ms. Andersen's reaction would have been. Somehow, someone accidently added the governor's speech to the video of the Mexican desert, and they put the video in the wrong case.

Soon Travis captured his love for the outdoors by painting what he saw on canvas, and at times, his paintings were so lifelike. On the other hand, Marci mastered the art of taking pictures with her father's old Kodak camera. Marci had pictures of her father painting the landscape, of her mother arranging the wildflowers she picked out in the desert, and she even had pictures of Caleb playing basketball, or cowboys and Indians with his friends.

She also took pictures of the wildlife and insects that make their home in the dry desert. Marci no longer longed to be near the water, and what used to be her favorite pastime activities in Virginia, took a turn toward a different direction in New Mexico.

Marci still read and kept up with her spelling, but taking pictures and staying outdoors were now her favorite pastime activities.

Reader's Digest

It was a warm and lazy summer day and everything was as perfect as it was going to get. The only problem was that Marci was restless and alone in the house. Looking for something to keep her occupied she thought of going outside. Then she saw her mother's Reader's Digest on the kitchen counter. Casually flipping through the pages, Marci came across a contest open to children her age and a bit older. The rules were simple enough. The story, essay, or comparison could be no more than seven hundred words. Entries would be judged on originality, creativeness, and how close the photo, picture or drawing related to what the entry dealt with. Winners would be notified by mail, and would receive a telephone call from the judge who read his or her entry. After that was done, the entry along with a photograph of the winner would be published in the Reader's Digest. Having read the rules, Marci put the magazine down and knew exactly what picture she would submit.

Now she had something to do and was ready to get started. With a cold glass of iced tea, her favorite pen, and a Big Chief Tablet, she decided to sit outside on the porch. This would help her think of the day she took the picture she was going to send.

Before Marci started writing her comparison: "How A Tarantula and I Are Alike," she wrote how she had a hard time deciding whether to write a comparison on how she and a tree were alike, or a spider, and the spider won.

"When I moved to New Mexico, I was scared, and could not hide from my fears. If there had been a cave somewhere nearby, it would not have been deep enough for me to escape into. Then my father introduced me to the desert, and I could not get enough of it. No longer did I want to crawl into a cave, because I wanted to be out in the sun where I could feel it warming my body. But like the female tarantula who stays in

its burrow, I knew I also had a place to hide if I had to. The first thing I saw when my father and I went exploring was a tarantula that was coming out of its hole. I think it too was feeling free, and for the duration the spider stayed out, the sun warmed it. As I walked a couple of feet, I saw another tarantula had shed the skin that covered its body, and the eight hairy legs. When I examined the molting, I saw how fuzzy the legs were. The tarantula needs the fur, and fuzz, but I shave my legs so they will be smooth, and not look like I have hair all over them. I thought how the tarantula stays in its burrow to prevent the sun from doing it harm. Just as the spider, I too tried to hide from the burning rays of the sun to protect my body. I also learned how to dress for the hot desert climate by shedding some of the clothing I wore. However, unlike the spider, I had to rub plenty of lotions and creams on my skin to protect my body.

Once the spider molts, it stretches the new skeleton to allow some room for new growth, and the new skeleton then hardens. When it molts, the tarantula lies on its back with its legs in the air to get rid of the excess skin. Because my eating habits changed, I gained weight. I had to buy larger size clothes as my bones grew along with my stomach. When I gained weight, I too wiggled my legs up in the air while I held my breath, and squeezed into a new pair of jeans. Yet, unlike the tarantula who can live for up to two years without eating a single thing, I would die if I did not eat.

The spider has many eyes and perfect vision. I have to wear glasses. These also help me see better, which gives me another set of eyes. Some tarantulas spin a web to catch their food. When it catches a fly, or a grasshopper, it twirls the insect around, and wraps it with the silk webbing like a cocoon. I cannot spin a web, but when I eat a burrito, I put meat and vegetables in a tortilla. I then get some foil to wrap it around my burrito. I either eat it, save it, or share my lunch with a friend.

The tarantula and I have to be careful of the dangers that surround us. She has to be on guard that birds of prey or humans do not kill her. I have to be careful my classmates, or other kids do not bully me, and that I am careful when I cross the streets.

I learned to appreciate what I see, to be friendlier, happier and to know it is okay to come out of my shell. I have learned that like the spider who cares for her children, so too do my parents protect us from things that are not good for us. I have also watched spiders leave their home in search of their own. One day I too will leave my family to explore my future. Eventually, I will meet someone and we will have our own family. I will have children and we will have to protect them, as did my parents. When we moved, I shed the city life styles, learned how to adjust to the climate and the country life, I have learned life does go on no matter what happens."

Marci could not think of anything else to add to her comparison; except that she hoped her entry would win. She also added a postscript letting the judges know she saved the molting the spider left behind. Counting every word to make sure she complied with the rules, Marci ran into her bedroom to get an envelope, stamp and the picture she took when she and her father were out exploring. When she put her entry in the mailbox, she kept her eye on it hoping the mail carrier would come before her mother returned. Seconds before her mother closed the back door her entry was on its way. Now all Marci had to do was to keep this a secret from her family. For weeks, Marci would check the mail to see if there was a letter for her, but after a month, she thought her entry was not selected and completely forgot about the contest.

The day was starting to get hotter when Marie was checking her prize winning rosebushes for aphids. When she saw the mail carrier stop at their mailbox, she motioned to her daughter to get the mail. Marie asked her if there were any letters for her. Marci fanned the mail and saw there was a magazine for Travis, a package for Caleb from Dell Comic books, utility bills, and the rest were letters for Marci from her friends. Letting her mother know there was no mail for her, she took the mail indoors.

The first letter Marci read was from Magdalene. Marci could not wait to read it, but when she did, she was shocked at how angry her friend was at her. Magdalene could not understand how Marci was getting used to living in the desert, and away from her friends. How she could be so happy when her friends missed her so much, and wondered why she did not write more often. She wanted to know what happened to the girl who was so upset at the thought of moving to a Third World Country. Marci couldn't figure what was going on with her friend, and why she was so angry that she liked her new state. Magdalene was always the one who was so positive, and wanted only the best for anyone. Marci wondered if her friend changed that much since she left, or if she was having a bad day when she wrote her letter. Having read Magdalene's letter, she opened Vanessa's, and tossed the rest aside, so she could read them later on in the day.

When her mother finished pruning, and checking her rosebushes, she checked in on her daughter. Marie was coming indoors when she heard Marci laughing, and knew she was reading Vanessa's letter. Vanessa was angry that Marci sent a picture of a tarantula, and thought she would like it. She continued by demanding Marci not send her pictures of the creepy crawlers she saw. If she did, she should write it on the outside of the envelope. This way she could shake the pictures out of the envelope, and read the letter without her mother running into the bedroom. Marci laughed even harder because she knew how dramatic Vanessa was and it did not take much for Marci to visualize her friend's reaction. Marci had completely forgotten she sent her friend a picture of the tarantula. Having read the letters from her friends, Marci got a boost of energy, and went for a walk. When she returned, Marci went into her bedroom to clear the clutter from her desk. While she was doing this, she saw the letter from The Reader's Digest. Marci took the letter and sat on the edge of her bed. Certain she did not win; she tossed the letter aside and opened the rest of the mail she received. Now all but one remained unopened, and she would now find out if she won the contest or not. Not wanting to read her entry had not won, Marci took her time opening it.

However, as she read the first sentence, she could not believe what she was reading.

"Dear Marci,

Let me be the first to congratulate you on your entry, "How a Tarantula and I Are Alike." We received over 2000 entries, and yours was judged as one of the best. The judge who read your essay thought it was the most amusing entry she had read in quite some time. She was so impressed; she shared it with the other judges. I am pleased to let you know she will be contacting you in a few days to get more information, and to confirm receipt of this letter."

There was more to this letter, but when Marci got to the part where the judge liked it, she did not continue reading. Marci jumped on her bed, and all around her room not believing a photo of a spider helped her win a contest. Now all Marci wanted to do was to bask in the light of her accomplishment before she told her family. She wanted to run all over the house shouting at the top of her lungs, but her mother was sitting in the den.

Tonight as the family took turns sharing what they did during the day, she would share her news. This was going to be the evening she would get all of the praise, and glory from her family. When Marci's turn came around, she was going to take her letter out of her pocket and hand it to her father. Sitting back, she would let the fireworks begin. With her head held high, Marci would answer their questions, and smile as big as she could. Until then, she had to find something to keep busy. There was no one she could share her wonderful news with, as she did not have a close friend she could call. Her room was clean, and it was too hot to go exploring, so keeping her news was proving to be more difficult than she thought.

As she was about to answer Vanessa and Magdalene's letters, her mother came into her bedroom. Knowing Vanessa had written to Marci, Marie asked what Vanessa had to say.

Marci replied, "Oh, not much, just that she has a boyfriend. Guess she forgot he was the one that had a crush on me." Marci also added she got a letter from Magdalene and she was angry I like living here.

"Is that why your face is so flushed," her mother asked.

Marci smiled and did not say anything. If her mother only knew how badly she wanted to blurt out her exciting news, but that surprise was what awaited her family.

"Sweetheart would you like to go to the mall."

Setting Vanessa's letter aside, Marci jumped off her bed and grabbed her purse. Could she really keep her news from her mother until it was time for the family to gather for dinner? When they were in the car, Marci did not want her mother to see the grin on her face so she looked out the window. Marie thought Marci was too quiet, and to break the silence, asked, "What else did Vanessa have to say?"

"Nothing much, other than she made friends with the girl that moved into our apartment. She says she misses me, and things have not been the same without me." Marci did not mention Magdalene's letter because it was still bothering her that her friend was so angry. Instead, she said, "Mom can you imagine me having a boyfriend?"

"Sure, I can, but I hope it won't be for a while," Marie told her daughter. Marci laughed, and changed the conversation by asking her mother why she was going to the mall.

"Do you remember the couple we met at church? Well they invited us to go to a movie and dinner on Saturday."

"Mom that is great, but you do know Caleb and I will be just fine right. We are too old to have a babysitter, so you and Dad just go out and have fun."

Marie and Marci went from one shop to the next, but Marie could not find anything she liked. But on the last dress shop they went to, a sales lady told Marie she might find the dress she wanted a couple of blocks down the road. Taking her advice Marie drove to the small shop. There, she found the summer dress she had in mind. Marci also tried a few dresses and for a while, it took her mind off her news. The trip to the mall and back home kept mother and daughter so preoccupied Marie never suspected her daughter was keeping a secret. Now all Marci had to do was wait a few more hours, but it would be like waiting for eternity.

The family was finally sitting at the dinner table, and Marci had to restrain her enthusiasm until it was her turn. Travis always had something to say, and this evening was no exception. Having read an article on how to draw children's faces, he thought he would use that piece of information on his students in August when school started. He wanted to teach the children how easy it was for them to draw. Marie told Travis and Caleb she and Marci had a pleasant day. How they went to a couple of dress shops until she was told to go to the boutique down the block. To add to her mother's comments, Marci told her father how pretty her mother looked. Travis smiled and winked his eye at his lovely wife. Marci was next, and she was getting ready to share her news with the family. Just then, Caleb asked if he could go next because he had something very important to tell the family. Even Marci was curious to find out what he had to say, but it was her turn.

"Little one is it okay if your brother goes next," her father asked.

Marci didn't know why she agreed to let Caleb take her turn, but she did, and Caleb now had their undivided attention.

"Guess what guys, I met another friend, and he also likes sports. Mom, I invited him to sleep over is that okay?" Marie nodded to let Caleb know it was all right. Caleb did not stop at that, as he had to tell the family he made a three-point granny shot. Pushing his chair away from the table, he got up and pretended he was shooting a basket to show the family how he did it. As his parents listened, they told Caleb that was wonderful news.

Marci could not believe what she was hearing. She actually agreed to give up her turn to hear this little twerp tell the family about his new friend, and their basketball game. When was this child going to grow up?

Finally, it was Marci's turn, and she did everything just as she planned. When she handed her father the letter her parents looked at one another not sure what Marci was up to. Marci now watched her father as he opened the letter. His eyes opened so wide she thought they were going to pop out of their sockets. Pushing his chair back, Travis stood up, and cleared his throat.

"Family," Travis said, "We have something so exciting to celebrate, and this special news is all about Marci." Travis then read his daughter's letter as she sat back and watched her family's reaction. When Travis read the letter, Marie came over and hugged her daughter.

"Honey, we are so proud of you. This is so exciting. What did you have to do to earn such an honor, and when did you find time to do this?"

Even Caleb told Marci how proud he was to have such a smart sister. Wow, a compliment from her brother, not even Marci was expecting something like this to happen. Marci's ego was so inflated, but she loved it and took everything in. Just as she was about to give Caleb credit for appreciating what she accomplished he blew it! Caleb laughed as he said, "Hey sis, is your spider friend going to show you how to spin a web?"

When Marie and Travis laughed, Marci's ego bubble burst. Wanting to get even, but trying not to show her anger, she replied, "By the way Caleb, what is a granny shot?" Before he could say anything Marie said, "It's one older people try when we don't know how to shoot a basketball into the net."

Now it was Caleb's turn to feel the bitter sting of ego deflation. Marci felt good as his mother put Caleb in his place. Why that little twerp, that should teach him to ruin his sisters moment of glory. Marie then asked Marci to tell them how she earned this honor, and not leave a single thing out.

"Yes, little one, tell us everything," Travis said with a gleam in his eye.

The attention was once again on Marci, and she told her family how she happened to be leafing through the Reader's Digest, and came across the contest. She told her family how she wrote the essay, and sent a picture of the tarantula along with her entry. Mom, Dad, it was so easy, but I never thought I would win. Now all I have to do is to wait for the phone call so I can find out what I won. Mom, remember when we went shopping to find you a dress? I wanted to tell you. It was so hard for me to keep my secret, but I wanted to share it with the family when we were all together. Once again, her father told Marci how proud he was of his little girl, and to show her, he said, "Come on everyone, leave the dishes. We are going to celebrate Marci's great accomplishment at the Dairy Queen."

The next day was just as exciting. Norma, the judge who read Marci's entry called to tell her, she would be going to her house to present her with her prizes. She also told Marci her name, along with her picture, and entry were going to be featured in the next issue of the Reader's Digest. Norma then asked Marci if she would be available to have her picture taken sometime during the week? Excited as Marci was, she told Norma any day would be good for her. Norma confirmed Marci had indeed won the contest, and asked Marci if she could speak to her mother. She needed to get permission to release her information.

Knowing she had to share her news, with Dr. Brewer, she called his office. When Doctor Brewer's nurse told him he had a call from Marci, he thought she was having a relapse. He immediately left the patient that was in his examining room so he could talk to her. Hearing the wonderful news, Doctor Brewer told Marci he was extremely proud of her, and was relieved to hear she was okay. He wanted Marci to show him the letter so he could show it to his wife and anyone who came into his office. Marci told him she would have her mom, or dad drive her to his office sometime that week.

Marci was anxious for the week to end so she could meet Norma. Yet, when she did, she was a nervous wreck. That day as she looked in the mirror, the first thing she saw was a huge pimple on the tip of her nose. Of all days, she broke out with the biggest and reddest pimple that was ready to burst. With that on her nose, Marci knew no one was going to see how happy she was when the photographer took her picture. Hard as she tried to hide it, nothing worked until Marie put makeup on her nose, and that seemed to help. However, Marci could not help but think of the hideous pimple.

Norma was a very nice woman, and for the few minutes Marci talked to her, she completely forgot about the pimple, and felt better about taking pictures. Once she was ready, the photographer took pictures of Marci taking the camera out of the box, and her showing the family what she won. It was beautiful, and Marci could not believe it was hers. She was so happy she started to cry, and hugged Norma and the photographer.

"That's only one of the surprises I told you about," and Norma handed her an envelope. When Marci opened the manila envelope, she saw a certificate, and was about to give it to her mother. Norma told her, "Take another look into the envelope."

When Marci looked, she saw a check for three-hundred dollars attached to it. Three hundred dollars was a lot of money, and Marci screamed at the top of her lungs. Not wanting to lose it, or spend it on something foolish, she asked her father to save it for her.

The last picture the photographer took was that of Marci hugging Norma as she wiped the tears from her eyes. That was one picture the photographer would definitely send Marci. Again, Caleb asked his sister why she was crying, but Marci did not bother to explain why she was so emotional because boys just do not understand. When Norma and the photographer left, Marci went into her bedroom, and wrote Vanessa a long letter.

Things changed between Caleb and Marci, but Caleb was still the little twerp he always was, and Marci was starting to appreciate her life in her new state, and her brother even more. Marci now realized her parents made the right decision to move to New Mexico, and she now wondered why it took her so long to accept what Caleb knew all along.

Anniversary

Travis and Marie's twelfth wedding anniversary was fast approaching, and Marci needed her prize money. Marci knew what she and Caleb wanted to buy their parents, but she didn't know how she was going to get it from her father.

What possible excuse could she come up with to get what she needed? The only thing she could think of was to talk to Caleb to see if he had any ideas. The first thing out of Caleb's mouth was that she wanted a computer so they could share it once school started. Why it was so simple, why did she not think of it? The next thing she needed was someone to help her make the final decision. Going to Sal, she told him what she had in mind, and she asked him if he would help her choose the right gift for her parents. Sal was happy to help Marci, and offered to take her to Sears in Belen.

Once again, Marci would have to come up with something clever to convince her mother to let her go. Sal told Marci not to worry. He would tell her mother he need her help to select a gift for his niece's birthday. Sure enough, everything went smoothly, and now it was up to Marci to ask her father for her prize money. She wanted it in case she should come across a computer she wanted to buy. Her father had no problem giving her the money, and the best thing of all was her parents had no clue what was in store for them. For Marci, that was the least she and Caleb could do to show their parents how much they appreciated all the sacrifices they had made for them.

It was a good thing Marci asked Sal Duran for his help. When the sales clerk at Sears asked what type of television, they were looking for Marci had no idea. There were so many to choose from and the sales clerk was very patient. Then the right television came into sight when Marci saw a 25-inch Admiral console.

The price tag was five hundred dollars, but was reduced to two hundred sixty eight dollars, and fifty-nine cents due to a small scratch on the top. Other than the scratch, nothing else was wrong with it.

Wanting to make room for the newer models the store wanted to get rid of the old TVs. Sal checked to see what features the television had and asked the sales clerk questions Marci never thought of asking. Talking it over with Marci, Sal told the sales clerk they would take it. When Marci came home, her mother and father were at the grocery store. This worked out for her because she would not have known what to say if they asked her if she found a computer.

A couple of hours later, Sal saw the Sears delivery truck drive up, so he went over to make sure they delivered the television he, and Marci selected. He also had them put the television where the old one was, and the old television went into Marci's bedroom. Then when Marci's parents returned, the television would be on, and waiting for them to see their big surprise.

As the Sears, truck turned the corner, Travis and Marie drove into their driveway. In the meantime, Sal ran out the backdoor so his neighbors would not know he was in on their surprise. When Marie was putting the groceries away, she went to replace the empty box of Kleenex in the den. Preoccupied as she was, Marie replaced the Kleenex box, and was about to go back into the kitchen when she turned around. She knew something was different, and that was when she saw the television. At first, she didn't notice it because they always had the television on.

"Travis, come here, hurry!" Travis thinking something was wrong ran into the den. Seeing Marie wide eyed, and holding her hand over her mouth he asked her what was wrong. All she could do was point to the television. Travis was just as surprised as was his wife, and when they read the card, Marci, and Caleb came out from behind the couch.

Knowing about the surprise that awaited them, Sal thought he would pay his neighbors a visit. When he rang the doorbell, Marie answered, and he asked her if she had a can of tomato paste, he could borrow. He was making Lasagna, and did not realize he was out. Before Marie gave Sal the tomato paste, she invited him into the den to show him the surprise their children had for them.

Pretending not to know what it was, Sal said, I was outside when the Sears delivery truck came to your house.

"Did they buy you a new recliner?"

"No, they bought us this television for our anniversary. Don't know if to get angry at them for spending their money on us, or just hug them to death," Marie replied.

"When we came home, the television was on as it normally is, and not until I was going to replace the box of Kleenex did I notice it was new. The kids waited until Travis and I were together before they came out of hiding," Marie commented.

"Wow! So when can I come over to watch Bonanza?"

"You can come over anytime you want, just make sure you bring the popcorn," Travis told his neighbor.

Marci smiled at Sal for going along with her plan. Travis then asked him a question about the television, and Sal accidently said, "The salesman said…." as he said this, Sal closed his eyes and pressed his lips tightly, as he had just tipped Travis off that he too was in on this surprise. Travis asked, "Sal, how did you know?" Then it dawned on him. "Was this the reason Marci asked for her money, and why she asked if she could go with you to Belen?" Sal smiled and nodded his head. "Well would you have let her go if she told you what she was up to?"

Marie now remembered what Sal had come for and went to the pantry to get a can of tomato paste. When Marie came back, Sal told her he had actually come over to see if they liked their surprise. Seeing the look on their faces, he knew they were thrilled at what awaited them, and that was all he needed. That evening the family ordered pizza, and watched their favorite programs on their new color television.

Wednesdays when *Bonanza" and "Little House on the Prairie* were on, Marci made sure the dishes were washed, and the kitchen floor swept. By 7 p.m., Marci, along with the rest of her family, and occasionally, a neighbor, or two were sitting in front of the new TV. Ben Cartwright was a man of wealth, and highly respected by the community, but that did not keep him from disciplining his sons.

Poor Hoss, while his father was scolding him, his brother, Little Joe was laughing, and teasing him. However, Little Joe did not fare any better because his father scolded him too. Although Marci laughed at Little Joe's antics, she compared it to the many times Caleb laughed at her, but he was a child.

Little House on the Prairie was another favorite TV series the family watched. Mr. Ingalls, a farmer, and father of 3 girls, and an adopted son was always getting his children out of whatever predicaments they got into. Half-Pint, his middle daughter was always with her father. She defended the children that were bullied, and often got in trouble. As Marci watched the episodes, she compared her, and her father's relationship to that of the Ingles.

The Olsen family, Nellie, Willie and their mother, Harriet were hateful, rich, and always got Marci angry. Nellie and Willie always wanted what others had, and most of the time they got what they demanded. When they did not get it, they played mean tricks on Half-Pint and her friends. By the end of the episode, the tricks any of the Olsen family played on anyone in Walnut Grove backfired on them. At the same time, Marci felt sorry for Mr. Olsen because he was so hen-pecked. Secretly he enjoyed seeing his spoiled family get what they deserved.

Sundays, Travis and his family gathered in the den and watched Bishop Sheen on the Catholic Hour. Bishop Sheen addressed issues that pertained to every age group, and when it was over; Travis turned the TV off so the family could discuss what Bishop Sheen talked about, including the jokes he made.

Excerpt from the Associated Press-Book Presents Best Messages of Bishop Sheen Clergyman's Words Called Timeless

The Divine Beloved speaks to the soul in a whisper, but because the soul is waiting for a trumpet it loses His command. Archbishop Fulton

Sheen By David Briggs Neither before nor since has an American Roman Catholic clergyman captivated the airways as Archbishop Fulton Sheen did in the middle of this century. Despite competition from Milton Berle, and with nothing more than a blackboard and a piece of chalk, the bishop garbed in a flowing cape reached some 30 million Americans of all faiths who watched his television program Life Is Worth Living. Cardinals would flock to this prelate when he was in Rome. Among the famous Americans he converted to Catholicism were Clare Booth Luce and Henry Ford II. Then came the Second Vatican Council in the early 1960s. Sheen was less than enthusiastic about some changes in a church that was changing rapidly, and he gradually faded from public view. He died in 1979. Now, on the 100th anniversary of his birth, a new book of his writings and television essays – From the Angel's Blackboard: The Best of Fulton J. Sheen – A Centennial Celebration – is being published by Triumph Books. What the book shows, in an age when books about taking care of the soul top religion best-seller lists, is how timeless Sheen's words are, said Patricia Kossmann, the book's editor. In rereading many of sheen's works, it becomes readily apparent that his voice can never be fully extinguished, she writes in the book's forward. There remains in his written and spoken words a keen insight into the universal human condition, and the universal quest for the divine in the ordinary. Born in El Paso, Ill., May 8, 1895, Sheen was ordained to the priesthood in the Diocese of Peoria in 1919. He received his doctorate from the University of Louvain in Belgium and taught philosophy of religion at the Catholic University of America. He began his broadcasting career in 1930 on the Catholic Hour on NBC. By 1950, the program's U.S. audience reached 4 million. In 1951, then Bishop Sheen was national director of the Society for the Propagation of the Faith and began his television series. At the height of its popularity, the prelate received as many as 9,000 letters a day. Kossmann remembered being mesmerized by Sheen as a grade schooler while watching his Tuesday evening program with her parents. When she first met Sheen as an editor of some of his later books, she expected an imposing figure, but was surprised as many were meeting him in person to discover a polite, slightly built man. But, oh, those eyes, she said, referring to the spellbinding way Sheen would look out at his audience. It was like he could read your soul, she said. He never did anything, in his words or otherwise, that ever made you feel less than special. In making selections for the book, Kossman said she went through dozens of books seeking the best, timeless wisdom. The book's chapters on subjects such as health and holiness, prayer and meditation and angels can be easily digested in a sitting. A common them of Sheen's writings and broadcasts was encouraging people to recognize the sacred in their lives. Courtesy is the homage of the heart to the sacredness of human worth and sanctity can be built out of patient endurance of a child's slurping of soup or one's inability to get rich, Sheen said. All of us would like to make our own crosses – tailor made trials, Sheen wrote. But not many of us welcome the crosses God sends. Yet it is in doing perfectly the little chores he sends that saints find holiness. The big, world-shattering things many of us imagine we would like to do for God might, in the end, feed only our egotism. On the other hand, to accept the crosses of our state of life because they come from an all-loving God is to have taken the most important step in the reformation of the world, namely, the reformation of the self. Elsewhere in the book, Sheen makes the connection between world peace and the peace of individual souls. World wars are only projections of the conflicts inside the souls of human beings, for nothing happens in the external world that has not first happened within a soul, Sheen said. Bishop William J. McCormack, the current national director of the Society for the Propagation of the Faith, said Sheen's message has increased in relevance overtime, particularly to people today who seek fulfillment everywhere but in their daily lives. Don't live in the past. Don't live in the future. This is the moment God has given us to be useful.

Route 66

Deejay Carlos Garcia happened to get a request from a listener to play Route 66, by Chuck Berry. Marci knew the words, and asked her father to turn the radio up so she could sing along. Marci sang at the top of her lungs, and when the song finished, Travis and Marie laughed when Caleb told his sister "She still sounded like a cat with a fur ball in its throat." It was true, Marci could not carry a tune if her life depended on it, but it did not matter. As a matter-of-fact, Caleb's smart remarks did not bother Marci anymore. She just continued singing until her father went through a dip in the road. The sign clearly indicated there was a dip up ahead, but Marci's father did not think much of it. Now the family was bouncing up to the roof of the car, and back down to their seat. Marci thought it felt like she was riding a roller coaster because she had to hold her stomach.

Suddenly everything she had eaten earlier came rushing to her throat. Holding her hand over her mouth, Marci was barely able to tell her father he had to stop the car. Marci jumped out of the car, and had just enough time to get down before she threw up. Seeing Marci was not feeling well, Marie had Caleb move to the front seat so she could take care of her daughter. Travis apologized, and said, "I'm sorry little one; I did not think the dips were so deep, and I thought they were spaced further apart than they are." Marie then told her husband to stop at the next Stuckey's and get Marci something to settle her stomach. After Marci drank her 7-up, she felt better. Then her bratty brother asked his father to turn around and drive through the dips one more time. He thought it was fun, and wanted to see his sister turn a darker shade of green. He was such a dork; always picking on her.

Marci was glad her mother was sitting in the backseat because once again she had to roll the window down, and stick her head out the window to get some fresh air. Travis had the air conditioner on, but Marci was still feeling the effects of the dips. With her mother taking care of her, she felt well enough to sit up, and focused her attention on the scenery. Seeing the vegetation on the side of the road zoom past her,

Marci again felt sick to her stomach. Travis continued to drive until he came to a bridge that crossed the Rio Puerco. Another driver was also about to cross the bridge, but thought twice about it. He too did not want to take the chance of not making it across without doing damage to his vehicle. When Travis drove past the other vehicle, the family waved to thank him for letting them through.

By this time, Marci was feeling better, and as she looked out the window, she saw dry yellow vegetation growing alongside, and up the flat mesas. She also saw the rocks and shale that had fallen, or slid down. Still feeling a bit woozy, Marci could visualize gladiators defending themselves from their enemies as they tossed the shale around, and left them where they landed. Driving past the mesas with the fallen shale, Marci saw other mesas whose color changed from a coffee brown on the top, to a light tan at the bottom. Just as she thought there was nothing else to see, something in the distance caught her eye.

“Dad, do you see that mountain over there?” “Yes honey, that is Mt. Taylor, and I was told it can be seen for hundreds of miles,” her father replied. “I was also told that in 1849 this mountain was named after President Zachary Taylor.”

While Travis was telling Marci what he learned, they drove past one of the Indian Reservations, and Marci saw a small church at the top of a hill with a dirt road leading to its front door. Nestled near the hill are pueblo homes that have been there for what seems like centuries. At the bottom are a dozen, or more adobe houses where Marci assumed some of the Native American Indians live, and could be caretakers of the church. Travis knew his daughter had also seen the church that was to their left, and told her it was the San Esteban Catholic Church. Maybe on our way back, we will stop and check it out. To add to this beautiful scenery, a freight train with many colorful boxcars, and flat cars was traveling down the tracks running alongside the mesas, and disappearing into the vast open countryside.

About to ask her father another question, Marci had to get some fresh air. Rolling the window down, Marci saw another mesa, but the rocks and shale on this one were almost red in color. Oddly enough, when she looked up, the clouds had also taken a pinkish hue. As the clouds floated over the mesas they cast a shadow over them, and Marci imagined them conversing with one another as friends do. She imagined them saying, “It is always good to see you my friend; I will see you on my way back,” and with that, the clouds slowly drifted away.

When Marci asked her father why the rocks on the landscape were so red, Caleb jumped in and said, “Don’t you know, that is where the wagon trains were traveling, and that is the mixture of the Indian, and white man’s blood.” Marci decided she would not ask her father any questions. She did not want to give Caleb a chance to add his opinion to what she knew would only be his sick sense of humor.

Marci’s father continued to drive, and in her mind, Marci tried to describe what she had seen, but that did not help. Then she thought, *if I can’t describe what I have seen, how am I going to write it so that Vanessa will know what I am talking about, and doesn’t think I’m crazy? There is so much more to these mesas, and the mountains other than their height. They are all so colorful. Each one different in shape, size and even the vegetation growing on, around and through it makes them very picturesque, but how do I tell Vanessa?*

Marci also thought about the shape of the mountains. She could see how through the years the winds shaped them into works of art. She thought how a mountain is never just a jagged, smooth, or high mountain. These are mighty giants taking care of the land, animals, and the humans living, and traveling around them.

As a newcomer to New Mexico, there is so much to see that it was difficult for Marci to take it all in. Marci now realized how much she had taken for granted when she was living back east. She never thought to appreciate the beauty that surrounded her. She just assumed that was part of her natural surroundings, and she would have the rest of her life to explore her state. How she wished she had taken the time to go to the lighthouses. Taken pictures of the landscape and enjoyed everything that surrounded her to share with her friends. Marci made herself a promise that she would never take anything for granted, and was not about to let that happen here. Besides, even if she wanted to she did not think she could. Seeing the landscape and scenery pass her by, she heard her father say, "Oh no," and pulled off the road and onto the shoulder. Something was wrong with the car, and Travis could not drive any further. The family was stranded in the middle of nowhere, and not a car was in sight.

Nearly an hour passed before anyone stopped to help. An old man in a yellow beat-up truck stopped and offered to pull the car to the nearest garage. Travis gladly accepted his offer where he would have the car checked. When the mechanic checked under the hood, he told Travis the water hose had a hole in it. Going into his garage, he went to check if he had one in stock. He knew he had received a new shipment, but he had been so busy, he did not have a chance to put them up. When he found the one he needed, he came out and told Travis, "He could replace it."

"Yes, do whatever you have to do. All I want is to get my family back home," Travis replied.

Knowing Travis and his family were safe, the man who towed the car to the garage got into his truck and was about to leave. Travis offered to pay him, but the man refused. Instead, he told Travis, "If ever you see anyone stranded, stop, and help them. "This," he said, "Will be how you will repay me for helping you, and your family." Travis agreed as he shook the man's hand and the man drove away.

A few minutes later, the mechanic replaced the water hose, and told Travis he could go anywhere he wanted without any problems. However, on that particular day, Travis did not feel good about going any further, so he headed back home. New Mexico was their state, and they were here to stay, and could travel to Gallup anytime they wanted.

Ms. Fastle

It was the beginning of another school year, and friends were happy to see each other, but Marci had no one. She was scared, and felt like crying. It was the same feeling she had when her father told her and Caleb they were moving to New Mexico.

For Marci, Monday, August 27 was her first day at a new school, and she felt like a complete oddball. Wanting to be the first to leave as soon as the bell rang, Marci chose the desk closest to the door. Even though some of the neighborhood kids knew her, they still thought she was a city snob. They continued to say Marci thought she was better than they were because she was from Virginia. Marci could not blame them for ignoring her because she had made it hard for them to get to know her when she moved into the neighborhood.

Marci's history teacher did not waste any time telling his students what he expected from them. He told them his class was a difficult one, but by the time the year was over, they were going to know many interesting facts about New Mexico. He continued to tell them they needed to take plenty of notes as he gave pop quizzes without notice. Anyone who thought they were going to pass his class by the seat of their pants had to think twice. This was refreshing to Marci because she knew she was going be too busy to feel sorry for herself. Having said that, Mr. Lopez started his lesson by telling his students they had to start taking notes.

"Some of you might not realize how lucky you are to have a school where you can get your education. According to some historians, there were no schools in New Mexico until the late 19th century. This means some of your grandparents never learned to read or write. Many might not have graduated because they could not go to school all day as you do. Your parents and grandparents had to help out in the fields, or take care of the children at home while their parents went to work."

Marci was stunned when she heard this, and could not imagine her parents having to work out in the fields in the middle of the day when it was so hot. As Mr. Lopez continued his lesson, he told his students the *Palace of the Governor* was built in 1609, and is located in Santa Fe, making it one of the oldest public buildings in America. The students also learned how Spanish explorers who hoped to find gold and wealth equal to Mexico's Aztec treasures named New Mexico.

New to New Mexico, Marci learned the governor was Democrat, Jerry Apodaca who was serving a second term. Thinking aloud she mumbled, "He must be a good governor to be re-elected so many times." Mr. Lopez overheard her remark and said the governor had done many things for the people of New Mexico.

"I hope the rest of you are also paying attention, and taking notes on what will certainly be one of the essay questions. Now pay attention as I tell you the events of how New Mexico came to be." Within fortyfive minutes, Mr. Lopez told his students how on January 6, 1912, the United States Congress admitted New Mexico as a state, and became the 47th state of the union. He also told them how the colors of the flag came to be, how Dr. Harry P. Mera drew the Zia symbol on the flag after he found it on a late 19th century water jar from the Zia Pueblo. How the Indians believe the number four does not only apply to the circle, but to the compass, the seasons, the four cycles of a day, and the seasons of life, childhood, youth, adult and old age.

Mr. Lopez was one instructor who did not believe in wasting time. Looking at the clock on the wall, he gave his students their first assignment. He wanted them to ask their parents what they did when they went to school.

"I know some of your parents, and we have shared information about our lives, so I will know if you took the time to ask them or not. If they did not have a chance to go to school, I want to know the reason for that as well. I don't want to hear any excuses as this will be part of your grade."

Class was over, and Marci knew she was going to like his class. She did not think Mr. Lopez was a strict man. Instead, she thought of Ms. Andersen who only wanted to educate her students.

As Marci was eating her lunch, a slightly overweight girl with a mouth full of braces, and neatly braided dark black hair asked Marci if she could join her. Looking around the cafeteria Marci saw there were a few empty tables. Not sure what this girl wanted, Marci told her she could sit if she wanted to. Knowing what the kids thought of her, Marci was very careful as she thought this might be a trick. Careful as to what she said, Marci lowered her voice, as she did not want to be too loud. She did not want to say anything that would make her stand out more than she already did. Having seen a group of girls sitting a few feet away from her bulling other kids she continued to eat her lunch. Sitting across from Marci, the girl told Marci her name was Juanita Gabaldon. When they were exchanging names, the girls from the other table came to where Juanita and Marci were sitting.

Jan, a tall slender girl with beautiful hazel green eyes, said, "Juanita, what are you doing eating with a city freak. Don't you know she is the city girl that lives in the big brown house, who won the Reader's Digest contest? She is the one who compared herself to a hairy spider. By the way city girl, your legs are long, skinny and hairy, do you need a machete to shave them? Maybe you will teach us how to write so we can take good notes, and won't fail our class."

The girls laughed and waited for Marci to say something. Marci knew girls like Jan Martinez and her friends at her old school and did not like them either. Marci stood up and was going to defend herself, but Juanita told the girls "to leave her alone because Marci was her friend."

"Well Miss Jan Martinez, at least she keeps her legs nice and clean. Not like your legs that always have stubbles and look like porcupine quills. Another thing, at least we know you can read," Juanita told her.

Juanita was not afraid to stand up to Jan and her gang, and they walked away. Yet, their laughter continued to ring in Marci's ears, and she didn't know how to make it go away. The sting of their laughter, and the remarks made toward her almost made Marci cry, but she was not going to give these bullies the satisfaction. Marci was still a bit skeptical as to what Juanita wanted. The one thing Marci did know was that no one put Juanita up to eating lunch with her, and that it was indeed Juanita's choice.

"Juanita, if you knew those girls were up to no good, why did you choose to have lunch with me? There are other girls, and a lot of empty tables you could sit at, so why me?"

"I heard Jan talking as to what they wanted to do to you, and I could not let that happen. But if you don't want me to sit with you, or be your friend that is okay, just tell me."

"No, please stay, and thank you for saving me from what could have been an embarrassing moment."

The girls talked for a long time, and Marci learned Juanita was in a couple of her classes. The reason she had not met her sooner was that Juanita was visiting her aunt in Colorado.

"I tried to talk to you before you left, but by the time I got my books, you were already out the door," Juanita also told Marci she lived but a couple of blocks from her house.

That afternoon Marci finally had a friend she could trust as she did Vanessa. However, she still missed her friends back home.

When Marci first saw her teacher Ms. Fastle, she wondered how she could walk on high heels all day long. Ms. Fastle was about five-feet-three inches tall, had a light tan; blue eyes, and wore her hair down. When she told the kids her name, she asked them to call her "Donna."

After she came back from lunch, Marci saw she had slipped out of her high heels and for the rest of the day wore flip-flops, one normally wore at home.

Throughout the year, Donna prepared her class for the science fair that was now less than a month away. This year she was going to do things different. Wanting to challenge her students to use the information they learned in all of their classes, Donna decided her students would have a choice of building an adobe house, an ant farm, a dam, a bird's nest, or a beehive.

As her students arrived, and were seated, she told them what their assignment was going to be. The majority of the students were excited to start their project. However, four students did not want to participate.

Ms. Fastle then selected five students to be the leaders for their class projects. Those five would choose five classmates to assist him or her. Once that was done, it would be up to the leader, and another student to build the project. The other four students would do the research, and write the report. The group as a whole would come up with twenty questions for the judges. However, they had to be simple enough for a third grader to understand. If anyone had problems with their part of the assignment, the leader would help. For those who did not want to participate in the science fair they would have a special assignment. The students knew whom she was referring to as they never took part in any class activities, and were always interrupting Ms. Fastle, yet, they always managed to pass every test.

Before the leaders chose their project, Ms. Fastle took the four students who did not want to be part of the science project out of the classroom. They thought their teacher was going to let them sit it out—but they were in for a rude awakening. Not wanting them to know which projects the leaders selected, Ms. Fastle took those students out of the classroom. As they were walking down the hall, Ernest Gallegos said, "Hey Donna, I'm hungry, are we going to the cafeteria?" Another one joked about not having to do the science project. When they walked into the library, Ernest asked Donna what they were doing there. She told the four, their assignment was to ask Ms. Rosenwald, the librarian for a book on judging projects. They were to find a book and read what it takes to be a judge. Hearing what they had to do, they now wanted to volunteer to be in one of the groups, but it was too late. The four did not know it, but this was just the beginning of their project. To their horror, they had the hardest assignment of all. However, Ms. Fastle told them she would help them with their project after school.

While Donna and the students were away, the group leaders choose the project they wanted to work on. They then split into groups and assigned tasks to each of the classmates they selected. Juanita of course, selected Marci to be on her team, and Marci, was very happy. Juanita told, "Her group, the project they would work on was going to be an easy one. My dad knows everything about building an adobe house, and I know he will help us. He can even help us with the questions, but we have to work together." When they were deciding where to meet, Marci insisted the meetings be at her house, and the group agreed.

By the time Donna, and the students returned, the bell was about to ring. Before she dismissed them, she reminded her students they needed to start on their projects right away. Marci wanted to tell her mother her classmates were coming to work on a school project, and could not wait to go home. Happy to hear her daughter invited her classmates over, Marie prepared a snack for the kids when they arrived. While they ate their snack, Juanita distributed the assignments, and they were ready to get started. Everyone had an idea as to what needed to be done, and time passed by quickly. After Marci's classmates went home, she now knew the house she hated was her home, and she loved every inch of it. As for the scorpions, tarantulas and other insects that were trying to find shelter, they never appeared. Marci often thought of the video she saw on the New Mexico desert and wondered who was in charge of doing the documentary. It just did not do justice to her beautiful acre of land. Of course, the video she saw was that of the insects who make their home in the dry desert in Mexico.

When Rafael Gabaldon came home from work, his daughter introduced him to her friend Marcy. Juanita then told her father what they needed. Rafael was tired, but he agreed to help the girls. This evening all he wanted to do was rest. Rafael told Juanita, "He would help them tomorrow as they did not have school, and he did not have to work. Marci, you have to be here by eight thirty."

Of all days, Marci slept late, and by the time she got there, Juanita and her father were waiting for her. Now that Marci was there, they were able to get started.

"The first thing you need to know, is when someone builds an adobe house, it is different then if it is built out of lumber. To make an adobe house you need four ingredients: straw, water, dirt, and people willing to work. We have what we need, and the material is all around us. We also have to let the sun do its job and dry the adobes. Now all we need is to mix it all together. This morning while you slept, I made some frames to pour the mix into them. When you know, what has to be done you will be able to make your project. So you girls can start by digging a hole," Rafael told the girls,

"Dad we're going to get all dirty!"

"Well Juanita that is part of making adobes. You have seen me make them, what did you think; I was going to do everything by myself while you watched?"

Rafael gave Marci her shovel, but she didn't know what to do with it. The only time she used one was to dig a hole at the beach. Of course, hers was plastic, and it did not look anything like the one she now had in her hands. Rafael Gabaldon chuckled as he showed Marci how to use the shovel, and he now knew he was going to enjoy teaching the girls how to make adobes. The first time Marci tried to push the shovel into the ground, her foot slipped, and she had to try again. Marci finally got the hang of what she had to do, and was eager to dig the hole.

Rafael told the girls the hole didn't have to be deep, but it had to be wide. To show them what had to be done, Rafael purposely had them dig a hole bigger than was necessary. He also told Marci that she would now learn what it took to build her house. The dirt was hard, and it took the girls some time before they actually dug the hole. Once that was done, Rafael threw the straw and dirt into the hole, and poured water so the girls could mix it. The next step for the girls was to mix what was in the hole with their hands.

"I want to make sure you get the feel of what people who build adobe homes have to do," he said. Having done that, Rafael had the girls get into the hole and mix the mud with their feet. Thinking Rafael was joking; Juanita and Marci looked at one another and started to laugh. They could not imagine what he wanted them to do. Their feet did not have fingers to mix the mud, but the girls did as they were told, because they knew Rafael had done this before.

Of course, Rafael had never mixed the mud with his feet, but he thought he would have fun with his daughter and her friend. On the other hand, he did not tell them he used a hoe to mix the mud. As the girls stepped into the mud, they now knew why the hole had to be wide.

By now, the temperature had risen, and Juanita and Marci thought the mud felt cool to their hands, but it was even more refreshing on their feet. While Marci was stumping the straw into the mud, she thought of the movie, *The Ten Commandments*. The scene where Moses and other Jews were mixing the straw, mud, and water to make the mortar needed for the *Pharos Pyramid*.

Seeing the girls were enjoying themselves, and about to start playing in the mud, Rafael told them to get out. Having experienced the feel of mixing the mud with their hands, and feet, Rafael told the girls they were ready to start making the adobes. When Juanita and Marci saw the twelve-by-six-by-four inch frames they had to fill, they didn't know how they were going to carry the house into the classroom. Rafael told them he made a couple of regular house frames so they would see how much mud it takes to make one adobe. With their frames, they could actually make twenty-two adobes at a time.

Rafael told Marci, and Juanita they had to put the mud they mixed into the large frames with their hands. Once that was done, they were to fill the small wooden ones. The girls were having fun, as they filled the frames with the mud. Not paying attention to what they were doing, they started to overfill them. Seeing they were doing a sloppy job, Rafael made them slow down, and gave them a plastic butter knife to scrape the excess mud off the top.

With Rafael's help and guidance, Marci and Juanita made enough small adobes for more than just one house. Once the two-by-one-by half-inch adobe frames were filled with mud, the frames were gently pulled up so they could continue to make more. Then they were left out in the sun to dry. The girls were now starting to scratch their legs, and feet as the mud was starting to dry. Seeing the girls were trying to scrape the mud off their legs with the butter knives, Rafael turned the water on, and had them wash their hands, legs, and feet. Being out in the sun all morning was too much for Marci, and she was exhausted. Making adobes was hard work, and for this to be a simple science project, it was requiring a lot of manual work.

Rafael knew they had been outside for some time, but did not realize how long it had been. That was until Juanita's mother called them in to eat lunch. Rosita Gabaldon did not have to ask them twice because she knew they were hungry. Having mopped the floor earlier in the day, Rosita had the girls rinse, and wipe their hands and feet because she did not want them to dirty her clean floor.

In the weeks Marci had known Juanita, this was the first time she was going to meet her mother. As soon as she walked into the kitchen all she could say was, "Oh my gosh, it's you!" Feeling her face burning with embarrassment, Marci apologized as Juanita and her mother looked at Marci as if she had lost her mind. Marci then told Rosita how she saw her in church. Unable to stop, Marci told her how pretty she looked in her pink fitted suit, and her veiled pillbox hat. "It looked like you had stepped out of a fashion magazine, and I could not stop staring at you." Marci knew she should stop before she went too far, but she couldn't.

"When you were scolding your boys, I got scared because you looked like a mean woman. I was glad my mother made me turn around and pay attention to the priest. However, you Rafael, I think you must be a nice man because your eyes are happy ones."

When Rosita heard this, she coughed and almost choked on the coffee she was drinking. Rafael smiled broadly, and said, "See honey, Marci is a smart girl. She knows a good man when she sees one."

Juanita knew Marci was babbling, and had gotten herself into something she could not get out of, so she kicked her foot. That was just what she needed, and Marci then told Rosita she was pleased to meet her. Rosita smiled and asked Marci how she wanted her hamburger. Marci replied she wanted it well done. Now that the awkward minute was over, everything was back to normal. As Marci was eating the hamburger, she told Rosita it was delicious, and better than any she had eaten at any restaurant.

While they were eating, Rafael told the girls if ever an ant bit them, mud could relieve the sting. Not knowing any better Marci asked if she had to mix the mud with the straw. Rafael chuckled, and said, "No, all you do is get a little bit of dirt, spit on it, and put it on the bite.

"Spit on it, oh that is gross. It's sick, and only boys do that!" Marci exclaimed as she continued eating.

Rosita told Rafael not to say anymore as Marci was eating, and he was upsetting her stomach. By the way Marci was eating, Rafael didn't think she was getting all that upset. The conversation then focused on what Juanita and Marci would do for the remainder of the day. Marci said she was going to go home to take a nap, as she was tired. She also had a couple of blisters on her hands from digging the hole and she needed to put a Band-Aid on them.

That evening the rain came and everything got a good soaking. When the rain started, Marci called Juanita so she would check on the adobes because she did not want anything happening to their science project. The rain continued for a couple of hours, but Rafael had already placed a plastic over the adobes.

Monday, Ms. Fastle asked her students if they had started their project. Some of the groups had, and she told the rest they didn't have much time. When class was over, Marci and Juanita went to check on their adobes. When they asked Rafael, if they were ready, he told them they would be completely dry by the weekend, and they would continue working on their project.

Friday evening, Marci went to sleep at Juanita's house so they could get up early and work on their project. Marci could not remember if she and Juanita talked all night, or if they watched TV until they fell asleep. All she knew was that they were finally going to get started on their adobe house. This time, Marci woke up very early, and went outside. However, it did her no good to get up so early because she was at a loss as to what the next step was. When it was time for them to continue working on their house, Marci asked, "If she should go for the glue, they were going to use." Rafael chuckled, and told Marci "They weren't going to use the kind of glue she was thinking he was going to use.""

Once again, Rafael had the girls mix the mud as they did the first time. This time, he had them use the hoe to get the work done. Having mixed the mud, the girls had to stack one adobe on top of the other with mud between the adobes to hold them together. To make it easier to understand, Rafael told them to pretend they were eating pancakes.

"To begin with, you put butter and syrup on the bottom pancake, and then you place the other one on the top. Because the syrup is runny, it goes all over and it allows you to position the pancake how you want it. That is how the mud you will put between the adobes will work except the mud is thicker."

Now that the girls understood, they started to build their science project. "Should you put too much mud between the adobes, it will ooze out on the sides. After you scrape it off, put it on the top of the next adobe."

Now that Juanita and Marci were building the adobe house, Marci asked Rafael several questions. By midafternoon, the girls had completed their project, and once again had to let the sun do its job and dry their house. When their house was completed, they could move it wherever they wanted. With the research done, and the report typed, it was time for the group to write their questions for their project. This was actually an easy task as they got most of their information from Rafael, but they also had information the other members of their team researched at the library. At their next meeting, a student drew a sketch of the regular adobe, and the ones they used on the house the girls built to include in their report.

On their final meeting, the group invited Rafael and Rosita to Marci's house, as she wanted them to meet her parents. "Besides, we need your help one more time." This time, the group wanted to know what he thought of the questions they came up with, and if he had anything to add. Rafael listened to the questions, and told them he thought they had all done an excellent job. He could not think of anything else to add to their report, or to their questions. Then Marci asked her father to take a picture of the group with Rafael to place in front of their project. After Travis took the picture, the kids thanked Mr. Gabaldon for his help, and Travis invited him to watch TV.

In the meantime, Rosita and Marci were in the kitchen drinking a cup of coffee while the kids put the final touches on their project. Days before it was due, Juanita and Marci hung curtains in the house, put a welcome mat outside the door, and put Popsicle sticks across the house to make a roof. The girls asked Rafael if he would take a picture of them standing next to it.

When the adobe house was brought into the classroom, the student judges had already read, and judged a couple of the projects. To everyone's surprise, these students were taking their assignment very serious. Now it was time for Marci's group to have the judges examine their project. Seeing how serious the student judges were about their assignment, anyone would have thought they were professionals. They even dressed the part. Even though there were two more projects to judge, the judges were confident they would have the results by the end of the week, if not by Tuesday. For the students whose projects were already judged, it was a big relief that it was over, and all they had to do was to wait for the results. As the judges examined the projects, they filled the forms they created. They didn't want to be doing everything at the last minute; after all, Ms. Fastle was counting on them to do a good job.

Friday school was dismissed early because of a school assembly, so the students in Ms. Fastle's class now had to wait until Tuesday before the judges disclosed their results. Once the judges were ready to report the results on the projects, Ms. Fastle wanted them to tell the class what they learned. Ernest being the spokesperson for the group said, "This has been an eye-opener for us, and to say it was boring would be a lie. We never knew how interesting learning could be, and from each of your projects we learned so much. Had it not been for Ms. Fastle's faith in us, we would probably be sitting in the back of the classroom making snide remarks. All that changed, thanks to our teacher who really cares for her students. When we meet with Ms. Fastle, we gave her our reasons for our decisions. She agreed with us, and this is how we rated your projects."

"Our fifth choice is the beehive. We think this group could have used something else other than cotton, and glue to make their project. The report was poorly written, and the group did not put much effort into their project. The fourth choice is the bird's nest. This was better than the beehive, but the materials used did not hold together when we put a marble in it. The research was good, but the questions were too complicated for children to understand. Our third choice is the ant farm. By the time, we were done checking it some of the ants got out of the cardboard maze, and bit us. The research was taken right out of the encyclopedia, and not much thought was put into the questions. Our second place is the beaver's dam. This was good, and could have been built by an actual beaver. When we ran water through, and over it, the water held, and any beaver would be proud to claim it as their own. Your downfall was that you didn't submit your report along with your questions. This left us with the adobe house. The judges, along with Ms. Fastle thought the adobe house was the best in every respect. Everything was so perfect from the Popsicle roof, down to the curtains, the welcome mat, and the family figures. Most of all, this team not only did their research at the library, but they got information from someone who actually had experience in building an adobe house. To add to their report, and their questions, they even took the time to draw a sketch of the adobes, and took a picture of Rafael Gabaldon who guided them. They also included the measurements of the adobes, and how many Popsicle sticks they used on the roof. As far as we could see, they were the only ones who actually used information they learned from their classes. Overall, this adobe house was rated excellent." When Juanita's group heard their project won they were extremely excited. They were even happier when Ms. Fastle gave them an A plus.

Parent-Teacher Conference was coming up, and after the judging was over, Ms. Fastle told her class all of their projects would be displayed so the parents could see what they did. Some of the students were not happy, but they had no choice. Juanita's group along with the second and third place winners wanted everyone to see how they used their skills. Now it was Ms. Fastle's turn to address the students, especially the student judges.

"I am extremely proud of all of you for working so hard on your projects. However, I am prouder of the judges who did not walk out on their assignment. Not only did Ernest and his group take it seriously, but they also taught me a lesson. I must tell you it has been a pleasure working with you. To let you know how pleased I am that you were so responsible with your assignment, not only am I giving you an A plus, but you do not have to take the final exam."

Ernest and his friends were shocked Ms. Fastle thought they deserved the grade she gave them. But they too learned how much fun learning could be, and they promised never to interrupt Ms. Fastle or any teacher ever again. The best thing about this science project was the sudden change in the four student judges. For the students who did not want to participate in the science fair, they actually taught their classmates a lesson. They were like the pebble that is tossed across a pond and sends ripples that grow.

Now that Marci and Caleb were in school, Marci truly believed they were closer as a family than when they lived in Virginia. Maybe it was because they were growing up and seeing things from a different perspective. Whatever it was, Marci was enjoying every minute of her new life, and saw her life taking a turn for the best.

Sewing Lesson

"Juanita, can you tell me where your mother buys your clothes?" I would like to ask my mother if she will take me there. Juanita thanked Marci for the compliment, and said, "Marci, you remind me of my mom's friend whose husband is a judge. She also asked mom where she buys our clothes because she has taken her daughters to the most expensive stores in Albuquerque, but they don't like the clothes because they aren't like the ones we wear." She then told her the clothes we wore were not store bought. "Mom makes most of our clothes. However, she also tailors what others give us. When my mom is done with the clothes given to us, no one can tell they were hand-me-downs. My mother loves to sew, and is a wonderful cook. Not only has she taught me how to sew, but how to cook and bake. Today is my birthday, and this is my birthday gift from my mother and father. Isn't it pretty," she asked as she twirled around to model her new skirt and blouse. Juanita having told Marci, it was her birthday, Marci wished her a happy birthday, and asked her "if her mother was going to give her a party." "No," Marci replied, "Mom is bringing my birthday cake to my homeroom class so that the kids in my class can share it with me."

After Juanita told Marci it was her birthday, "she asked her friend if she knew how to sew and cook." Marci was very impressed with Juanita's talents and told her she never thought she needed to learn how to do either. Being the only girl, she did not think it was necessary. All Marci had to do was go to the department stores and selected whatever she wanted.

"Gee Marci, if you really want to learn, I can teach you how to sew." Marci jumped at the idea that Juanita could teach her something she never thought of doing. She even stopped walking, and looked at Juanita.

"Are you serious, do you really think I can learn," she asked. "It sure would be great if I could surprise my mother."

"Well we shall soon find out. If you want, we can start anytime you are ready. I can show you how to do needlepoint, and after you finish it, you can hang it up in your room. Then, I will show you how to use a sewing machine."

As the girls resumed their walk, Juanita told Marci "The first thing she would teach her was how to thread a needle, and then she would show her how to follow instructions on patterns. Once I learned to sew, the first thing I made my mom was an apron, and she still has it. If you want, you too can make one for your mother, and when you finish it, you can give it to her. She will probably be as surprised as my mother was when I gave it to her."

Juanita was going too fast for Marci, but she loved every minute, and Marci could hardly wait to get started.

The remainder of the day, Marci thought of nothing else, but that she was going to learn something not even her mother knew how to do. Knowing she was going to learn how to sew made everything else so unimportant. Could she be any happier? Maybe, but Marci was not going to ruin her mood by thinking what could possibly go wrong. This was an extremely wonderful day for her, and she wanted the mood to last. For as much as Marci hated Mondays, today she didn't care if Jan and her friends bullied her when they came her way.

When Marci got home, her mother took her books as she normally did, and asked Marci if she wanted to go to the corner store to get a coke. "Yes, Mom, I would love to go with you." Marie was not used to seeing her daughter so happy and asked, her if she had a good day at school. "Why do you ask?" "You just seem to be extremely happy. It seems like you have something special on your mind." "Well I was the only one too ace my math test, and I'm happy about that."

That week, Tuesday and Wednesday came around rather quickly, but Thursday and Friday were so slow in coming. Then it was Friday evening, and Marci wasn't sure if she could sleep that night, but that did not matter. Tomorrow she was going to learn how to sew. Saturday morning, Marci got up, cleaned her room, took a shower, ate breakfast, and went to Juanita's house. As she rounded the corner, Marci saw Rafael was feeding his chickens. When Rafael saw Marci get off her bike, he asked her, "What are you doing there so early in the morning. "Juanita is asleep, and she normally sleeps late on Saturday."

"Asleep? How can she be sleeping so late, it's already eight-thirty."

"Well you know Juanita; she can sleep all day if we let her. So what brings you here so early in the morning?"

Without a moment's hesitation, Marci told Rafael, "Juanita was going to teach her how to sew. I'm so excited because I don't even know how to thread a needle much less sew a button." "Well, Juanita will be a good teacher, and you will learn a lot."

Rafael then asked Marci, "if she would like to have a cup of coffee." "I would love the company, and this will give me a chance to know Juanita's friend better." Again, this was something new for Marci.

Having fed his chickens, Rafael and Marci went in to drink a cup of coffee. "So how do you like your coffee?" Rafael asked. "I don't know I have never had a cup of coffee, but it sure smells good. Mother always told my brother and me it would stunt our growth. Besides, I do not want to shrink, so I have stayed away from things that are not good for me. Sometimes the aroma of coffee smells so good, but I have never asked if I could have some."

"Hum, well do you think your mother will get angry if you drink half a cup of coffee with me?"

"If you think it will be okay, but do you think that it will stunt my growth?"

"Well I have been drinking coffee since I was two years old, and it did not stop me from growing," Rafael replied.

Marci watched Rafael pour a small amount of coffee in one cup, and fill another cup for himself. Two teaspoons of sugar and some canned Carnation milk went into his cup. Marci's coffee had fresh milk and looked more like chocolate milk, but she was able to taste the coffee, and it wasn't bad. In fact, after her second sip, she thought it was very good. Before Marci finished drinking her coffee, she told Rafael,

"I won't tell my mother I had a cup of coffee if you don't. Maybe we can keep this a secret between us." Rafael smiled at the little girl who sat across from him, and he promised he would keep her secret. He could not remember when he was asked to keep a secret from anyone other than his children, and it made him feel special.

Having woken up, and curious as to who Rafael was talking to, Rosita walked into the kitchen. When she saw Marci, and after Rafael poured her a cup of coffee, she started preparing breakfast for the family. "So Marci, how long have you been here?" Rosita asked.

"I got here at eight-thirty," Marci replied.

Juanita finally woke up, and was surprised to see Marci sitting at the kitchen table drinking coffee with her father. Up until that day, Marci had no idea Juanita came from a large family. Marci always thought the boys and girls walking with her were Juanita's friends. On that day, Marci was introduced to the entire Gabaldon family.

After the family had eaten breakfast, Juanita asked her friend if she wanted to go outside to play. Marci exclaimed, "Go outside and play! Juanita don't you remember you're going to teach me how to sew." "Oh Marci, I'm so sorry, I completely forgot all about it. Let me get my sewing basket so we can get started." Going to the closet to get her sewing basket, Juanita told her friend, "She was going to start by teaching her how to thread a needle.""

"There's a lot to learn, but we will go slow, and before you know it, you are going to be an expert," Juanita told Marci. "First, I want you to get the hang of threading a needle and learn how to follow instructions. With that, the girls went into the living room where the lighting was better.

Threading a needle was not as easy as Juanita made it seem. Again, and again, Marci tried to thread the needle. First, she put the thread into her mouth, moistened it, and as she was pulling it out of her mouth, she had to flatten it with her teeth. Then she had to poke it through the eye of the needle.

"Juanita, I can't even see the eye, how am I to thread it?"

"You'll learn in no time," Juanita responded.

When Marci was finally able to push the thread through the needle, Juanita showed her how to use a needle threader. "Gee Juanita, why didn't you show me this trick in the first place? Then I wouldn't have had such a hard time."

"If you want to learn how to sew, you have to start from the beginning, just like I was taught," Juanita replied.

Going back to her closet Juanita brought a blouse that had a couple of buttons missing. "Okay Marci, now you are going to learn how to sew buttons on a blouse. The first thing you have to do is line the missing buttons with the buttonhole. Other than learning how to thread a needle, knowing how to sew buttons is one of the most important lessons you will learn. When you finish sewing the buttons on my blouse, you can go home and do the same on whatever item of clothing you have."

While Juanita was teaching Marci how to sew buttons on a blouse, she told Marci her dream was to one day be a fashion designer. "I want to learn all I can about the latest fashion, and see what clothes other women wear," she said. Juanita then showed Marci some of her sketches, and asked Marci to tell her what she thought. Not knowing what to expect, Marci was surprised that Juanita could draw something so beautiful. Juanita, "I love them. When I become rich and famous, will you design my dresses?" Juanita laughed, and told Marci she would. Marci got back to her sewing lesson, and following Juanita's instructions, she placed the needle on the reverse side of the blouse and pushed it through. Instead of the needle going through the buttonhole, it went into Marci's thumb and it bled for a second so Juanita gave her a Band-Aid. Marci continued, and she pricked her finger a couple more times. That was when Juanita taught her how to use a thimble. This was just another safety device to help Marci from pricking her finger again.

"Juanita, I think I am doing something wrong because the button is not staying on the blouse the thread keeps coming out."

"Let me see what is going on. Marci, I'm so sorry," Juanita replied. "I forgot to teach you how to make a knot at the end of the thread. This is good that it happened because as you saw, the thread was just going in and out of the material. Get the thread and twirl the thread around the needle. Once you do that slide the thread down the needle, and you have your knot. But sometimes the knot doesn't take, and you have to repeat the process."

No matter how long Marci tried, this was harder than threading the needle, but she finally got the hang of that too. When Marci finished sewing the missing buttons on the blouse, Juanita inspected her work.

"Marci this is very good. You are a good student."

Marci was so excited at having completed her first sewing lesson, she was ready to go home and do the same for her blouses. Marci's first sewing lesson was over, and before she got ready to leave, Juanita gave her a needlepoint kit plus regular needles to sew her buttons. This was so she could continue practicing her sewing. Juanita opened the package, and showed Marci how to read the instructions. She said, "This is yours to do at home, and there is no rush because this is your project. If you have any problems, come over and I will help you. It isn't as hard as you might think. All you need to do is to pay attention to what you are doing," Juanita told Marci. Once Marci was done, she was to show it to her, and then Juanita would teach her how to embroider.

When Marci got home, her mother asked her what she had done at Juanita's house.

"Not much, we just sat around, talked, washed dishes, and I helped Juanita clean her room," Marci replied. She knew this was not true, but she could not tell her mother what she did. She wanted to surprise her. Days Marci was not learning how to sew, she looked forward to the weekends. That was when she could sleep as late as she wanted. However, on this particular Saturday, Marci's mother woke her up from a delightfully sound sleep.

Tía Lupe Castillo

"Marci, wake up. Juanita's on the phone, and wants to talk to you, and she said it is urgent."

"Mom, what time is it?"

"Seven o'clock and you know Juanita likes to sleep as much as you do, so it must be serious."

When Marci answered the telephone, Juanita was crying. She asked Mari if she could please go over because she had to talk to her.

"Juanita, give me a couple of minutes to get dressed, and I will be right over." After she hung up, Marci told her mother she had to go to Juanita's house because something was wrong.

"I'm not sure what time I will be home, but I will call you."

With that, Marci got on her bike, and peddled as fast as she could to meet Juanita down the road. However, Juanita had not left her house, and Marci saw her friend sitting on the porch step. Marci sat next to her friend, and Juanita told Marci about the phone call her mother received last night. "She said the person who called her mother, said she was going to hurt herself. Marci, I heard Mom say, "Lupe, is that you?" She begged her not to do anything, as she would be right over. Mother was so scared, she ran out of the house in her pajamas. As mother rushed out of the house, I got up, and put a pot of coffee on the stove. I also swept, and mopped the floors as I waited for her to get back. Mom did not get back for several hours, and when she came home, she looked tired, and extremely worried. Mom was glad I had made a fresh pot of coffee because she said she needed it. I poured her a cup of coffee, and asked her what was going on. Mom told me about the phone call, and said the caller laughed and hung up. Thinking Tía Lupe was having a relapse my mom drove to her house. When she arrived, Tía Lupe was looking out the window as if she was waiting for someone. Tía Lupe heard Mom pounding on the door, and when she opened the door, Tía Lupe had a knife in her hand. She claimed she was cutting meat for supper so she wouldn't have to do it later. My mother was scared because Tía Lupe kept looking at her, and then at the door, as if she thought Mom was going to run. Mom was scared because she didn't know what my Tía was thinking, but pretended she wasn't. My mother also said, Tía Lupe 'told her that she was ironing', "but the ironing board wasn't up, and the basket was empty." When my aunt asked her why she was there so late at night, my mom told her about the phone call, and my aunt laughed. She told, her, "To go home because she was okay and very tired." Mom knew she couldn't do anything so she got in the car and started to drive home. Something made mom turn around, and when she passed by the house my Tía was sitting outside with her dog. My mother didn't know what Tía Lupe was doing, but since her son was thrown off a bull and trampled to death, she hasn't been the same.

After Dr. Brewer examined Tía Lupe, he told her family Lupe had a nervous breakdown. After she saw her son die participating in a sport he loved, and one she had asked him not to join, she couldn't take it."

Tía Lupe must have thought everyone had abandoned her when she was taken to the hospital. The doctor asked the family to stay away from the hospital until they were able to evaluate my aunt. From that day forward, my aunt changed and she blamed the family for everything that happened to her. Until my mom told me what happened to my Tía Lupe, I didn't know why my aunt acted as she did, but now that I know, that hasn't change my love for her. By the time my mom told me what happened, I was angry because if someone thought it was funny to pull such a horrible prank on my mother, I did not think it was funny. Marci, I just had to call you because I don't know what to do. I think my aunt is very sick, and I need you to go with me.

Juanita told Marci "they had to go to her Tía Lupe's house right away, as she may have done something to herself." The girls peddled as fast as they could, and Juanita told Marci how her Tía Lupe suffers from severe depression and migraine headaches since she lost her son, and was admitted to the psychiatric ward. "On several occasions, she has told us she is going to harm herself, and we never know if she is serious. Tía Lupe has been very depressed lately, and I am afraid she might do something bad."

Normally it took Juanita a half hour to reach her aunt's house, but today the girls were there in less time. When they arrived, Tía Lupe's dog Gonzo, started to bark and tipped her someone was outside. Soon as the girls were near the elm tree, they could see Tía Lupe in the kitchen, and Juanita jumped off her bike. Marci leaned hers against the tree, but Juanita didn't care if her bike fell down, or not, all she wanted was to make sure her aunt was okay. As she banged on the door, Juanita yelled, "Tía Lupe, it's me Juanita," but Lupe took her time opening the door. When she did, she had a smirk on her face. "Come in Juanita, what's wrong?" As Juanita and Marci went indoors they saw the ironing board was up, and a basket full of clothes next to it. Juanita had seen Tía Lupe standing by the sink, and she now thought she was probably pouring water into the steam iron. Juanita composed herself, and as she did, she saw Tía Lupe still had a smirk on her face, and Juanita didn't like how her aunt was looking and talking to them. Seemed as if Tía Lupe was taunting them as she asked Juanita what was going on. Juanita then told her aunt about the phone call her mother got last night. "No wonder your mother was scared when she came over. You know me, when I cannot sleep I start ironing, and last night was one of those nights. I told your mother I was all right, and she knows I would never do anything to hurt my family, or friends by hurting myself. I just don't know what

Rosita was thinking when she came, but I don't think she believed me," Lupe told Juanita. Knowing Tía Lupe wasn't telling them the truth, Juanita didn't say anything. Marci was not sure what to believe, as she did not know what was going on. Lupe did not seem to be distressed, or concerned about anything other than getting her clothes ironed. Not convinced her aunt was all right, Juanita helped her with her ironing. When she had ironed all of the clothes in the basket, the girls had no choice but to leave. Convinced her aunt was okay the girls then said good-bye and left.

This time Rosita was the one who had to wait for her daughter to come home. When the girls walked into the kitchen, Rosita told Juanita to tell her everything she had seen. Juanita told her mother she didn't see anything different, and that she helped her aunt iron the clothes. When Rosita saw her daughter was visibly shaken, and was crying, she put her arms around her daughter. Everyone knew Tía Lupe was Juanita's favorite aunt.

Later that afternoon Rosita sent Juanita and Marci to Tía Lupe's house with some red chili. Not wanting to arouse suspicion, Rosita told the girls to tell Lupe, the chili was for her supper. But when the girls arrived, Tía Lupe was sitting outside on the children's swing. Marci saw Tía Lupe had a faraway look on her face, and it sent shivers down her spine. It even made the hair on the back of her neck stand up. Marci didn't know if Juanita was scared, but she was, and Marci was hoping Lupe had not noticed. Not wanting Tía Lupe to see how scared she was, Marci asked her how she was doing. "I know why you are here, and you can't fool me. I learned a lot when I was in the mental hospital, and I am not afraid to tell you what I feel," She told the girls, "You are all liars and I hate all of you." Juanita did not care what her aunt said as she went up to her, and hugged her. She told her she still loved her, and was not afraid of hearing anything she had to say. An hour or so passed, and the girls left with Tía Lupe still sitting on the swing. As the girls left, they waved good-bye, and Tía Lupe managed to smile and wave back. Juanita and Marci never talked about it, but Marci wondered if Tía

Lupe had indeed made the telephone call to see who loved her enough to go check on her.

County & State Fair

Our Lady of Belen fiestas was just the beginning of events for the residents of Valencia County. Soon the residents would bring their arts, crafts, canned fruits, vegetables, chili, salsa, clothing, art displays, and other items they wanted to enter. Each one hoping his or her entry would be the one to win them a blue ribbon.

By this time, Marci's parents had practically adopted Ernest, Isaiah and Isidro into the family, and it was as if Marci now had to put up with three immature boys. Travis and his family had never seen so many items in one small building. Of course, they had never been to a County Fair, and were amazed at the beautiful things the residents brought. Looking around they saw many blue, red, yellow, white, and Best of Show Ribbons on the entries the judges selected.

On the day Travis and his family went to the County Fair, five judges were sampling pies to see which pie would win the Best of Show Ribbon. The room was full as the contestants waited for the judges to announce whose pie they liked the best. Tension mounted even higher, and the contestants looked nervous as the last pie was being judged. After the pie was sampled, the judge announced there was a tie between the caramel pecan pie, and the banana cream pie. The tension mounted higher, and no one spoke a word, as the two pies were sampled one more time.

After much deliberation, the judges returned, and this time everyone would find out which pie the judges liked best. Returning to the table the head judge picked up the Best of Show ribbon, and two blue ribbons. Clearing his throat and speaking into the microphone the judge told the contestants how much they enjoyed sampling all of the pies. "I know any of us would be happy to have a slice of your pie with our morning coffee, but we also agreed there is one pie that melted in our mouths. So we would like to meet the individual who baked the banana coconut cream pie."

When seventy-two-year old Urban Montoya heard his pie won, he was overwhelmed. Both he and his wife made their way through the crowd to accept his prize winning ribbons. When the judge was going to present him with the award, his wife, who was just as excited, slapped her husband on his butt. As she did this, he sneezed, and his toupee slid down his face, and fell on top of the pie the judge was holding. Instead of shaking the winner's hand, the judge instinctively caught Urban's toupee as he was going to accept his ribbons. With the judge holding on to the toupee, Urban reclaimed his hair and the ribbons from the judge.

Once it was back on his head, he was asked the secret to his flaky piecrust and filling. He told the judge it was his wife's secret recipe, and that this was the second time he had tried his hand at baking. The scene created such a comical sight everyone including the old man and the judge laughed. The second blue ribbon went to Marie Nadine who baked the caramel pecan pie. Laughing at what had taken place, the girls went into the clothing section. While Juanita and Marci were looking at the entries on display, Marci came across Juanita's entry. "Juanita, your entry has two blue ribbons!" Marci exclaimed. Juanita rushed to see which ribbons she had actually been awarded. When she saw her entry had indeed won both a blue ribbon, and the Best of Show, Juanita screamed at the top of her lungs.

"Juanita, that is beautiful, do you think if I continue to practice my sewing I will be able to sew like you?" Marci asked. Smiling, Juanita replied, "Only if you practice like I do."

As the girls exited the building, they had seen all the entries, and now it was time for Isaiah to compete in the rodeo competition. By this time, the bleachers were filling up as children five to ten-years-old were going to participate in the Mutton riding event. Unlike the older competitors, the children were not allowed to use spurs, but were required to wear helmets to prevent head injuries. This, like any of the other competitions required skill from the children who rode the sheep and rams. To the children participating, this could be their first event for possible future rodeo competitions. As the children competed for the mutton buckle, many were thrown from the sheep or rams. Fortunately, the animals had plenty of wool for the children to hold on too. Yet, some of the younger children cried as they were tossed to the ground, and butted by the sheep. While some cried, others dusted themselves off and went to sit with their parents.

When the clowns saw children crying they went to comfort the child, and walked him or her to the bleachers where their parents were sitting. For the children who entered the Mutton completion but did not ride the sheep or rams; they competed in a race to see who ran the fastest; the animal, or the child. When these events were over, all of the contestants waited to see who scored the highest points.

Once the Mutton competition was over the horse, and bull riders were ready and anxious to compete. Unlike the younger children, the older contestants had no wool to hold on to, and they were anxious to start the competition. Earlier in the day, Ernest explained how riding a wild horse is like riding a bike over extremely rough terrain. "This requires a lot of work and dedication, but we compete for a new saddle; the championship belt buckle; a trophy, and cash up to three-thousand dollars." Then Ernest told them how they are only allowed to use a rig made out of leather which has a handle to help get on the horse. How riding any horse demands precise timing between the rider, and the horse. In the meantime, the horse tries its best to buck the rider off his back. But the most dangerous of all events is riding a bull like Thunderbolt, Insanity, or Tornado who could weigh anywhere from 2000 pounds and up."

After a dozen or so riders had ridden their horse, it was Ernest's turn. As he mounted the horse assigned to him, Ernest had a serious and determined look on his face. The horse wasn't happy to have anyone mount him, and before Ernest got the horse out of the pen, it was kicking his hind legs up in the air. Ernest knew he could not let the horse feel how anxious he was to get this over with and how badly he wanted to break the winning score. After Ernest mounted the horse, and the gate swung opened, the horse burst out of the pen. This is what Ernest had trained for all year, and his time to enter a high score started. Marci could hardly take her eyes off Ernest as the horse tried his best to buck him off his back. Marci watched as the horses' feet kicked the dirt, and his hind legs went up as far back as they could. All the while Ernest held the reigns with one hand as tight as he could. At the same time, his other hand was waving wildly in the air. Ernest tried his best so he wouldn't be thrown off and kicked by the horse as others had been. It seemed as if Ernest was on the horse for more than eight seconds. Yet, Marci could not get over how Ernest's hat remained on his head while the horses kicked, and bucked.

Hours passed, and when the competition ended, Ernest knew his score wasn't good enough for first place. Even though he had his heart on winning the grand prize, second place, and one thousand dollars was not bad. Ernest may not have won this time, but he was already thinking of next year's competition and what he would do different. The final event was the bull riding competition. To Marci, only those whose brains were so rattled and didn't have enough sense to stay away rode Thunderbolt, Tornado, or Insanity. Riding a horse is rattling enough, but riding a bull is like using a jackhammer when you have no experience. When the bull riding competition started, Marci was amazed to see how high the bull's hind legs kicked; how quickly he jumped up; and with little effort turned from one side to the other. This time, the clowns sought extra protection from the bulls as they got into barrels to protect themselves from the bull kicking them, and possibly stomping him to death. The clowns were ready to distract the bull when he bucked the rider off his back. No matter how much the clowns tried to protect the riders, several of the contestants were injured, by the bull's dangerous horns, and rushed to the hospital. Ohers went into the safety zone limping, but that didn't stop the competition. Even though the bull's horns were cut at the tip to prevent him from stabbing the cowboys, Thunderbolt managed to toss one of the clowns into the air and cracked his ribs. Insanity stomped on another clown, and he too, was rushed to the nearest hospital. News from the hospital filtered down letting the spectators know the condition of the injured contestants, or clowns, as the last bull rider had his turn.

As Travis was driving home, Juanita commented how the state fair was coming up in September. "The New Mexico State Fair is held in Albuquerque, and runs for seventeen days. It kicks off as the county fair did in Belen, but the state fair is much bigger. This is where residents from throughout the state bring their arts, crafts, flowers, livestock, and much more. The Midway is many, many times bigger, and for me it is hard to choose which ride I like best. My parents have taken us every year, and we have so much fun. But this year is going to be even better because I can take you to the Midway where the rides are, and we can eat from the different food booths," Juanita told Marci.

Months passed since Marci had written to Vanessa and this time, she told her about the things Juanita taught her. About Tía Lupe, and how wrong she was in not wanting to move to New Mexico. How extremely hot New Mexico is, and how living in the desert was not all-bad. In fact, she liked many things about her new state. Marci included how she wished Vanessa could come visit her, but left the part out where she wanted to go back to Virginia. Instead, she told her about the evening her parents took her and Caleb through an Indian village. How scared she was when her mother told her they were going to a pueblo to see 'real live Indians' who were celebrating an important feast day.

By the time we arrived, it was late in the afternoon, and I was scared because I did not know what was going to happen to us. I even made Caleb hide, and for as much as he bugs me, I did not want him to get hurt. Of course, he wanted to see who was going to be scalped. I could not hold him down, and I remembered how the Indians used to scalp the men in the movies we watched. How they took the women and children, as their hostages, and I was afraid that was going to happen to us. When I was brave enough to look out the window, I saw Indian men carrying wood, and piling it near what looked like a gray doghouse.

There was also smoke coming out, and the Indian women were taking things out of the doghouse. As we drove around the outskirts of the village, I continued to hide so the Indians would not see me. Then dad turned a corner and Caleb screamed, "Dad, I saw a dog drag something away." Father told Caleb to stop scaring me because nothing happened. Caleb laughed as he told daddy he didn't see what he saw. He was too busy keeping his eyes on the road so he wouldn't run over anyone. Dad finally parked the car, and we walked to the center of the village where we heard drums, and Native American Indians chanting. There, we saw other visitors watching the Indians dance in their traditional clothing. Some of the Indians were half-naked with red and black lightning streaks painted on their faces like those on TV. Others had feathers on their hair, and some of the younger children had a beaded headband around their forehead with a feather on the back. While I was watching the eagle dancers, I watched how they moved as freely, and graceful as a bird in flight. If their arms were wings, I know they would have flown into the sky, and soared gracefully into the clouds, and above the dancers. Vanessa, I was so intrigued with the dancers I forgot how scared I was until the dancing stopped. When Caleb nudged me to move, two Indian boys walked to where we were standing. One boy was dressed in his traditional clothing with many tiny bells around his ankles. The other boy was the eagle dancer. Not able to see his face, I looked into his eyes. Vanessa, he talked to me and said, "Hi. We heard you moved here not too long ago. I have seen you in my math class, and tried to talk to you. Do you know I have never seen anyone with hair as red, and skin as white as yours? With the sun going down, your skin looks like snow. Are you what people call an albino?" Not knowing what to do or say, I froze. My feet felt as if they were made of lead, and my mouth felt as if it was glued shut, as I continued to look into his eyes. The Indian boy said, "I hope you aren't afraid of us." To add to my fear, his friend asked, "If I could hear how the drums and my heart have the same rhythm. We think that is good because we know you can be one of us," the masked Indian boy said. He must have seen the horrified look on my face because he started to laugh as they walked back to the dancing circle. Turning around the dancer told me, "He would come get me." Vanessa, you will never know how scared I was! I thought he had selected me as his sacrifice to their god, and I didn't know what to do. I knew they have special powers no one else has because we watched that on TV. Petrified as I was, I could not move, and at that moment, I remembered the story our teacher Ms. Andersen told us about the Indians who held up a stagecoach. Remember how she told us about the renegade Indians who killed some of the white men, and took the gold, and hid it so that others would not find it? With my red hair, and my fair skin, I was afraid I was going to be held hostage. I thought he wanted to exchange me for information to the gold. Then I looked up, and saw dark clouds looming in the distance ready to take the souls of those of us chosen as their sacrifice. Guess God heard my plea to be rescued because Mom showed up, and told me it was time to go home. Now I know how the white women on TV felt when they were taken from their family, and the wagon train. Vanessa, my heart was beating so fast I thought I was going to faint so I held mother's hand as tight as I could. I wanted her to know when I let go should the Indian boy change his mind, and come after me for his sacrifice.

As we were getting into our car, and on our way home, my mom asked if I was sick. "You are as white as a sheet," she said, all I could say was that "I was okay". Now that I was with my mother and father, I knew I was safe, and they would protect me. Caleb would have handed me to the Indian boy just to hear me beg him to save me. Vanessa, you just do not know how thankful I was to be alive, and with my parents. When I was in the car, I sat back, and relaxed. I looked up to see the stars, but the clouds were starting to cover them. Never have I been so happy to be where I felt safe. Then I decided I had to write everything that happened should I happen to disappear. I never want to forget how sacred I was so I went into my bedroom, and started to write my letter. Vanessa, I know much of what I wrote probably makes no sense to you, but I just want to tell you what I am doing. If my parents ever contact you and ask if you know where I am, you will know who took me, and why. Well my dearest friend, I have to end my letter because I am very sleepy. Please write back. With that, Marci ended her letter to her friend, and went to bed.

Thinking she had left her fears in the letter she wrote, Marci found that was not so. Now that she was going to sleep, the wind started to blow, and the lightning lit up the starless night. Thunder boomed, and lightning continued to light up the dark sky as Marci hid under the blankets. As the thunder and lightning moved further into the distance, Marci was able to relax. No sooner had she fallen asleep than she heard unusual noises coming from the kitchen. She also heard something, or someone trying to get in. Frantically, Marci knocked on her parent's bedroom door, and told her father she heard someone trying to break in. Travis jumped out of bed, and ran into the kitchen. Turning the kitchen lights on, he saw the door was locked, but the screen door was open. Cautiously, Travis looked out to see if anyone was outside. When he opened the kitchen door, he realized he had not locked it. With the wind blowing as hard as it was, it caused the screen door to open and close.

To reassure Marci it was only the wind, he took her into Caleb's room. As Travis opened the drapes, a flash of lightning streaked across the sky, and the rain came down. Travis then saw the tree branches were scratching against the house. Marci wasn't convinced it was nothing more than the wind, so she asked her mother if she would sleep with her.

"Honey what's wrong," her mother asked.

"Nothing, guess the thunder, lightning and wind are making so much noise I am not able to sleep."

The truth was that Marci did not want to be alone as she thought someone was coming after her, and this was what was scaring her. How could she be certain it was the trees scratching the wall, and not something or someone else? How could it be the wind opening, and closing the kitchen door when she locked it? Marci did not want to tell her mother about the Indian god who was angry and coming for her. How could she tell her mother what she was really thinking? Putting that aside, Marci wanted to make sure what her father told her last night was true. She wanted to see the tree branch that was rubbing against the house that scared her, and could not wait to go outside. Last night's rain made every thing smell so clean and fresh.

Sunday when Travis took his family to church Marci thanked the saints for taking care of her and her family. The weekend was over and it was a new week at school. When Marci went to get her books from her locker, she saw some Indian boys standing by the wall. She smiled at them, and was glad her class was a few feet away from her locker. How she wished she had gotten her books earlier because she was afraid of what might happen. She knew she had to walk away pretending she was not afraid of any of them.

One of the Indian boys said, "Hey guys, this is the white girl I was telling you about. Her skin is even whiter, and her hair redder in daylight."

Marci recognized the voice and knew it belonged to the Indian boy who came to talk to her. Hurriedly she walked into her classroom before they saw how scared she was, and saw the tears that were filling her eyes.

When class was over, Marci looked for Juanita and saw the Indian boys talking to her. Marci froze and thought he had also chosen Juanita to be his next sacrifice. Could this be his way of getting even with her for going home before he could offer her as his sacrifice to his god? Afraid the Indian boy had seen Juanita and Marci together; Marci thought he was going to make her beg for her friend's life. Not wanting anyone to hurt her friend, Marci was going to rescue her as her mother rescued her. As Marci got closer, she heard the Indian boy tell Juanita he would be at her house later that night and left. He also wanted to know if Marci was going to be there. During their lunch break, Marci asked Juanita if she knew the Indian boy, she was talking too. Juanita told her she did, and that he was her cousin Marcos Lucero. "He's your cousin, are you sure?"

"Yes, of course I'm sure. My sister married his uncle."

Marci remained as calm as she could because she now knew Juanita was giving Marcos information about her. There was no way Marci could possibly express how scared this made her feel. By the time, their lunch was over, Marci learned all about the Indian boy who scared her. The one she thought wanted to sacrifice her to his Indian god. Marcos was an honor student who would never hurt anyone. He wanted to know who Marci was because Caleb invited him to go to their house. Marcos knew Caleb had a sister, so he wanted to be ahead of the game. He wanted to avoid that awkward moment of having to ask a girl her name. Marci also learned he was a star athlete and belonged to the Rodeo Club.

After Juanita told Marci all about Marcos, she felt so silly, and knew better than to mention what she thought Marcos wanted to do. How could she possibly believe everything she saw on television? She also learned what she thought were doghouses were actually outside hornos/oven and the men were taking wood so the women could bake their bread.

Marci's life took on a different meaning after that episode. She now decided to be herself. No longer was she going to let her imagination take over before she had a chance to get to know the person. Marci was also glad she did not tell Juanita what she thought because Juanita would have laughed so hard she would have peed her pants. Then she thought of the letter she sent Vanessa, and she laughed. How was she going to tell her friend in Virginia what she wrote was all a big mistake?

On the second Saturday in September, Marci and her family were on their way to watch the New Mexico State Fair Parade. The streets from Louisiana Avenue to Central had New Mexicans, and tourists along with Travis and his family looking for a place to sit. Finding a spot away from their families, Marci and Juanita managed to squeeze in with the rest of the crowd. The onlookers waited for the parade to start as they looked up at the overcast sky. By this time, they started to open their umbrellas in anticipation of what was to come. Soon everyone heard sirens in the distance, and they knew the New Mexico State Fair Parade was on its way.

The blaring sirens pierced the air and babies started to cry, while some of the children and older generation placed their hands over their ears. Men and women from the Armed Forces proudly carried the United States, Prisoner of War, New Mexico, and the Veteran Flags. As the color guard passed, the crowd stood to show their loyalty, and respect for the men and women who defended and continue to defend our Country. As the Color Guard went by, cheers, were heard up and down the street.

Next in line was the Parade Marshall and his wife followed by the New Mexico State Fair Queen, and her escorts, school bands, colorful floats, horses, and the clowns who entertained the crowd. The miniature horses were a big hit, but the clowns scared some of the children. Yet, all of these entries were hoping they would win the grand prize.

As the parade was about to end, the rain came. This happened every year, so it was something New Mexicans were used to. Earlier the sun was beating down on the crowd, but parents were now scrambling to get their children, blankets and other items they brought with them and the crowd was dispersing as fast as they could. However, the rain was not going to put a damper on the thousands of fair goers, who were on their way to the New Mexico State Fairgrounds.

If Marci thought there were many items at the Valencia County Fair, she was amazed to see the entries at the New Mexico State Fair. Once again, Juanita and Marci went to see the clothing; and sure enough, Juanita's satin baptismal dress, bonnet, cape, booties, and blanket had earned her a purple and blue ribbon. The girls looked at all of the entries, and later went to the *Manuel Lujan Building*. There, Marci and Juanita saw paintings from not only the children in the local schools, but paintings from many of the local artists.

When Marie went to see the flowers that were on display, she made a huge mistake. She was like a humming bird that flies from one flower to the next not knowing which one she liked best. This time Marci and Juanita had to pull her away from the floral arrangements, as she wanted to take them all home. However, Marie's next option was to buy seeds and bulbs to add to her flowerbed, and she was happy with that.

Marci could not get over how friendly everyone was, but most alluring of all was the aroma of the food. There was fry bread with honey or powdered sugar from the Indian Village, burritos, enchilada plates, and hamburgers with red or green chili from the Spanish Village, not to mention the corn on the cob, barbecued turkey legs, funnel cakes, cotton candy, candied apples and so much more from the other vendors. Yet, at every corner, and up and down the sidewalks, booths were set up to entice children with their items. When Marci was paying for the fry bread, she asked the woman if she had been making fry bread for a long time.

"I have made them since I was a very young girl, but Native Americans have been making fry bread since 1864," she said. Having bought something to eat, Juanita and Marci sat on the grass and watched people toss rings on coke bottles, or throw baseballs at bowling pins hoping to win a prize. Then they saw Caleb, Ernest, Isaiah, Isidro, Marcos, and their friends heading toward the basketball hoop to try their luck. Caleb and his friends had no problem shooting the basketball into the hoop, and by the time the girls walked up to the booth, Caleb managed to win two huge teddy bears. Seems the boys were showing others how easy it was to win a prize, so they were asked to leave.

Marci and Juanita went to the Midway where they rode the Ferris wheel, roller coaster, the tubs and anything that took the screaming kids up, down, and in many directions. The kids had their chance at riding every ride they could possibly get on. The girls also went into the house of mirrors where they laughed at their distorted image until Caleb, Ernest, Isidro and Marcos walked in on them. The boys laughed at what they saw, and to get away, the girls went to listen, and watch the various singers and dancers. As they approached the Indian Village,

Marci heard the drums beating, but this time, she was not afraid some Indian god was going to come after her.

When the girls caught up to Marci's parents, Travis wanted seeds from every chili he saw. He knew he could plant a garden that would produce chili as beautiful as the ones in the baskets that had blue ribbons. Travis asked the farmers at the state fair many questions and he learned about the different types of chili. Now, Travis was anxious to get started on a garden of his own. And by the time Travis gathered his family and their friends, the kids were tired, and ready to go home. Exhausted from the all-day event, the only thing Marci remembered going home was that she was talking to Juanita and a minute or so later, she was asleep.

Once the State Fair was over, Marci's father decided, he wanted to plant a garden. Knowing Rafael knew all about gardens, he went to talk to him. Walking to Rafael's house, Travis saw him outside. When Rafael saw Travis, he asked him what he was doing on his side of the neighborhood. Travis told Rafael he had come over so he could tell him what he had to do to plant a garden in the summer. Rafael then invited him indoors where they went into the kitchen. After Rafael made a fresh pot of coffee, Rafael told Travis the first thing he had to do was to turn the soil over so it will be ready for planting. Rafael offered to give Travis some of his chili seeds, and volunteered to lend him his Rotor Tiller.

By the time Travis was ready to go home, he knew all he needed to plant his garden. He thanked Rafael for all of his advice, and said he would take the chili seeds, but thought it would be best if he bought a Rotor Tiller of his own. This way he could have it handy at all times. After all this would be his very first garden in his new home.

The following morning Travis got up very early, and drove to Albuquerque. By the time he got back, Marci was waiting so she could help her father. Both wanting to try their hand at gardening, they selected a section in the backyard. Assembling the Rotor Tiller, Travis tried to turn the soil over, but the ground was hard and clayish, and to his surprise, the Rotor Tiller bounced all over the place. Exhausted, Travis sat down to rest. "Let me try," Marci told her father. Marci did not know what came over her. What made her think she could handle a piece of equipment her father had a difficult time handling. A few seconds after she started the Rotor Tiller she turned it off. Travis was not about to let a piece of machinery get the best of him so once again he went to talk to Rafael. He needed an expert's advice and who better than from an experienced gardener.

Marci's father spent the rest of the afternoon at the neighbors, and when he came home, he told Marci what Rafael told him to do. He said Rafael told him 'they had to dig a well, because if he used the city water for the garden it would create a huge bill. If he was to dig a well, and that would save him a lot of money.' When Caleb heard his father say they had to dig a well, he said he could not help because his hands would get blisters, and he would not be able to play sports.

Later that afternoon, when the family had eaten lunch, Travis and Marci went to the spot they selected for their garden. When they cleared the dead leaves and other debris the wind blew into the yard, Travis spread the fertilizer and started to soak the ground just as Rafael told him to do. So he watered his garden with the hose until he dug his well. Once that was done, Marci and her father went indoors and waited several hours so the water could soak into the ground. Opening the door the moist fertilizer filled her nostrils, and Marci decided to stay indoors.

Besides, tomorrow was another day and the awful smell would hopefully, go away. The next day Marci watched her father as he maneuvered the Rotor Tiller. This time the ground was easier to work with as it had soaked all night. She knew this was going to be her father's garden, so she waited until he invited her to help. Marci had never had so much fun, and both she and her father were now looking forward to summer. However, they had to wait until late February, or early April to start their garden.

The Queen & Her Royal Court

"Hey Marci, do you want to go visit my grandmother?" Juanita asked. "Grandma called my mom and she has some errands she wants me to do."

Never having met Marci's, grandmother, Marci agreed to go. What Marci thought was going to be a lazy and boring afternoon was going to be anything but thatThe girls had a great time talking and laughing as they peddled their bikes to Grandma's house. When they walked in, Juanita said, "Hi, Gramma, my mom said you needed me to help you. My friend Marci moved here from Virginia, and she wanted to meet you so I brought her with me."

"Hello Marci, it is nice to meet you, and thank you for coming to help Juanita," Grandma replied. Grandma turned to Juanita and told her, "Your cousins are coming today, and I want everything to look nice, and clean. I want you to sweep the patio, bring the eggs in from the chicken coop, and be sure you don't leave the broom outside the coop when you finish." Juanita's grandmother told her what it was she needed done, and Juanita went outside,

"You can get the other broom that's in the chicken coop, but be careful the rooster doesn't come after you, "Which one is the rooster?" Marci asked.

"He is the bigger one with the prettier feathers and his comb is fatter," Juanita replied. There was a moment of silence, and the look on Marci's face told Juanita, Marci didn't know the difference between a chicken and a rooster. Of course, Juanita failed to tell Marci chickens also have red combs. Still confused, Marci went into the chicken coop, and looked for a rooster with pretty feathers and a fatter red comb on its head. Not seeing one, she found the broom and walked outside. Thinking she closed the door behind her, Marci did the one thing Grandma told them not to do. She forgot to close the door to the chicken coop, and the rooster, along with the chickens saw their way to freedom. While Grandma was washing the dishes, she looked out the window and saw the girls chasing her chickens. The one thing Grandma did not like was for anyone to chase her chickens. Wiping her hands on her apron, she ran outside and scolded the girls. Grandma thought the girls were making a game of chasing the chickens that got out, but all they were trying to do was to get them back into the coop. As Grandma was about to close the door to the chicken coop; the rooster escaped. This made her even angrier. Taking the broom away from Marci, Grandma chased the rooster, and as she lifted the broom, the rooster attacked her leg. All Juanita and Marci could do was look in horror as the blood ran down Grandma's knee. The girls ran to tell Grandma her knee was bleeding. Looking down at her knee, she said, "Oh that's nothing," and taking her apron off she wiped the blood. With Grandma's help, the girls managed to get the chickens where they belonged. Once the rooster, and the chickens were in their coop, and before Grandma went indoors, she told Juanita they should gather the eggs.

Later her knee started to swell, and being a midwife, Grandma knew what herbs she had to put on her knee to help with the swelling. No matter what herbs she used, it didn't help the swelling, and after a week went by, Grandma had to see a doctor. With the penicillin, and the herbs Grandma's knee healed, but the rooster left a bad scar on her knee. Anytime her knee started to hurt, she blamed it on the rooster who attacked her knee. Whenever anyone mentioned they had a sore knee, or other parts of their body hurt, Grandma would tell them how the rooster attacked her. After she finished telling her story, she would laugh and tell them how good the rooster tasted after she caught and fried it. She made sure that rooster never attacked anyone ever again.

Once they completed their first chore, Juanita and Marci started on the next one, which was to sweep the patio. All this was new to Marci, and she watched Juanita as she started to sweep the dirt. Juanita then showed Marci what they had to do. When that was done, they primed the red hand pump that was about a hundred feet from the house until the cold, clear water started to flow. While Marci pumped the water, Juanita filled the bucket they were going to use to carry the water in. Again, Juanita showed Marci how they were to walk backwards or sideways while they sprinkled the water on the ground. They could not throw it because the water would just make a puddle, and it would undo the nice sweeping strokes they made when they swept the patio. When Marci understood what they were going to do, she started to sprinkle the water on the ground. Marci commented how the ground smelled like it had just rained, and how everything smelled so fresh. That is exactly what Grandma wants the Albuquerque cousins to think. Sure, the smell of rain was in the air, but on this day, it only existed at Grandma's house.

When their chores were done they told Grandma they were leaving, and the girls got on their bikes and peddled back home. At the stop sign, Juanita saw the cousins arrive, and waved as they drove past them.

Then Marci asked Juanita, "Why do you have to sweep the patio, and sprinkle water on the ground from the well, when your relatives from Albuquerque come to visit?"

"Oh, this is something we have done since I can remember. We come to Grandmas while my mom and dad work, or go to their meetings. We even come on Saturdays to do what you just helped me do—by the way, thank you. Mom had already told me today was not going to be any different, so I knew what to expect. One would think the queen and her royal court were coming," Juanita remarked as she laughed.

Every time Marci saw Juanita and her sisters going to their grandmother's house, she knew the royal family was visiting, and they had to sweep the patio. To Marci, it was odd they did this so their grandmother could hear her grandchildren say how very fresh it smelled. *Of course it rained* Marci thought, the only rain cloud somehow found its way from the well onto the ground that was swept at Grandma's house. Marci was constantly amazed at the things New Mexicans did, however, no one thought it strange but her. Every time Juanita had to go to Grandma's house Marci went to help.

Eventually, Marci got to know Grandma and her ways. Now when she told her to get the eggs, and not let the rooster out, Marci now knew what a rooster looked like, and made sure she didn't let him out.

Time passed, and after a while, Marci did not think the things Juanita had to do were so strange.

Halloween

Everything was going better than Marci had ever thought it would. She was adjusting to the move, and doing well in school. Now that the state fair was over, everything went on as before. The main topic of conversation both at school and at home, was what to wear for Halloween. Marci, Caleb and their friends were now looking forward to Halloween so they could wear their homemade costumes. The week before Halloween, Marci invited some of her friends over for a pajama party. While they were making the final adjustments to their costumes, Marie brought them freshly popped buttered popcorn. Hoping Marie had ideas to stimulate their imagination Marci said, "Mom, we know what we are going to wear, but we were wondering if you have any ideas that would help us get into the mood."

"Let me think about that," Marie replied. As Marie left Marci's bedroom, she went to the den where Travis was watching TV.

"Sweetheart, the girls want suggestions as to what they can do to get ready for Halloween, can you think of any?"

"Well they can go outside and tell scary stories, or we could take them to the movie Friday evening", Travis replied.

Marie thought about it, and once again, she went into her daughter's bedroom. She asked the girls if they would like to go to a movie on Friday evening, and they replied, "They would."

It just happened that Nieto's Theatre was featuring "Carrie," as the main feature of the month. The previews they had seen were enough to know it was going to be a hair rising, nail, biting movie. Now all they had to do was to call their parents and get their permission to go.

Forgetting the second feature was *"Count Dracula,"* with *Christopher Lee,* Travis knew the girls would need nothing more to stimulate their imagination.

The following week Travis and Marie took the kids to the movie, and having waited a half-hour or so, the audience started to clap their hands, and stomp their feet. They were anxious to see *"Count Dracula"* bite some unsuspecting woman and see blood dripping from his fangs and her neck. The double feature was exactly what the girls wanted; however, they did not realize how scary it was going to be. From the beginning to the end, kids screamed at the top of their lungs, and held on to each other. By the time the movie was over, the sun was going down, and the setting sun was casting mysterious shadows wherever the kids looked. As they walked to the car, the kids were discussing what part of the movie they thought was the scariest. When it came time for Marci to say which part scared her the most, her father placed his hand on her shoulder. Marci let out a scream that started a domino effect, which started with the girls and ended with the boys. Travis apologized, but nothing he said calmed them down. He did not realize how scared the kids were, and knew the girls needed nothing more to keep their imagination active for Halloween.

When Travis drove Juanita and her brother's home, Travis walked them to the door. About to leave, Rafael invited him to stay, as he wanted them to meet his mother. Of course, Travis was not going to refuse an invitation from Rafael. Hoping Rosita had some fresh coffee, and salsa, he accepted the invitation. Travis then went to get Marie and the kids from the car.

The October sun was starting to set, and after several minutes, Travis asked Marie if she was ready to go home. "Why don't you wait a few more minutes, and I will ask mamá if she will tell the kids the story of *La Llorona,"* Rafael told Travis. Rafael's mother agreed, and Rafael said, "Mamá, before you start, let me get the boys. I know they went down the street to play basketball so I won't be long." While Rafael went to get the boys, mamá, thought it would be a good idea to tell her story out on the porch. She asked the girls if they would like to go to a movie on Friday evening, and they replied, "They would." When Rafael came back, he brought Caleb, Juanita's brothers and some of the neighborhood kids with him because they never got tired of listening to Grandma's stories. While some of the kids joined Juanita and Marci on the grass, others sat with the adults on the open porch. Grandma was quite a storyteller, and after what the kids had been through, the mood was just perfect. With the twinkling stars, and the moon in and out of the clouds, Grandma started her story of "*La Llorona*."

The story I am about to tell you is a story my grandmother told me, and her grandmother told her. Some of you might not think it is true, but you need to listen carefully. When she saw the children and adults were comfortable, Grandma pulled her shawl over her head. As she did this, her facial features seemed to change, and grandma started her story.

When Serafina was a young girl in school, she and her friend, Carmen were always bullied. The kids made fun of them, and no matter how hard they tried to fit in, nothing worked. Serafina was not pretty like the other girls. She was fat, had acne and pimples on her face and it did not matter how hard she tried to lose weight, and clear her face, nothing worked.

One day, Serafina's biology class was studying frogs when one of the kids said, "This one looks like Serafina, and the skinny one looks like Carmen." The majority of the kids laughed, but the teacher did not think it was funny, so he escorted the student to the principal's office. From that day on, some girls and boys called her "bullfrog." Serafina was hurt that the kids could be so cruel, and hateful. But, as the years passed, Serafina matured and she learned to take better care of herself, as her features changed. Now the kids that used to call her bullfrog couldn't believe how pretty she was.

By the time Serafina and her classmates graduated from high school, the boys that called her names were asking her for a date. No matter how many times the boys asked her to go out with him, Serafina turned them down, and now it was her time to laugh at them. Even the girls were jealous of the once ugly "bullfrog Serafina." There was one boy Serafina, and the rest of the girls wished he would ask them for a date.

Tomás Montoya was a handsome young caballero, with dark black hair, well built, and rich. Anytime he went into town, the girls gathered around him, as they wanted him to pay attention to her, and only her. At first, Tomás never paid attention to Serafina because she was not like the other girls. She was not pretty, and shapely. Months passed, and even Tomás started to notice how Serafina was maturing, and how her face no longer had the ugly pimples and acne. However, Serafina ignored him, as he had ignored her in the past, but she so wanted him to ask her for a date. Knowing that would never happen, she would walk home. Now every time she saw him, she did everything in her power to make Tomás think she did not want his attention. As many of the girls in the village, Serafina thought Tomás was handsome, and she told her friend Carmen she knew he was the young man she wanted to marry. The difference between Serafina and the rest was that she ignored Tomás' flirtatious advances.

Tomás had never met a girl who ignored him and this bothered him. He knew he had to win Serafina's attention so he went back to the ranch, to think of ways to win her attention. When Tomás asked his mother for her advice, she was appalled that he would lower his standards and date a girl from the village. She scolded him, and wanted to know what he was thinking. But, his father did not see anything wrong with that.

Months passed, and Tomás was still trying to get Serafina's attention. On a warm and breezy evening as the sun was going down, Serafina was going home after a walk around the neighborhood. Tomás made his usual, appearance in the village, but this time he did not see Serafina so he decided to go home. On his way back home, he spotted Serafina and followed her. Tomás was determined to get her to notice him because he wanted to know everything about her. When Serafina heard Tomás call her, she decided it was time she stop and talk to him. Tomás and Serafina talked, laughed, and had a good time. When Serafina said, she had to get home, Tomás walked with her, as he wanted to know where she lived. By the time he left her, he knew all he wanted to know. Going home, Tomás knew he was going to take Serafina to meet his parents. After Serafina went indoors, she ran to her mother and hugged her because Serafina was happy her plan was working.

Tomás and Serafina dated for a couple of years and on the day he was going to propose to her, he showed his father the ring he bought his fiancé. His father was pleased that his son found the girl he wanted to marry, yet when he showed his mother the ring, she spat on it, and told Tomás she hoped Serafina would not accept his proposal. "Mama, why would you do that," he asked. Shocked his mother would react that way, he ran outside, mounted his horse and rode off into the edge of the pasture to think of what had taken place. Tomás sat on a tree stump thinking of ways to change his mother's mind until the sun started to go down. When he entered the house, his mother would not speak to him. Not able to change his mother's mind, Tomás did what he started out to do.

The following day was cloudy, and gloomy, but Tomás did not want to wait any longer to propose to Serafina. It did not matter if his mother did not approve, he loved Serafina enough to go against her wishes. From the day his mother meet Serafina, she despised, and cursed the day her son meet her. His father thought she was a pretty girl, and told Tomás to treat her with respect. He wanted to get to know her better so he wanted Tomás to bring her to the ranch more often. After Tomás proposed, he and Serafina were seen all over town, and throughout the ranch. Months later, they made plans to get married, and all Tomás wanted was to make sure his fiancé was happy. I want you to find the finest gown money can buy Tomás told Serafina, even though his mother objected to everything he did. On the day of their wedding, everyone, but his mother attended Serafina and Tomás' wedding. Their wedding and their reception was the talk of the town for months. Tomás father was happy to see his son so happy that he built them a house where they could live, and raise a family. Tomás and Serafina were as happy as any young couple could be, but Tomás' mother was jealous, and she would do anything to ruin their marriage. That was how much she despised her daughter-in-law.

It was a gloomy day as sleet was coming down when Serafina was told she was going to have a baby. Happy as she was, Serafina could not wait to tell her husband, and as any young man would be, Tomás was extremely excited at the prospect of being a father. Now all they had to do was to make sure Serafina did everything the doctor told her to do.

Nine months later, Serafina surprised Tomás when the doctor told him his wife had given birth to twin boys. To his joy, Tomás shared the news with his parents, and Tomás's father was thrilled that he was a grandfather. But, his mother saw the birth of twins as something evil, and warned her son to stay away from them. Her son did not listen to his mother; nor did he believe his sons were evil.

Days after the boys were born and sent home; they were colicky and required plenty of attention. Tomás and his father loved being with the twins, but as time went on; he got tired of hearing them cry. Serafina no longer paid attention to Tomás, as her children needed her. After months of hearing his boys cry, and demand their mother's attention, Tomás no longer wanted the responsibility of a family, so he left Serafina and his children. On the day he went back to the ranch, Tomás' father could not believe his son could abandon his children, but his mother rejoiced by inviting a certain young woman Anita Peralta, to dine with them. She always thought her son was going to marry Anita before he met the horrible Serafina. After many months of dating, Tomás fell in love with Anita, and they were now the ones everyone saw around town. Once that happened, Anita was a frequent guest at the ranch, and Tomás' mother even suggested Anita spend the night with Tomás.

In the meantime, Serafina could not understand why Tomás left her and their children, and cried all the time. She could not sleep, eat, or even take care of the twins as she used to. Not even her mother could console her daughter as Serafina was beyond being consoled.

Winter was coming, and the days were getting colder. Serafina needed to get out of the house, and decided to take the children out for a stroll. They had not gone far when Serafina saw Tomás ride past her, and her children with a woman as beautiful as she used to be, but dressed even more elegant than Serafina could ever dress. When Anita looked at Serafina, she laughed and raised an eyebrow in disapproval. As Tomás and Anita rode past them, Serafina heard her say, "Tomás, how could you possibly marry a girl like her?"

Angry as Serafina was, all she could think of was what the woman said. Now, all she wanted was to get even with her husband, and thought she would teach both his mother and Tomás a lesson. She would take the boys to the ranch where Tomás would have to look after his children for a month or so. After this, Serafina stopped taking care of her appearance. She no longer cared how she looked and after a week or so, her face broke out with pimples she scratched and scared her face. Her hair grew and became tangled and unruly, but she did not care. Now when she picked the boys up, she would scratch them with her nails because they were long, split and cracked. She even stopped talking to Carmen, the only true friend she had.

Months passed, and the boys had not been outdoors for a while, so Serafina's mother asked her daughter if she wanted her to take the boys out. Telling her mother she would take them, Serafina wrapped the boys up, and put them in the carriage. When she was a block from her house, Tomás and Anita rode passed her. Neither one recognized Serafina, but she recognized them, and as they rode past her, she yelled out his name. Curious as to who the old hag was that called him, Tomás turned the carriage around. When Tomás realized who the old woman was, he was shocked; got back in the carriage laughed, and continued on his way. Serafina was so furious and angry; she did not realize she had taken the wrong path home. Seeing that she was on the bridge that crossed over, the Rio Grande, and in her depressed state of mind, she stopped to check on the boys. As they looked at their mother with their big brown eyes, they reminded her of Tomás. Leaning over her children, they started to cry, as they were cold and hungry. With the thought of Tomás laughing at her, she didn't hear the boys cry. Instead, she thought they were laughing at her. Without thinking, angry and distraught, Serafina took her boys out of their carriage and threw them into the river. A few of the village residents were standing at the riverbank because they had never seen the river with so much water. When they saw, Serafina throw her babies into the river the residents were stunned and could not believe what they were witnessing. Several of the men jumped into the icy river to save the babies, but the current was so strong the children were immediately pulled down into the icy cold water, never to be seen again. When Serafina realized what she had done, she started to scream, and jumped into the river to rescue her children, but it was too late. Yet, other men jumped in to help her before she too was dragged down into the river. The people who were there tried to help Serafina, but after she was rescued all she did was to walk up and down the riverbank searching for her children. The rescue team responded, but could not find the boys. Serafina cried, "Ayyy, Ayyy, my children, my children, where are you? Please come back". No matter how many times she called out to them, her children did not answer.

When Tomás' mother was told her grandchildren were dead, she was happy Tomás no longer had children with that woman who wasn't worthy of her son. His father was devastated that he no longer had grandchildren, and mourned their death. "Why are you crying?" his wife asked, but he did not respond. Instead, he got into his carriage, and went to see how Serafina and her mother were doing. He wanted to know what happened that made her throw his grandchildren into the icy river. Of course, when he saw Serafina, he too was shocked at how she looked. Yet, that was of no concern to him because he was worried as to Serafina's wellbeing.

Days and months passed, and Serafina was seen walking the ditch, and riverbanks. She thought the water might have taken her children into one of the ditches, but no matter how long she searched for her children, she never found them. On an extremely cold, foggy, and wintery day in November, Serafina was found frozen under a blanket of snow near the river where her children drowned. When Tomás heard his wife threw his children into the river, he was angry, and never returned to the village, until the day she was buried. As Serafina's mother tried to cope with the loss of her grandchildren and now her daughter, the neighbors comforted her as much as they could. When they saw Tomás had come to pay his respects to his wife, everyone was watching his every move. Standing before Serafina's coffin, Tomás saw Serafina was dressed in her wedding gown and looked as beautiful as the day she married him. As he lowered his head, the mourners saw Tomás spit on Serafina's face. Having done that, he turned around and told her mother, "He prayed her daughter would burn in hell, and cursed the day he ever married her." No one moved as the mourners were in shock. How could he come and disrespect his wife and his mother-in-law as he did? Where was he when Serafina and his children needed him? Why did he not take responsibility for abandoning them? Having done what he did, Tomás left, and after that, no one knew what happened to Tomás.

Throughout the years, the villagers started to hear stories of a woman looking for her children. One evening some neighbors were talking about the woman who was said, "Sounded as if she was crying." After that, word spread and the residents now called the wailing woman, "*La Llorona*." Everyone knew it was Serafina searching for her children, and they knew she would not rest until she found them.

On a brisk spring evening, a young couple was sitting by the riverbank when they heard a strange wailing. Thinking it was the wind, they paid little attention. Again, they heard someone crying, and this time they thought it was a baby. Getting up, the couple saw a woman dressed in a white gown crying, "Ayyy, Ayyy my children, where are you; where are you my children?" Wanting to help her, the couple walked toward the woman. Then it dawned on them who this woman was, and they didn't know what to do. Scared they held on to each other, as the woman tried to grab them. When she reached for them, she scratched their arms with her long nails, and they watched her walk past them. Having walked a few feet away from the couple, Serafina let out a high-pitched, scream that made the hair on the back of their necks stand up. The moment she disappeared, they could smell sulfur as if someone had lit a match. Some of the residents said that was what someone would smell when the devil was around. The couple never went back to the river because they were afraid they might encounter the woman who the residents were calling, *"La Llorona."*

To this day, the villagers say Serafina cries like a baby to lure children to her. Others say she walks along the road so that someone can give her a ride. Yet others say her punishment is to wonder along the ditches, and riverbanks looking for children, so she can claim them as her own. The one thing everyone agreed on was that anytime anyone saw Serafina, a strong odor of sulfur lingered after she was gone.

Grandma told the children not to think "*La Llorona*" only walks the ditch, or riverbanks. She also appears to children who are out late at night misbehaving, or doing something they should not be doing. Some have said she also appears during the day because that is when the children of the village play outside. "When we were children, our parents warned us Serafina would take us thinking we were her lost children, and were told to be careful," she said.

Do you boys remember how Julio drowned a couple of years ago? "Well his mother told me that when she went to identify him, one of the employees asked her if he had run into a barbed wire fence while he was burning weeds. When Julio's mother asked why he would ask such a question, the employee told her it was because he smelled like sulfur." Then his mother knew *"La Llorona"* had claimed him as her own to replace her children.

I know you kids think this is just another story, but when you go out on Halloween, make sure to stay away from the ditches, and if you see someone dressed in white, run, run as fast as you can. Grandma finished her story, and no one moved. Travis broke the silence when he asked if they would like to hear the story he, and his friends were told when they were children. "Yes, we would love to hear it," Grandma replied..

According to my father, and grandfather the legend of *"The Jersey Devil'* has been around since 1735. Just as the one Grandma told us about *La Llorona,* we were told to watch out for the *Jersey Devil.* This too has many versions, and many residents from Jersey claim they have seen it, but I seem to be getting ahead of myself, Travis said. The place this happened on has many trees with patches of swamp water, and a lot of sandy soil—like quicksand. Having said that, let me tell you what we were warned about when I was about six, or seven. This is about a woman whose name was Mrs. Leeds who had twelve children. Father said, "The day Mrs. Leeds found out she was pregnant with her thirteenth child, she was extremely angry. Anytime the women in Pine Barrens asked her how she was doing, she would complain because she was pregnant, and having to feed another child. Not a day went by that someone wouldn't hear Mrs. Leeds say, "If the devil wants this child, he can have it." At the same time she would laugh, and say, "If it were not for him, I would not have the powers he gave me." Mrs. Leeds would practice witchcraft, and believed the devil was her best friend. If she asked him for a special power, she would try it on the people she didn't like.

On a cold and stormy evening, Mrs. Leeds neighbors gathered at her house to take the other children to their houses. This way the midwife and her husband could do their job without having to worry about the other children being in the way. Besides, they were afraid of what Mrs. Leeds might do to them after the baby was born if they didn't help her. As the evening progressed, the wind, lightning, and rain came with the vengeance of a tornado. At the same time, Mrs. Leeds was having a horrible time. Never had she experienced the pain she was going through with any of the other children. No matter how the midwife tried to help her, or what herbs she had Mrs. Leeds drink to ease the pain; nothing worked. Throughout the storm, the neighbors could hear Mrs. Leeds scream in agony, and they sympathized with her.

After thirteen excruciating hours, Mrs. Leeds finally gave birth to her thirteenth child. While the midwife was cleaning the baby, he looked like a normal baby boy, but within a few minutes, the baby's appearance changed. It changed from a normal baby to that of a creature with hooves, a goats head, huge bat wings, and a forked tail. When he saw the midwife, it growled and screamed at her. "He was going to kill her for bringing him into the world if she didn't run out of the house." He then turned to his father and told him to leave. Once the baby and his mother were alone, he stood on his hooved feet, turned around, and in a rough and snarly voice laughed, and said, "Mamma." As he turned around, he saw an open window, and before he flew out into the storm, he told his mother, "One day he would come back." The story of this thirteenth child spread quickly, and everyone was afraid to go out at night. Many said the *Jersey Devil* would swoop down and take dogs, cats, small livestock, and would even take children. After the *"Jersey Devil"* ate the animals, their bones could be found scattered about, but the children's bones were never found. The residents of Pine Barrens thought the remains were thrown into the sandy soil where they sank to the bottom. No one tried to search for their children because they knew they would be sucked down to the bottom within minutes, and they left the remains at the bottom of the swamp. Shortly after the creature was born and fled from his mother, the residents started to report sightings of what they were now calling, *"The Jersey Devil."*

One year the residents asked a local minister to exorcise the monster, but he couldn't. Anytime anyone said he saw the devil, he would tell Mrs. Leeds. However, when the thirteenth child saw them, he let out a horrible scream, and would disappear into the night. On the day Mrs. Leeds died, her demon baby came for her and took his revenge on his mother as he tore her to pieces. She did not want him, and gave him to the devil, so, the devil's son left her remains scattered for the wild animals to devour. He would then cut the animals that ate his mother's remains into small pieces so nothing remained of her and threw them into the sandy soil where they sank to the bottom.

When our father told us that tale, my friends and I never went out alone. We were in before dusk, and made sure we were never alone when we walked next to the swampy patches of Pine Barrens. We were always told to be on the watch for Mrs. Leeds because no matter how deep her devil son threw her into the swamp, she always came up. So like you, we were told not to go out at night because we never knew when the *"Jersey Devil"* or his mother might take us away from our parents. Even my father and grandfather were afraid to go out at night. "I know we no longer live in Jersey, but one never knows what follows you, or comes out at night that can get you," Travis told the kids.

By the time he finished his story, Grandma's eyes were as wide as those of the boys and girls whose mouths were frozen as if they were ready to scream, but unable to do so. That night the neighborhood boys did not know what awaited them as they walked home, but they did not want to find out. Afraid to go home, one of the younger boys asked Rafael if he would go with them. As Rafael and Travis took the boys home, Travis asked Rafael if the story his mother told was true. "Mamá has told us that story since I was a kid and she has never changed anything. I have never asked her, but others have told similar stories," Rafael replied. In turn, Rafael asked Travis if his story was true. "Well for us it was. Here, the females tell of La Llorona, but the males in the families are the ones who tell the story of the Jersey Devil and his mother because we are the ones who go hunting in the forest of the Pine Barrens. We are the ones who have to warn our children of the danger that lurks in the swamps, and what could happen to them."

Juanita, Marci, and the adults went indoors to warm up as the evening was starting to get cooler and the men took the neighbor kids home. When the men returned, they stayed outside enjoying the cool evening breeze until it was time for Travis and his family to go home.

Grandma told many stories that sent chills up and down Marci's spine; like the night, she was walking home, and saw her dead sister follow her home; however, she was not sure it was her sister or if it was the Llorona, because she appeared once she passed a ditch. Marci heard many of grandma's stories, but none compared to "La Llorona," and her father's story of the "Jersey Devil."

Halloween was here and Caleb and Marci dressed up in their costumes, and went to Juanita's house. When they arrived, Juanita's brothers and sisters had already left, so the trio went from house to house trick-or-treating. Everyone was having fun, and the trio was almost at the elementary school when other kids joined them. But, there was one more stop to make before going to the carnival at the Raymond Gabaldon Elementary School.

Ms. Webb's house was the last one in the neighborhood, and the only one near a small ditch. No one knew if Ms. Webb was ever married, or had children because she never spoke to any of the neighbors. All everyone ever saw her do was rake her yard, and burn weeds. As the kids neared her house, Juanita told Marci and Caleb, "Ms. Webb was strange, but meant no harm. She was someone who lived in the neighborhood long before Marci moved to New Mexico." Juanita remarked, "She thought Ms. Webb was there even before she was born because she could not remember anyone else living there."

Ms. Webb's house was the last one on the street, and before they headed to the carnival, other kids joined Juanita, Marci, Caleb, Ernest, and Isidro as they went to knock on her door. When Ms. Webb did not answer, the kids started to leave. As they were walking away, she told them to wait as she had a trick for them, but the kids did not hear she had a trick, instead they heard she had a treat, and the children gathered around the door, ready for the treat. Greedy Caleb decided he wanted to be the first in line so he would get the best candies Ms. Webb was going to give them. Teasing the rest of the kids, he told them he wasn't going to share with them. Caleb could not wait to open his pillowcase as wide as he could so none of the candies would fall to the ground. As the children heard Ms. Webb's footsteps, they opened their bags and pillowcases eagerly awaiting their treat. Again, the children shouted as loud as they could, "Trick-or-Treat," and Ms. Webb responded, "Get ready, I'm coming."

When Ms. Webb said she was coming, the children thought she was going to give them candy just as the other neighbors had given them. As she came to the door, Caleb screamed, *"Run it's the Llorona,"* and did not wait for anyone as he screamed his way past his friends. The children were not prepared to see a seventy-year-old woman dressed in a witch's costume, with her hair all a mess coming at them with a pitchfork. Her long narrow nose, beady eyes, and tight thin pressed lips only made her look more evil under the witch's hat. It was not as if she was walking toward them—she was literally running. How a word could possibly come out of a mouth whose lips were pressed together so tight was a mystery to the kids.

Tonight, unlike the scarecrow in *The Wizard of Oz* who was given courage, Caleb lost his to an old woman with a pitchfork. His courage, the straw he had tucked into his costume, a pillowcase full of candy, apples, popcorn balls and everything else he collected throughout the night now belonged to Ms. Webb. The children scattered as fast as their legs could take them and no one looked back. One of the kids screamed, she stabbed me; I'm bleeding! The poor kid was so scared he peed his pants, and thought it was blood running down his legs. The rest of the kids saw her coming, and they did not wait to see what this old woman was going to do with her pitchfork. Kids screamed as they thought *"La Llorona"* was walking down the ditch, thinking she was going to come after them. However, what they saw was a plastic bag hanging from a tree branch blowing in the breeze. Yet Caleb said he saw the *"Jersey Devil"* fly over him.

On this Halloween night the children's imagination was so active nothing could compare with what had just taken place. None of the kids could ever make up what was happening because this was even scarier than any movie they had seen. Once they were a safe distance from Ms. Webb's house, some of them stopped running so they could catch their breath. The rest ran until they got to the school gymnasium where the

Halloween Carnival was taking place. When it was time for the kids to go home, they knew they had to pass Ms. Webb's house. Deciding to go as a group they ran until, one-by-one they arrived at their house, and the group got smaller and smaller. Juanita, Marci, and Caleb were alone and they still had to get home in the dark of the night wondering if "Ms. Webb," *La Llorona,"* the *"Jersey Devil,"* and his mother or anything else was out to get them.

Sunday Marci and Juanita were going to the Dairy Queen when they saw Ms. Webb raking the leaves in her front yard. When she saw the girls on her side of the street, she raised the pitchfork, and started to laugh. Afraid to walk by her house, the girls held hands as they ran to the opposite side of the street. If they had to, they could run to the neighbor's house, and Ms. Webb could not hurt them. Yet, the girls could not escape from her view. As they ran, they heard her say, "Trick-or-treat, I have a lot of candy to give away if you want some, come, and get it."

San Clemente Fiestas

When Father Gene read the weekly announcements, he reminded his parishioners the fiestas of "San Clemente" would be celebrated in a couple of weeks. On November 23, we will be celebrating our "Patron Pope Saint Clemente's Feast Day." You kids know some of the adults as teachers, policemen, firemen, and farmers. Well, Saint Clemente is known as the patron of boatmen, marble workers, marines, sailors, sick children, and stonecutters. Did you ever think of praying to a saint when you get sick? Well now, you know you can ask him to help you get well."

The six young ladies who are running for fiesta queen have another two weeks to raise as much money as they possibly can. The majordomos have been collecting the money, and keeping a tally of how much each girl has raised. Saturday after the money is counted, the girl who raised the most money will be our new queen. Sunday the old majordomos will be relieved of their responsibility, and, the new majordomos will also start their duties on Sunday, and they too will be in charge for one year. For those of you who do not know what a majordomo is, they are the church stewards, or guardians of the church. They help with the activities, maintenance and assist the parishioners as much as possible. In the meantime, these young ladies have had bake sales, washed cars, babysat for donations, and done whatever they can to raise money for our parish.

"Remember," Father Gene, said, "the money these young ladies raise will help the parishioners in our community." Most of you know how the candidates have gone to different parishes to sell baked goods, hoping she will raise the most amount of money to be our next fiesta queen. This morning, some of the candidates are selling raffle tickets, and baked goods outside in the courtyard. The bischitos (sugar cookies) I bought after the eight o'clock Mass, were delicious. Too bad I didn't have a cup of coffee to go with it. As in the past, there will be plenty of food booths, games, and a carnival for the kids. We will also have several bands for your dancing pleasure. Both the Spanish bands and deejay Carlos G will entertain both the young at heart, and the older generation.

Once Mass was over Travis took his family to eat breakfast at one of the restaurants. They still had a few more boxes to unpack, but the boxes could always wait for another day. After a big breakfast, the family spent the entire day indoors enjoying their new home as no one felt like working. Not even Caleb went outdoors to play basketball, which was unlike him. This cold November Sunday must have set the relaxing mood for the following week because the family forgot about the boxes in the garage. All week the contestants went door-to-door asking the community for their help so she could be the next fiesta queen. A few went to Marci's house, and Marie did not hesitate to help them.

Saturday when Sal was driving past Travis house, he saw Travis and Marie sitting out on the porch enjoying the sunset. Going around the neighborhood, Sal stopped and asked,"If they were going to the fiestas?

They started last night and I don't think you want to miss all of the excitement," he said.

Marie then turned to Travis and said, "Let's go. It will do the family good to leave the house. Besides, we are now parishioners of San Clemente and we need to support our church."

Soon as Travis and his family arrived at the fiestas, one of the candidates came running toward them. She told Travis she had three more books left to sell, and there was still time for her to turn the money in before they stopped counting it. Travis helped the young girl and bought the remaining raffle tickets. There were some great prizes, and they had as much of a chance to win as anyone else. Happy she had sold all of her raffle tickets, the girl ran to turn in the last of the money, and the ticket stubs. Another girl saw Travis and his family, but by the time, she counted the remaining tickets she had to sell, Travis was already buying tickets from the other contestant.

Counting the money took time, but when that was done, it was time to announce the name of the new fiesta queen. By this time, the girls and their families gathered around the announcer. Tension mounted as the nervous girls waited hoping she would be the next reigning queen. Before the majordomos announced the name of the third runner up, they asked for a drumroll. "And the third runner up is, Helen Sanchez." Happy as she was, Helen was disappointed she had not raised enough money to be the next fiesta queen. For the remaining contestants the few minutes were extremely tense. Once again, a drumroll was requested, and "Josephine Sanchez was named as second runner up" The name of the runner-up was announced, and now there were four girls who had their hands over their mouth in anticipation of who would be this year's queen.

Okay, Carlos, we need a long drumroll. I know the girls are anxious to hear who will be crowned queen, but we need to make it more exciting for them. Once the drumroll was over, "Sophia Garcia was proclaimed as the fiesta queen." In shock and overjoyed she couldn't say anything. She cried while the other girls congratulated her. Sophia screamed while her family surrounded her. The parishioners who were at the fiestas now knew who the next San Clemente fiesta queen was, and they were happy for her. However, Travis and his family had already left, so they did not hear, or see which girl had won. Tomorrow during the 11 a.m. Mass, the parishioners that were not there would find out which of the contestants won.

Sunday, Travis and his family got ready to go to Mass. When the family found a place to sit, Marci wanted to see which girl had won, and how a fiesta queen dressed. Today everyone would find out who the new reigning queen was, but more important, everyone would find out how much money she raised. The music was lively and Marci felt herself moving to the rhythm of the music. She did not understand what the choir was singing, but liked how the music made her feel. It did not have the same effect as the music deejay Carlos G played last night, but it still sounded good. Marie thinking Marci was nervous nudged her so she would stop squirming. At the same time, the choir stopped singing, and when Marci turned around, she saw the altar servers entering the church. The choir waited for a few minutes before they resumed singing, and a few minutes later, everyone stood up as the procession started down the aisle.

The old and the new mayordomo's carried San Clemente's statue on a colorfully decorated processional litter. Following were the reigning queen, her escorts, and last year's queen. The last in the procession to enter the church were the deacons and Father Gene. As everyone remained standing, Father Gene stepped onto the altar and started the Mass.

Sitting between her parents, Marci leaned toward her father and told him the girl he bought the tickets from was the one who won. Travis smiled and said, "He was happy he bought the remaining tickets because that might have been what helped her."

After the sermon, Father Gene said it was time to let the parishioners know how much money the queen and her attendants raised he got Marci's attention. First, he thanked the old mayordomo's for all the work they did the past year. Father then introduced the new mayordomo's, and congratulated them for accepting the role of stewardship. Next, he introduced the young girls who worked so hard to raise the amount of money they did. As each one stood up and introduced, she was given a bouquet of red roses. Then as last year's queen put the tiara on Sophia Garcia's head, the new mayordomo's draped the red robe over her shoulders, and gave her a dozen white roses. Now that the competition was over, and after six months of hard work everyone now knew who San Clemente's Fiesta Queen was.

Sophia thanked everyone who helped her win, but she especially thanked her family for helping her with the bake sales, and car washes that helped her win. While Marci listened to Sophia, she tried to figure how old she was. Marci liked that Sophia was wearing a knee length yellow beaded party dress that looked very pretty on her. She thought Sophia was about fourteen years old, and was in the eighth or ninth grade. Although she was a little on the chubby side, the dress made Sophia look thinner. Sophia also had a natural tan, and a very pretty smile. After Sophia sat down, Father Gene congratulated the young girls, and told his parishioners they had raised eight-thousand dollars with Sophia and her family raising a whopping four-thousand. And, as you know, the money raised will help many of the families in the community. Father Gene was very proud of the young ladies, who worked so hard to raise as much money as they did. He also thanked the parishioners and the community who made this year's fiesta so successful. He then challenged the females both young and old to beat the amount of money raised this year. Marci thought by then she would know some of the neighbors, and it might be fun to try her luck. The coronation of the queen was over, and Father Gene proceeded with the Mass. Before he gave his parishioners the final blessing, the winners of the raffle tickets were announced, and to Caleb's surprise, his name was selected as having won one of the prizes.

Sophia and her royal court followed the altar boys who led the procession outdoors, and once Father Gene was outside the rest of the parishioners followed. As Marci and her family left the church, they too congratulated Sophia, and her attendants, along with the new mayordomos.

By now, the aroma of the food filled the air, and everyone was ready to get to the food booths. Travis headed right to the savory green chili burritos. He and his family had been in New Mexico but for a few months, and he could not get his fill of the chili. When Marci told the woman what she wanted on her hamburger, the woman asked her if she also wanted green chili. Seems chili was what everyone topped their food with, but Marci could not get used to eating their spicy food—at least not yet, so she wanted hers with plenty of mustard. Having had their fill, Travis and his family went to the cakewalks; tried their luck at the bingos, looked at the arts and crafts where they had a butterfly painted on their cheeks. Having visited all of the booths, and sampled the various foods, Marci and Caleb went to the amusement rides. All this was new to them, and Marci had to admit if only to herself, she was having fun. For a little while, she forgot everything, and everyone she left behind as she enjoyed herself.

Once they ate and walked around, Travis, Marie and the kids went to listen to the Brown River Band who was playing their last song. Those who were ready to dance had to wait for the musicians to set up their instruments. Once the music started, Travis and Marie got the urge to dance. Watching how the others moved to the music, Travis and Marie knew they could dance to the Spanish music the band was playing. Marci didn't think her parents knew what they were doing, but they followed the rhythm of the music. Seeing her parents were having fun, Marci asked Caleb if he wanted to get something to eat, and ride the Ferris wheel.

By the time Marci and Caleb got back, Travis and Marie were talking to the couple they had gone out to dinner with in the summer. Travis tried to get Marci to talk to the couple's daughters, but she had a bad feeling about them. Marci was not sure why she was acting like this, but she felt she owed it to her friends in Virginia. She felt she was not ready to have her father force her into making new friends.

Laundry

While Rafael and Rosita were in Albuquerque, the rest of the family was helping fill the Thanksgiving baskets for the needy at the San Clemente Parish Hall. Juanita, who did not volunteer to help stayed at home and did her chores. Once she was done, she did not know what to do, so she gave her dog Rascal a bath. Walking into the laundry to put the wet towels into the hamper Juanita got an idea. It was a warm Saturday in November, and a perfect morning to wash clothes and hang it outside on the clothesline. She then called Marci to ask if she wanted to help her with a project. Thinking Juanita's cousins were coming to the ranch, Marci was about to decline the invitation. Juanita then told her she was going to surprise her mom and do the family laundry and Marci quickly changed her mind. By the time Marci arrived at Juanita's house, Juanita had the Maytag washing machine in the middle of the kitchen. Marci had never seen a washing machine like the one she was looking at because her mother always took their laundry to the Laundromat.

As Marci watched Juanita plug the cord from the washing machine into the wall socket, Juanita told her they didn't have much time. "We have to finish before mom and dad get back from Albuquerque," Juanita told her friend. Marci had no idea what she was doing, but she did what Juanita told her to do. When Marci screwed the hose to the kitchen faucet, water squirted all over the kitchen, because she did not screw it on right. Juanita's surprise was getting to be more difficult than either girl thought it would be. Never having actually washed clothes, Juanita was doing what she had seen her mother and sisters do so many times. While Marci filled the washing machine with cold water, Juanita sorted the clothes. First, she separated the clothes into three piles; whites included socks, underwear, and sheets. Light colored clothes were next and the last pile were the dark clothes, shirts and pants.

Having sorted the clothes, the girls put the first load into the washing machine. Because the boy's socks were included, they let the clothes soak in Clorox. When they checked the kitchen clock, the girls knew the white clothes had soaked for exactly a half hour. Then they emptied the water out of the machine and threw the water outside. Juanita then had Marci fill the washing machine with hot water, while she poured the Tide into the water. Marci also had to fill the aluminum tub with cold water because that is where they would rinse the clothes. Turning the knob on the washing machine, the girls watched the agitator dissolve the soap, and swish the clothes around in the soapy water. Everything was going just as Juanita was hoping it would. Juanita did not want to burn her hands, as the water was very hot, so she got the fork her mother used to take the clothes out of the hot water.

Once the clothes was rinsed, and put through the wringer, the clothes went into a basket where it was taken outside to hang on the clothesline. The girls were feeling so good because it made them feel grown-up. By the time they came in from hanging the white clothes, it was time to take the light colored clothes out of the washing machine, and put it through the wringer so they could rinse it.

By this time, the water had cooled a little and Juanita did not have to use the fork. As Juanita was guiding the clothes through the wringer, Marci asked her a question. Juanita took her eyes away from what she was doing for a split second, and only a second; however, when she did, she let out a horrible scream. Marci thought Juanita was joking when she said her hand was going through the rollers. That was until she saw Juanita's hand, her wrist, and part of her arm on the opposite side. By this time, Juanita's face was turning quite pale from the pain. Yet, she managed to tell Marci to unplug the cord from the wall socket. Marci stood motionless, and in shock until Juanita yelled, "Damn it Marci, pull the damn cord before my body goes through and squeezes me to death." Marci heard Juanita tell her what she had to do, but she could not move. Once again, Juanita yelled, "Marci, pull the damn cord," and this time Marci did as she was told. Juanita then hit the red bar that released the rollers and they pulled her arm out. As they did this, Juanita's body went limp, and she let out a sigh of relief.

Seemed like hours had passed while the girls were trying to release Juanita's arm from the tight grip of the rollers, but in actuality, it was but a few minutes. Shortly after that, Juanita's older sister came in and asked her what they were doing. The girls told her what happened and she checked Juanita's arm. She saw red marks where the rollers pressed on her arm, but nothing was broken. Juanita was told to take an aspirin, and go to bed. Marci was told to go home, and as scared, as she was she ran out of the house so fast she forgot she had ridden her bike.

Marci ran into her house and trying to catch her breath, Marie asked her, "What's wrong?" Once she was able to breathe, Marci told her mother how she was helping Juanita wash clothes and the rollers on the washing machine tried to squeeze the life out of her friend. Seeing how scared Marci was, her mother assured her Juanita was going to be all right. Marie then told her daughter she would take her to Juanita's house to make sure she was okay. When they arrived, Marci saw Juanita was helping her older sister wash the rest of the clothes. Relieved her friend was not hurt and able to use her arm Marci ran and hugged her.

Monday when Marci went to school, she looked for Juanita. When she found her, Juanita told Marci her mother told her never to do the laundry when no one was there to supervise her. On the other hand, she praised her for trying to help. Marci tried to tell Juanita how scared she was that her whole body was going to be squeezed through the wringers, and they laughed until their sides ached. Their friends asked what was so funny, but Juanita and Marci looked at each other and laughed even more.

The thought of Juanita going through the twelve-inch rollers was so outrageous they laughed until the tears were rolling down their faces. When Jan and Elaine came to join them, the girls tried to tell them what took place, but it was one of those times where they had to be there to appreciate why they were laughing. Never again did Juanita and Marci try to do the laundry by themselves. Instead, they compared socks to see whose was the whitest. Marci's who had hers done at the Laundromat, or Juanita's whose socks were washed at home.

Thanksgiving

Travis and his family were going to celebrate their first Thanksgiving in New Mexico, with Rafael, Rosita and their extended family. When Rosita invited Marie and her family, Rosita told Marie not to take anything as there would be plenty of food, but Marie decided to bake some pies. Not sure what she did different, Marie was pleasantly surprised when her piecrusts came out extra flaky and the meringue so fluffy. When Marie and her family arrived, Rosita commented on how beautiful the pies looked. With a compliment from Rosita, Marie no longer had to worry her pies would be a flop. When Marci saw all the food on the table, she thought the entire neighborhood was coming to Juanita's house. How wrong she was, as Juanita told Marci that was what her mother prepared for any gathering. If Marci thought there was a lot of food, she soon changed her mind when Grandma, Tiá Lupe, the Albuquerque cousins, neighbors, and friends arrived. Before anyone started to eat, they gathered in the dining room and Rafael, and Rosita blessed their friends and family who gathered to share this special meal. Silently, Marci also gave special thanks for having survived the move to New Mexico, and able to share this day with her family and new friends.

Other than the turkey, mashed potatoes, gravy, salads, and desserts, nothing was the same as the Thanksgiving dinners Marci was accustomed too. In Virginia, families served gravy over their mashed potatoes; however, here in New Mexico, their choice was red or green chili along with gravy. Seeing how some of the children were also eating chili, Marci did the same as did her father. The amount she served was about the size of a pea; however, the chili was spicier than what she was used to eating. Not wanting the kids to make fun of her, she ate the food with chili first. The food was delicious, and Marci ate until she felt she was about to burst the seams on her pants. Everyone had their fill of food, and the children went out to play. Juanita's family did not have fancy toys, but the toys they did have were a lot better than those bought at any store.

When asked if she knew how to walk on stilts, Marci said, "She did."

Ready to show them how good she was; she wanted to know where the stilts were. Juanita then ran to the woodpile, to retrieve the two rough homemade stilts. As she snickered, one of the Albuquerque cousins said, "Okay Marci, show us what you can do." Marci could not believe these were the stilts. Where were the nice shiny store bought ones, she thought Juanita was talking about, and the ones she was going to show-off with? Caleb came to her rescue and asked if he could try them. Soon the boys took over, and the girls had to think of something else to play with. Again, Juanita came up with another idea, and said, "That's okay we can walk around with our high heels." Marci was used to walking with her mother's shoes, so once again she felt very comfortable. Again, she was surprised that they were not going to wear real shoes. Running to the trash pile, Juanita got a couple of cans of Pet milk. Putting a piece of baling wire through the holes on the top of the can, she told Marci those were their high heels. Marci laughed thinking Juanita was joking. When she wrapped the wire over her shoe, Marci saw Juanita stand on the cans. Juanita then proceeded to show Marci how she learned to walk on homemade high heels. "The best thing is, that we can use any size and height we want," Juanita said. It looked so easy, so Marci asked if she could try them.

What Juanita made look so easy was more difficult than Marci thought. Once she tied them around her shoes and stood up, Marci lost her balance and fell. Having fallen a few times, Juanita told her what she was doing wrong. Marci managed to get the hang of the Pet milk high heels, and had no trouble balancing, and walking on them. Marci then saw Juanita's brothers and other boys throwing corncobs with a feather stuck in it into the air. "What are they playing with?" Marci asked Juanita. "Why those are, our helicopters and we see who can throw it up the highest. Then we watch as the corncob comes twirling down," Juanita replied.

Marci and Caleb had so much fun playing with homemade toys, and were amazed at the things Juanita and her brothers had. Caleb's favorite was the cowboys chasing the Indians. All he had to do was drop a magnet on the dirt, and whatever particles stuck to the magnet, that is what was placed on any piece of paper. When he put the magnet underneath the paper, he moved it back and forth to make the magnetic particles move. Depending on which direction the magnet moved, that was where the Indians and cowboys chased each other.

This time when it came to playing basketball, Caleb had competition. Felix was just as talented as was Caleb, and for a while it was a one-on-one. They were having so much fun the men decided to join them. A few minutes into the game, the men decided to challenge the boys, and the basketball game turned into a free for all. Not wanting to admit they could not keep up with the boys, the men decided it was time for them to go indoors and play poker. As the sun went down the kids decided to play hide-n-seek, and they did this until it was time for the Albuquerque family to leave. Of course, nobody ever left Rosita's house without taking something to carry the family over for at least another meal. When Travis and his family were getting ready to leave, he saw Rosita put a jar of her delicious homemade salsa into their goody bag. Marie and the rest of the family could not eat a lot of the salsa because it was too spicy for them, but that did not bother Travis.

Now that Thanksgiving was over, the local stores were getting ready for Christmas. The churches were preparing for their yearly tradition of "*Las Posadas*," and the schoolchildren were looking forward to their two-week Christmas break. Marci had given thanks for everything she gained since they moved to New Mexico, and not Mexico, and now her family would start preparing for Christmas. Soon they would start to decorate their house inside and outside with Christmas lights and other decorations.

As New Mexican's have done for centuries, Travis's family would see parishioners from San Clemente do a nine-day re-enactment of Mary and Joseph searching for a place where Mary will give birth to her Son. For nine evenings, parishioners from San Clement and other parishes then go to designated houses seeking shelter for Mary. While the pilgrimage continues, the parishioners sing Christmas Carols as they walk down the street. When Joseph and Mary are denied entrance, the entire group is invited indoors for refreshments. Then on Christmas Eve, children from the parish re-enact the birth of Jesus, and at this time the Posadas have come to an end and Christmas is celebrated.

Christmas

By this time, many of the residents decorated their homes with Christmas lights and set Luminarias out to show Joseph and Mary the way. Once again, this was something Travis and his family had never seen. When Travis asked Sal to tell him what Luminarias are, Sal told him "Luminarias are nothing more than a votive candle placed on sand inside a brown paper bag. Some will tell you they are Farolitos, and others say Luminarias. What they are called really does not matter. Anyway, when the Luminarias are all in place, the neighbors wait until the sun starts to go down to start lighting the candles. It is not an easy task, and it takes time to light them. Once you see how beautiful they look, and the calming effect they have on the people is all that counts," he said. "Some of us also do the same thing to welcome the New Year."

When Travis was told about this tradition, he did not tell his wife or his children because he wanted to surprise them. So on Christmas Eve, Travis and his neighbors lined hundreds and hundreds of Luminarias up and down the sidewalks and their homes. By the time this was done, the sun was starting to go down, and it was up to Travis to light the Luminarias at his house. When they were lit, the entire neighborhood took on a peaceful and calm atmosphere just as Sal told Travis it would, and Travis now understood what he meant.

Throughout the day, Marie and her children were busy getting ready for Christmas and too busy to notice Travis was not indoors. When he went inside, he asked his family to go outside because he had a surprise for them. Not sure what the surprise was, Marie and the children followed him. Marie and the kids could not get over how beautiful the neighborhood and their yard looked. They had never seen anything so beautiful. By the time the family came indoors, Marci was tired, as it had been a long day. She tried taking a nap so she would stay awake during the Midnight Mass, but she could not. As she looked out her bedroom window, Marci saw the Luminarias emit their soft glow. Happy her father had done that for her family, she knew he helped guide the Infant Jesus to their home, and she took a nap. Marci had barely closed her eyes when her mother was waking her up to get ready for Mass. Rubbing her eyes, and getting out of bed, Marci went to her bedroom window to see if the Luminarias were still lit. When she saw they were still giving off their glow, she started to get dressed.

Tonight, Marci would wear her new dress, nylons, shoes, and gloves she and her mother bought at the mall. When she combed her hair, she wove the shimmering blue ribbon in her hair that matched her dress. Once dressed and her hair combed, she looked in the mirror, and could not believe how pretty, and grown-up she looked. Tonight she was pleased with the young girl in the mirror who was looking back at her. By the time Travis and his family entered the church, it was hard to find a place to sit.

Decorating the sides of the altar were two-twelve-foot Christmas trees with miniature strings of lights on them that sparkled like the stars on a dark moonless night. When Marci knelt down to pray, she saw the church lights were dimmed. For Marci that only added to the beauty of Christmas Eve. As the choir sang, "It Came upon a Midnight Clear," the feeling that came over her was like the light from the luminarias, calming and peaceful, and she felt so blessed. Her heart was overflowing with joy. When Father Gene gave his sermon, Marci listened to everything he had to say. She even joined the choir and sang along with them. For

Marci, nothing was more important than to participate wholly in the Mass, and to thank God for sending the Infant Child.

On this holy night, Mary gave birth to the Infant Jesus, and no matter where anyone sat, the peaceful Crèche welcomed the parishioners. Once Mass was over and the doors leading out of the church were opened, someone yelled, "It's snowing!" Marci could not wait to go outside and see the snow, and just as beautiful as everything had been, this too was a wonderful sight. The snow gave the luminarias that decorated the sidewalks and the roof of San Clement Catholic Church a mystical glow.

Midnight Mass was over and as their tradition back in Virginia; Travis drove around the neighborhood to see the lights and the decorations. Driving through the neighborhood, the swirling snow made the Christmas lights on the houses shine brighter. However, the luminarias around the Nativity sets, driveways, and sidewalks were starting to go out. As Travis drove into their driveway, their luminarias still had the same peaceful, and magical glow about them, as did those at the church.

Even though Marci and her family were now New Mexico, residents the same traditions they shared in Virginia, would be followed here. As in Virginia, Caleb begged his father to let him open all of his presents. However, Travis reminded his son this was their way of celebrating Christmas. Just because the family moved to a new state, nothing changed. Having said this, Travis told Marci and Caleb to select the present they were going to open, but the rest were to remain under the Christmas tree. Caleb tore open Santa's present, and saw Santa gave him Spiderman pajamas. Wanting to show them off to his family, he ran into the bathroom; put his pajamas on, and paraded around the room.

Marci was delighted Santa brought her the gold bracelet she had seen at the jewelry store. This one had her name on it and it came with a pair of earrings. Going to the mirror, Marci put her earrings on, as she wanted to see how they looked on her. Then it was Marie and Travis' turn to open their gifts, and they were pleased Santa knew they needed knitted hats, scarves and gloves, and Santa even gave Cleopatra some toys. Having opened their gifts, the family went to bed. After Marci put her pajamas on, she set her new clothes aside for Christmas. Once again, she thanked Jesus for bringing her to New Mexico and making her so happy. Too excited to sleep, Marci thought she would lie down and read. Getting a book off her bookshelf, Marci got into bed and as she lowered her head on the pillow, she fell asleep.

Christmas morning, Caleb woke the family up so they could open their presents. "Come on everybody wake up. It's Christmas," he yelled. Marci jumped out of bed and ran to the Christmas tree where Caleb was opening the rest of his presents. Marci had some catching up to do but both she and Caleb opened one gift after another. From her father, Marci got a new bike as she had outgrown the old one. Her mother gave her a new bedspread for her bed, and a matching one for Cleopatra. From Caleb, she received a carrying case for her camera, and Cleopatra gave her some film. Everything was just so perfect Marci had to pinch herself to make sure she was awake. Marci gave Caleb a new basketball and a basketball net. His mother gave him a Spiderman sleeping bag and flashlight.

Now when it was time for Caleb to open his father's present, he had to go outside. Caleb did not want to go out because it was bitterly cold, but did what his father asked him to do. Once he was outside, Caleb asked his father, "Why couldn't you bring my gift inside." "Well son, Travis said, your Christmas gift is too big for me to bring inside. Besides, you have to look for it," Travis replied. Caleb looked all around, but the falling snow prevented him from seeing what his father had given him. Then Marci saw what Caleb was trying so hard to find. Next to the wall was a doghouse with a big blue ribbon on it. Yet Caleb did not see it. Back in Virginia, the family could not have a dog because the yard was too small. Now their new house had a backyard that was so big, Caleb could have as many dogs as he wanted. When Caleb saw the doghouse, he did not know what to do. Then it dawned on him there might be a dog inside, and he wanted to see what it looked like. When he looked inside, the doghouse was empty.

"Dad, where's my dog?"

"Well son," Travis replied, "I thought we would go to the dog pound where you can pick the one you want. He is going to be your dog, and it's important you like him."

"Hey Dad, do you think we can go on Monday? I think I know what type of dog I want."

"Sure son, we can all go. No! Dad, this is my dog, and I want you and me to go get him."

Marie agreed with Caleb. "It should be the men of the family to go get the dog who will be protecting this family," she said. Travis agreed to his son's suggestion and everyone went indoors to eat breakfast and enjoy the family's first Christmas in New Mexico. While Marci was eating breakfast, she asked her father if after the holidays were over he would paint her old bike. "Now that I have a new one, I want to give the old one to Juanita's family so they can have two bikes. One bike for so many kids just isn't enough." Her father agreed to her suggestion and this made Marci's Christmas even better.

Breakfast was over and Caleb went to play with his toys; Marci went to her room to watch TV, and enjoy the gifts she received from her family, and Travis and Marie took their coffee into the den to enjoy their first Christmas in their new home.

The wind had died down, but snow continued to fall as Travis and his family went to visit their friends and deliver Christmas gifts. No matter where the family went, they were invited to eat. It was like Thanksgiving where everyone ate until they could eat no more. However, on this their first Christmas, Travis's family did not stay long at Rafael and Rosita's house, nor at any of the neighbors. This was their time to be together as a family in their new state, and their new home.

Of course, that did not stop any of the family members from snacking all day long. Travis, Marie, and Caleb eventually fell asleep, but for Marci, it was another day where she would write Vanessa a letter. Marci wanted to tell her friend all about Christmas in New Mexico, but she could not find the right words. For as much as she wanted to describe the Christmas traditions she could only write it was a beautiful sight, and she wished Vanessa had been here to see it—but that just did not sound right. Throwing a few sheets of paper into her wastebasket, and putting her pen down, Marci had to think how she was going to write what she had to say. Having taken a few minutes, Marci started her letter by telling Vanessa how surprised she was when she saw a snowman made out of tumbleweeds. Knowing Vanessa had no idea what tumbleweeds are, Marci tried to tell her how some snowmen in New Mexico, are different from the ones in the display windows at the mall.

Trying to describe what they looked like, she wrote how one big round brown weed with a million small thorns is placed on top of the other. Once it is sprayed with white paint, or snow from a spray can, a scarf, mouth, eyes and a nose are added to it. Marci knew none of this would make any sense to Vanessa, but she tried to describe the snowman as best she could. She even sent her a picture of Grandma's snowman. Marci told her friend about the long-standing tradition of *Las Posadas* that start two weeks before Christmas and end on Christmas Eve. She also wrote how during the day for Christmas Eve, she and some of the kids went around the neighborhood shouting, "Mis Crismes, Mis Crismes" (My Christmas, My Christmas), until they were given something to celebrate Christmas Eve. It was sort of like Halloween except they did not go to Ms. Webb's house.

When other kids came to Marci's house, her mother was prepared because the neighbors had already told her about this tradition. When Juanita invited Marci to go with her, and her friends to her grandmother's house, Marci was not sure what they were going to do, but she went anyway. When they entered Grandma's house, the neighborhood kids were kneeling. Marci asked Juanita what was going on, and Juanita told her they were waiting for Grandma to bless them.

Once Grandma blessed the kids, she gave them a winter pear from a large bowl and they went around the neighborhood to see what the other neighbors would give them. Marci told Vanessa, how she and Juanita had a great time as they went from house to house filling their pillowcases with fruits, candy, and how some of the neighbors even gave them money. Marci also told her friend she never thought she would have a friend who would be generous enough to share her grandmother with her. Now she wished she had known her grandmothers, but that was not to be.

By the time, Marci finished writing the letter to Vanessa; it was as if she had written in her journal. The letter was seven pages long, and that did not include the pictures she sent. Having written her letter, Marci sat back on her chair. She then wondered why she was finding it hard to describe what Christmas was like in New Mexico. Maybe she did want to be selfish, and wanted to keep her first New Mexico Christmas where it belonged…in her heart. She then realized she just did not want Vanessa to understand what it was she was trying to say.

Shredder

The weekend was over, and Travis and Caleb went to the dog pound to find the dog they were going to adopt. When Caleb saw all of the dogs that were there, his choice suddenly became more difficult. Seems Caleb was not the only one who was promised a dog or a cat. Boys were looking for the special dog that was going to protect their family he selected. The girls were looking for the kitten that would purr on her lap when she sat down. There were dogs and cats of every size, with short hair, long hair, no hair, and all of them trying their best for someone to take them to their home. Some boys and girls found the animal they wanted right away, while others walked up and down until they left with a very excited and happy puppy or kitten.

Many of the dogs were adopted and Caleb did not think he was going to find the one he wanted. The remaining dogs barked, and jumped to get Caleb's attention, which made it more difficult for him to choose one. Then Caleb saw the dog he wanted. He was a beige medium size boxer with big brown eyes. As he was about to reach for the dog, another boy took him. Why had he not seen the dog sooner? Caleb did not know what to do as the dog that was going to protect their home left the dog pound. Once more, Caleb and Travis walked up and down the aisles, but none of the other dogs appealed to him. As Caleb was about to choose another dog, the boy who took his dog came back.

"I'd like to trade this dog for another one," the boy told the employee, "Can I do that?" The boy was told he could and with that, he selected the small black, and white Terrier, Caleb was standing next to the Terrier, and as the boxer was about to go back into his cage, Caleb said "he wanted to take that dog home." "I'm happy this dog is going to a good home because this was the second time he was returned. I can see by the look on your face you will be a good owner," the employee told Caleb.

"Dad, this is the one I want! I know he will make a good watchdog, and I will take good care of him. See how he is looking at me. I know he likes me," Caleb told his father.

"Okay son let's see what we have to do to take him home."

As if that was his cue, the Boxer licked Caleb's face. Soon the adoption papers were filled, and Caleb adopted the first family dog. Travis didn't know if Caleb or the dog was more excited about finding a partner. As Travis drove home, he asked his son if he had a name for his dog. Caleb looked at the dog, and could not think of one.

Marie was flipping through a magazine that came in the mail when she saw Travis coming up the driveway. Soon as Travis stopped the car, and Caleb opened the car door, the dog jumped out. Marie, anxious to welcome the newest member of their family stood up, and opened the door. She did not have a chance to see what he looked like because the dog ran past her, and ran to the Christmas tree. As Caleb and Travis were hanging their jackets in the closet, they heard a loud crash. Marie ran into the den to see what the commotion was all about. As they walked into the den, they saw Caleb's dog wagging his tail next to a fallen Christmas tree.

Cleopatra ran off hissing as she was rudely woken up from her nap. Seeing the scared dog, there was no way Marie could get angry. After all, he was just a pup who was excited to have a home and all they could do was laugh.

For Marci, all this commotion was the perfect opportunity for her to use her new camera and she took a picture of Caleb's dog next to the Christmas tree. Marie had not intended to take the tree down for another week, but she figured she might as well do it now. After the tree was up, Marie asked Travis to bring the trunk from the garage as she started taking the remaining decorations down. Not looking where she was stepping, Marie's foot stepped on something soft. Afraid to look down to see what she had stepped on Marie was relieved to see it was not dog poop. Instead, Marie saw it was a present that had not been opened, and she picked it up. Turning it over, she saw it was something her daughter had given her. When she called Marci to ask her what it was, Marci said, "Oh mom, I forgot to give it to you. I made it all by myself." Eager to see what her daughter had made, Marie tore the wrapping paper and saw it was an apron. Once she unfolded the apron, she could not believe Marci had made it and asked her who taught her to sew.

"Mom, do you remember when I first met Juanita? Well one day I asked her who made her clothes and she told me her mother made them. She also told me, she knew how to sew, and asked me if I wanted to learn. I told her I did, and I had been hiding this for almost a year. Do you like it?"

"Honey, I love it. Thank you for this special gift." Then as Marie went around the tree to unplug the lights, she called Caleb.

"Okay son, this is the first lesson in having a dog. You need to get the bucket, mop, and wipe up what your dog did."

" Oh mom, that is gross. Why do I have to clean it up? I didn't do it."

"No, but he is your dog, and this is why you need to train him to live outside in his doghouse," Marie told her son.

Caleb cleaned up the mess his dog made, and pulled on the pup's leash, however, the pup was as stubborn as any dog could be. Caleb was trying to take his dog outside, but it was more difficult then he thought. Frustrated, Caleb kicked him because he would not listen. When the dog let out a yelp, Marie turned around and asked, "What happened?" "I kicked him so he would get up," Caleb told his mother. Angry that he kicked the dog, Marie told him, "He was never, ever to kick an animal just because he would not obey. We can take him back to the pound if that is how you are going to treat him," Marie told her son. "Mom, I'm sorry, I just got angry. I promise never to do that again and I promise I will try to train him," Caleb said as he petted his dog. Caleb then took the dog outside and released him from his leash to do his business.

That night the dog howled and scratched at the garage door so someone would let him in, but no one did. The following morning, Caleb went outside to check on the dog because like the rest of the family, he was not able to sleep. Caleb had not thought of a name for his dog, but he knew it would come to him. As he stood out on the porch, he called his dog to see if he would respond to any of the names he thought of naming him.

"Here Lucky, here Butch, come on Sandy, here Rover, here Buster," but the dog did not respond. Wondering where he was, Caleb walked out to the back yard. Sure enough, there he was wagging the stub of a tail, and sitting next to Marie's rosebushes, happy as any dog could be. Caleb yelled," Oh no, Mom, Dad come here!"

Travis and Marie did not know what was going on, but rushed to the backyard to see why Caleb was so upset. Rushing outdoors, Travis and Marie were shocked at what they saw. Their beautiful backyard was full of holes, and Caleb's pup was next to Marie's favorite rosebush chewing on Caleb's new basketball. Marie stood speechless as she saw the damage the dog had done. The puppy managed to dig up most of her rosebushes in the middle of winter. Travis also did not know what to say until Caleb broke the silence. "Hey dad, I know what I am going to call my dog. His name is Shredder," Caleb announced ever so proudly. Travis and Marie laughed, and Caleb moved Shredder's doghouse to the other side of the house where he couldn't damage the remaining rosebushes. Because the ground was frozen, the rose bushes were taken indoors where they would be wrapped and placed in containers.

Once the ground warmed up, the roses would be replanted. Shredder was a quick learner, and he knew what he could, and could not do. He was a kind and gentle dog, and wherever Caleb went, Shredder was at his side. As the days passed, Shredder and Caleb became best friends. However, if Shredder thought someone was harming a member of his family, he would growl and bare his teeth. In the meantime, Cleopatra stayed indoors, and refused to make friends with the newest member of the family. For several days, Cleopatra did not come out of the bedroom she shared with Marci. A month or so later, Shredder was trained and times when the weatherman advised the animals be brought indoors, Shredder would run upstairs to sleep in Caleb's bedroom.

There were many more Halloween, Thanksgiving, and Christmases' for her family and her friends including many trips throughout New Mexico, but nothing would compare to their first Christmas in New Mexico. This time when Marci wrote Vanessa a letter, she included the family's experience with Caleb's dog. Marci would gladly have written to her other friends, but Vanessa was the only one who answered.

Spring Break

During spring break, Juanita and Marci went to visit Grandma on a daily basis. One morning when they went to Grandma's house Marci knew she had made her rice pudding. As Marci opened the kitchen door, the aroma of cinnamon lingered. Grandma had just served herself some rice pudding and invited the girls to eat with her. Marci had never eaten rice pudding and asked Grandma for the recipe because she wanted her mother to make her some. When Grandma gave Marci her recipe, she could not believe it was so simple to prepare and so delicious. Having eaten their dessert and the dishes washed, Grandma asked the girls to sit outside so they could visit under the oak tree.

The next day the girls again went to visit Grandma and this time she was making tortillas. Grandma saw Marci was watching her every move and asked her, "If she wanted to make one." Marci tried as hard as she could but she never mastered the art of making them round as Grandma did.

Juanita already knew how to make tortillas as her mother taught her so she sat and watched. Grandma loved the girls and never favored one over the other. Yet they were always on their toes trying to duplicate grandma's recipes but that never happened. Juanita and Marci did not have the magic ingredients grandma had–love and experience.

While Juanita was in Albuquerque with her mother Marci was alone with nothing to do. Getting on her bike, she peddled her way to Grandma Wright's house. When she got there, Grandma was crocheting as she sat on the porch swing.

"What are you doing Grandma?" Marci asked.

" Oh, I'm just finishing a doily for a friend of mine."

Sitting next to Grandma, Marci watched what she was doing. After a few minutes, Marci asked grandma if she would teach her to do what she was doing.

"I want to learn everything you can teach me because one day I will have children and I want to teach them everything you have taught me."

Delighted at the prospect of teaching a child the art of crocheting she learned when she was young; Grandma told Marci she would teach her how to crochet if she was serious about learning. Having said she was Marci learned the basic steps to crocheting. It took Marci several lessons before she caught on to what Grandma was trying to teach her. Once she learned how to crochet, she made her mother a doily for her coffee table. Proud of what she had done Marci went to show it to grandma. Examining the doily grandma told her the next step was to learn how to starch it. This too was another lesson for Marci, and with grandma's help, she completed the task. When the doily dried, Marci was not very happy because it was so limp—but Grandma was very pleased. Knowing what she had to do Marci asked Grandma for the box of Faultless starch so she could starch it some more.

Peddling her bike as fast as she could, Marci rushed home so she could starch her doily the way she wanted. Forgetting how much starch to add to the water Marci decided to pour the remainder of the box into the pan. Leaving the doily in the pan of water and starch Marci went to make herself a sandwich. She forgot all about her project when her mother came into the kitchen and sat down to eat. A half-hour or so later Marci remembered her doily and went back into her bedroom. By this time, the starch had thickened and Marci had a mess on her hands. Later when Marci took the doily out, she realized she had starched it too much. Removing as much of the white clumped starch, Marci stretched it on a towel, and left it to dry. Even though there were white clumps on the doily, she was proud of what she had done. She then placed it on the coffee table as she went to get her mother. She wanted to show her what Grandma taught her to do. However, Marci never expected Caleb to rush into the den and see the doily. Seeing it, Caleb thought it was a huge spider web with insects. When Marci was taking her mother to show her what Grandma taught her, she saw Caleb holding the stiff doily in his hands. Happy as he was he asked his mother if it was something she bought him for his birthday. When Marie told Caleb, "his sister made it" all he heard was that "it was a surprise" and he hugged his sister.

Caleb's birthday was a couple of days away and he thought Marci made it for him. Marci did not have the heart to tell him it was not his and all she could do was to wish her brother an early happy birthday. Caleb said, "Thanks sis now I have a spider web for my Spiderman" and ran outside to show his friends. While Caleb was showing his black spider web to his friends, they wanted Marci to tell them where she bought it. Caleb told his friends his sister made it for him and they wanted one too. "She can't" Caleb told them "she made it for me for my birthday and she used up all of her string." Caleb never heard his mother tell him it was something Marci made her. Now her beautiful stiff doily was hanging from a tree limb swaying back and forth like a spider web with insects wrapped in a silk cocoon. After that experience, Marci never attempted to crochet again.

Daddy's Garden

Now that the planting season was almost here, Marci and her father were busy cleaning the area their bountiful garden would grow. While Travis was busy tuning up the Rotor Tiller he bought last year, Marci started to clear the debris left by the wind, rain, and snow.

Several months passed, and once again, Travis and Marci were excited as they worked on their garden. Travis made sure he spread the fertilizer evenly as he went over the soil several times. Having completed the task she started, Marci sat on the ground, and could smell the moist soil. Satisfied with the way the soil looked, Travis made enough rows to plant the chili and vegetable seeds he saved from the previous year. When the rows were ready, Travis pushed the soil aside so Marci could put a couple of seeds into the hole. She would then cover the seed with the soil Travis pushed aside. Having planted the seeds, Travis pulled the switch to the well they installed, and watered the garden. Sitting on the ground, Travis and Marci watched the water break through the rows, and shoveled the dirt to stop any leakage. By the time they finished, father and daughter were tired, and sweaty.

When they went indoors, they took a shower, and relaxed. As they sat in the den drinking a tall glass of iced tea, Marci and her father talked about their garden. They knew it was going to be the most beautiful garden in the neighborhood; that is next to Rafael's garden. However, he lived four blocks from Travis and his family.

April and May passed, and Marci started to lose interest until her father called her to the garden. Stumbling on her shoelaces as she ran outdoors, Marci was excited to see why her father was calling her. Getting up, Marci ran to where her father was standing. Knowing they had done everything right, Marci hugged her father as he pointed to four green plants protruding out from the ground. From that day forward, they watered, hoed, and waited for their garden to yield the vegetables. Marci had gotten into a routine of checking the plants, yet nothing was happening. When she was about to give up on her routine, she saw the plants were flowering, and ready to grow the vegetables they would be eating.

One evening while Marci was checking her mother's flowers, she saw there was something else growing. Forgetting she too wanted to try her hand at planting, Marci had poked holes in the ground, and put chili seeds in the flowerbed. To her surprise, her hidden chili plants were growing along with the flowers. After months of hard work, the family was now enjoying fresh vegetables from the garden. Marci loved the taste of the fresh, crisp carrots and the earthly aroma of the soil as she pulled the vegetables from the ground. It was a mystery to her how a huge tomato plant would grow from a teeny tiny seed, and that a single seed could produce so many cucumbers and watermelons.

What a great summer Marci had with her father as they watched their garden grow. Marie also enjoyed going to the garden to gather the fresh vegetables to make salads for dinner. She also had enough vegetables she needed to make salsa like Rosita taught her. In the meantime, Caleb and his friends sat in the garden eating the tomatoes and cucumbers. Caleb was quick to eat what was growing, but not once did he lift a finger to hoe the garden.

One evening before the sun went down; Travis and Marci were hoeing the garden when he came across cigarette butts near the cucumber plants.

"I wonder how these got here," Travis said. Marci thought he was talking to her, and told her father "she had seen Caleb, Ernest and Isidro smoking. However, she was not sure they were the ones who left the cigarette butts." When they were done hoeing, they went indoors and washed their hands. Travis then called Caleb and Marci into the den where Marie was watching Julia Child on TV.

Caleb, Marci told me she saw you and your friends smoking in the garden, is this true? Travis asked. Marci saw the anger on Caleb's face as he admitted he and his friends were smoking. "Dad," Caleb said, "My friends and I did smoke, but I didn't like how it left a bitter taste in my mouth. My friends would smoke while I ate a tomato or cucumber, and that's why the cigarette butts were there."

Turning the TV off, Marie listened as Travis told his children how smoking could ruin their health, and how some of his friends died from it. The lecture was over, and Travis made his children promise they would never smoke. However, as they swore not to smoke, Marci saw Caleb cross his fingers so she knew he did not mean it. For the rest of the summer, Travis tended his garden, but by this time, Marci had lost interest.

The following week while Travis and Marie were at the supermarket, Caleb took Marci to the shed and forced her to smoke two cigarettes. Standing at the doorway, Caleb laughed at Marci, as she got sick to her stomach.

"If you tell Mom, or Dad I forced you to smoke, I'll make you smoke the whole pack. I am doing you a favor, as I want you to see what it is like to smoke, and the awful taste it leaves in your mouth," he said. When their parents came home, Marie asked her daughter if she was ill. Marci told her she had a bad stomachache— which was no lie. Thanks to Caleb, Marci never took up smoking, and even the thought of a cigarette made her stomach turn.

Another summer had come and gone, and at the end of August, Marci went to the garden, and saw the chili hanging from the plants was turning red. Curious, Marci went to ask her neighbor Emily if she knew why the chilies on the plants were turning color. Emily told her "the chili that is left on the plants turn red as it starts to dry. That is what I make the chili ristra's that are hanging on my porch," Emily told her.

"If I pick all of the chili that is on the plant, will you teach me how to make a ristra?" I want to surprise my father and I do not want the chili to go to waste.

"Sure," Emily said. "Go pick the chili even if it isn't red and bring it to me."

Running home, Marci picked all of the chili, and to her surprise, it filled a five gallon bucket. When Marci returned, Emily was waiting for her with string and bailing wire so she could teach Marci how to make a ristra.

"Okay Marci, watch what I do, and you will see how easy it is," Emily told her. Marci watched as Emily showed her how to string the chili, and then it was her turn. What Marci thought would be easy—was not. It took her several tries before she felt somewhat comfortable doing what Emily did. Then Marci realized it was in knowing how to pull the string around the chili stems that held the ristra together. Once she had the hang of it, Marci emptied the chili from the five-gallon bucket she brought. Marci strung the chili on the bailing wire, and saw what she had accomplished.

Eager to show her father what she did with the chili that was left in the garden. Marci could not believe it was her work hanging on Emily's porch. It was the most beautiful ristra in the whole neighborhood. Emily then took the ristra down and handed it to Marci. What a proud moment that was for Marci when her father told her he wanted to take her picture before he hung the ristra outside to dry.

"Dad, when I had to string the chili, I thought it was like roping a calf. First, I put the rope around the calf's neck. Then I brought the calf's legs together, and tied a loop around them." Travis laughed as he patted his daughter's head, and took the ristra from her.

Chicken Dinner

Then there was the time Juanita and a younger sister, Cynthia decided to surprise the family by preparing supper. Neither one knew what they wanted, but both agreed they wanted to surprise their parents. Cynthia asked Juanita what she had in mind, and Juanita thought and thought, and finally said, "How about chicken, mashed potatoes with gravy, tossed salad, and Jell-O? That is easy, and we can prepare it before Mom and Dad come home." The only problem with that suggestion was that the chicken was still alive. Of course, they didn't think that was a problem. All they had to do was catch the chicken, and kill it. Juanita and her sister knew what they had to do as they had seen their father do it many times. With that in mind, the girls chased the chickens to see which one they could catch. Twenty, then thirty-minutes passed when they realized they had been chasing the chickens for over an hour. Time was going by faster than they realized, but the girls did get plenty of exercise. As they cornered and caught the nice fat chicken, Marci stopped by. She saw Juanita grab the chicken from its legs, and swing it round and round, but the chicken would not die. The only thing that did was to make both Juanita and the chicken dizzy. Not able to hold on to the chicken, Juanita finally let go as she staggered, and fell to the ground. The chicken fared better; it was dizzy, but able to walk.

Seeing what her sisters were trying to do, Juanita's sister, Martha could not help but to sit down with Marci and laugh. She could not believe her sisters were actually trying to kill a chicken by getting it dizzy.

Curious to see what else, they were going to do; she sat down on the porch steps, and watched the sideshow. By this time, the chicken was easy prey for anyone to catch so out of nowhere; Martha figured it was time to take the chicken out of its misery. Before anyone could stop her, Martha caught the chicken, put it on the tree stump and whacked its head off with Rafael's small hatchet. Oddly enough when the chicken was released, it was still walking around. This scared the daylights out of

Marci, as she had never seen a chicken walking without its head. Marci also thought she never wanted to get Martha angry, as she did not know what she would do to her. Without its head attached to its body, the chicken was an easy catch for Cynthia. When the headless chicken was caught, Juanita asked Marci if she wanted to help. Reluctantly, Marci agreed, and helped fill an aluminum tub with boiling water. As Marci brought the first pail of water, Juanita put the chicken into the tub and started to pluck its feathers. Never in Marci's life had she seen a chicken get its head chopped off, nor had she ever smelled anything so horrible. Having plucked the chicken's feathers, removed everything the chicken had inside, it was time for Juanita to cut the chicken so they could fry it. As disgusted as Marci was, she was unable to pull herself away from what Juanita and Bess were doing. Having killed, plucked, cut and fried the chicken, everything went smoothly, and by the time Rosita and Rafael came home, Martha was setting the table.

That evening when Marci went home, she couldn't eat anything that resembled meat. While the rest of the family was eating homemade hamburgers, Marci decided to fix herself a plain salad as her stomach was upset. Marci's hands smelled like wet chicken feathers, and no matter what she did, she could not get rid of the smell, nor could she stop thinking how the chicken got its head chopped off with no remorse.

Anytime Travis's family was invited to Rafael's house for dinner, Marci wondered how this animal was butchered, and who did it. So long as Marci did not see the animal get slaughtered, she was okay eating what was placed before her—so long as it was not fried chicken. That was something she just could not eat, and chicken was no longer one of her favorite meals. Even when her mother prepared fried chicken, Marci tried forgetting the headless chicken, but that was hard to do.

Butchering a pig and preparing the meat is a tradition within the New Mexico Spanish population. When Marci's family was invited to attend a Matanza at Rafael's house, the family got up around four o'clock in the morning. Cold and windy as it was, Marci got dressed in her warmest clothing. When they arrived, Marci saw men from the neighborhood throwing wood into the blazing fire. Other men were laughing and greeting each other as they stood around drinking coffee trying to warm up.

By this time, Juanita, Ernest, and Isidro's family along with Sal, and some of the other neighbors had been up for several hours, and Marci was now going to see a thousand pound pig be shot right between the eyes. If she thought it was cruel to see a chicken get its head chopped off, seeing a pig shot was very sad. All Marci could think of was that somewhere there were piglets that were fatherless; and no longer did they have a father. When the pig's jugular was slit, blood squirted out, and someone was holding a pan so it would drain into it. As soon as the blood stopped dripping into the pan, it was rushed into the kitchen where the women were waiting to cook it. This took precise stirring and the person cooking the blood did not want it to burn. Almost cooked to perfection it was seasoned with chopped onions, chili hearts, and chili seeds, salt, garlic, and other spices if desired. Even the pig's head was put in the freezer to make tamales later on in the year, as nothing went to waste.

Watching the men put the pig into a tub full of boiling water to shave it, Marci asked Juanita, "Why the pig had to be shaved. Was it because it was male?" Juanita laughed, and told her, "It was so the neighbors and their friends would not get a mouth full of pig bristles when they ate the Chicharrones." (Pork skins.)

When the men slaughtered, and skinned the pig, the medium size pieces of meat were cooked in a large brass pot, full of grease. While the men were busy butchering the hog and preparing the meat, Rosita and her daughters were inside the house making tortillas so the neighbors and guests could eat. When Marci got the courage to taste the pork skin, she thought it was okay, until she ate one with bristles on it. Now she understood what Juanita told her about chewing on pig bristles, and she spit it out.

The sun was now poking through the clouds, but it was still very cold. Throughout the day, Juanita and Marci went with plates full of meat to the relatives and neighbors who could not make it. Around noon, everything was done and the meat from the pig had been cut, distributed, and put into the freezer. Those who came early in the morning to help were now going home to rest, as it had been a long day. Soon everyone except, Travis family, Tía Lupe, Sal and Ernest's family remained. Rafael and the men were tired, and hungry; as were the women who made sure the supply of coffee and fresh tortillas didn't run out for the Chicharrones.

Now it was time for those who were still at Rafael's to eat. When Marci sat at the table, the blood was placed next to the beans and Marci thought it not only looked horrible, but it smelled awful. Hearing someone at the table say, "Please pass the blood," she had to leave the table. Marci could not believe Juanita's family, neighbors, and friends were vampires. She also could not believe she was eating parts of a pig that earlier she had seen butchered. How could someone from the south forget her upbringing and become a cannibal? By the time, she finished eating; Marci forgot everything and enjoyed the food.

Now whenever Travis and his family were invited to Rafael's for a gathering, they could not refuse an invitation to go to any of the Matanzas Rafael had at his house. Of course, Marci was happy none of her pets ever met their maker the way some of Juanita's farm animals did.

After this experience, Marci decided she would sample the food before she refused to eat it.

One morning, Marci and Marie were eating breakfast when they heard someone honking the horn on Rafael's yellow Chevrolet truck, and Bess was yelling at the top of her lungs as they drove by. Opening the front door, Marci heard, "Vote for Bess as your next Possum Queen."

By this time, Marie came outside and saw Bess was wearing her pajamas and pink rollers on her hair, riding in the back of the pickup truck. She was waving her hands wildly as she shouted, "Hi Marci, be sure to vote for me as the next "Possum Queen." With that, they took off down the dirt road raising dust clouds as they drove to the next house.

"What is going on?" Marie asked her daughter. "Bess, Juanita's sister likes the Beverly Hillbillies and she wants to imitate Allie Mae," Marci replied. Marie laughed as she went indoors to finish her breakfast, and drink her coffee before everything cooled down.

Many times, Marci went to sleep over at Juanita's, and they would spy on the neighbor they were told practiced witchcraft, and had risen to the highest level of witchcraft. The neighborhood kids had seen her out late at night mixing her herbs and, brews in a black caldron, and were afraid of her. Her neighbors knew, and respected her, and those who practiced witchcraft went to her for advice. One by one, Juanita's sisters and Marci would climb the trees, and without turning her head, the neighbor would tell them she knew they were watching her. She yelled at the girls, and as she did, the flames beneath the pot got brighter, and sparks flew all around her.

There were many interesting characters living in the community, and Rafael's family along with some of the other neighbors and residents had nicknames for them. Along with the neighbor witch, there was "Superman, Blondie, the Staring Man, Mr. and Mrs. Jiggs and Lee Marvin." They were given these nicknames because they resembled movie stars, or comic strip characters. But we can't forget "Tara-Ta-Ta" who was given this nickname because he used to stutter, and "Ms. Mudaply." Ms. Multiply was a grade school teacher who could not pronounce the word "multiply" and she would say, "Mudaply." As usual, Rafael's younger brother, Lulo would say, "There's never a dull moment in this family," and he was so right!

One day, Rafael told Sal, Blondie had died.

"Oh no, what happened," he asked.

"He was hit by a car."

Sal then asked him how the wife was doing. Rafael and Lulo laughed as they realized Sal thought it was the man, and not the dog that died. Hearing it was the dog, Sal was upset and told Rafael he should have told him from the beginning it was the dog, but Sal was happy it wasn't their friend Blonde.

Carlsbad Caverns

Travis and his family were now celebrating their twelfth year in New Mexico, and he wanted to take his family on a vacation. Throughout the year, he had asked his neighbors and the other teachers where they had gone on their vacation. One of the teachers asked him if he had taken his family to the Carlsbad Caverns.

Before Travis decided to take his family there, he called to inquire what there was that the family could enjoy while they were there. The receptionist told him they could stop at White Sands National Monument. There were various activities they could do that included sledding down the dunes. Having heard this, Travis thought they might try it. Depending on what time they left the house, and arrived. As Travis and his family were on their way to Carlsbad Caverns, the scenery, and landscape was no different from what the family was now accustomed to seeing. However, as they neared White Sands, Marci started to see something white on the ground, and on the vegetation. Reaching their destination, Travis and his family were utterly amazed as the scenery changed.

Elaine tried to tell "Marci how the sand could fool anyone into thinking they were seeing snow," but Marci could not imagine what she was trying to tell her. Hard as Marci tried to imagining white sand, she could not. Elaine had told her to picture miles and miles of salt out in the open, but for Marci, that just did not make sense. Never in Marci's wildest dream could she have imagined what she saw. Elaine was right when she told Marci New Mexico has snow that never melts. Had Elaine not told Marci about the white sand, she would have thought they were coming upon a huge snowstorm.

The family finally arrived at White Sands, and after Travis parked the car, everyone got out. Anxious to run in the sand, Caleb and Marci could not wait to get out. Caleb was the first to take his shoes off, and run barefooted in the warm gypsum sand, leaving the rest of the family behind him. Catching up to her brother, Marci then decided to wait for her parents. When the family was together, they walked for several hours.

At about 3 p.m. Marie told Marci it was time to go. Looking around, she realized they wondered far from the car, and she could not see her husband or her son. Marci saw her father waving to get their attention, but Caleb was nowhere in sight.

Prankster that he was, Caleb pulled his white tee shirt over his head, and from a distance, no one could see him. Marie was frantic, and Travis had her sit down while he and Marci went to search for Caleb. For a split second, Marci thought she had lost her brother, but that would have been too good to be true. When Marie saw her little boy, she hugged, and kissed him as if he had been gone for months. Marci wanted to gag as she heard her mother treat Caleb as if he were a baby. As Marie took hold of his hand, Marci started to walk toward the car making sure her mother could see her—not that it would make a difference. Marci knew if she had done what Caleb did; her mother would have scolded her, but not Caleb. Oh, no, Caleb could do no wrong. He was the baby, and needed to be treated as one.

So what was Caleb going to do when they went sledding down the dunes? Was he going to be the clown that he is, and show off like he always did, or was he going to be a normal twelve-year-old idiot? Catching up to her brother, Marci didn't have to wait long to have her answer. Soon as Travis rented the waxed plastic saucer, Caleb let everyone there know what an idiot he was. Instead of lying flat on his stomach as the rest were doing, Caleb stood on the saucer. The minute he stood on the saucer, both he and the saucer went down the slope. Caleb and the saucer traveled a few feet before he was tossed on his head. Caleb rolled a distance, and when he stood up, he had to shake off all the sand from his body. He also had sand in his mouth and spitting it out as fast as he could. The other kids, along with the adults could not help but laugh at him. Marci laughed along with the rest, and it was now her turn to tease Caleb, and he had no way of getting out of this.

It was getting late and the family still had a ways to go before they arrived at their destination. Once in the car, Marci had a chance to remove the sand between her toes, and drink more water. She was tired, and knew she had to take care of her sunburn, but for her, it was well worth it. Nothing she had seen, and done earlier in the day could be duplicated anywhere, other than, in New Mexico.

Travis did manage to get his family to the motel before it filled up and Marci went straight to bed. Still burning from the sunburn she got earlier in the day, Marci did not bother to take a shower. Although she was aching, and feeling bad, she slept through the night.

The following day after they ate breakfast, Travis drove his family to Carlsbad Caverns. By the time they arrived, the temperature had risen to a high of one-hundred and four degrees, and that did not help Marci's sunburn. She knew it had to be cooler in the cavern than outside in the heat, and was ready to go down. Before the visitors entered the cavern, Ranger Bobby would give the tourist some interesting facts about the caverns and the bats that live in them. Not having a choice, the visitors listened to what the ranger had to say. Of course, it did not help that the temperature was rising and everyone wanted to go where it was nice and cool.

Ranger Bobby had a job to do, and no matter how hot it was, he had to educate the visitors about Carlsbad Caverns National Park. He told the tourists how the caverns were designated a National Monument on October 25, 1923. That the Park contains eighty-three separate caves, including the nation's deepest limestone cave that is 1,597 feet and third longest. He told them Carlsbad Cavern has one of the world's largest underground chambers and countless formations. How a variety of tours are offered year round, and is decorated with stalactites, stalagmites and a variety of formations that began more than 500,000 years ago after much of the cavern had been carved out. The ranger continued as he told the tourist how Carlsbad Cavern is a sanctuary for about one million bats. During the day, the bats crowd together on the ceiling of Bat Cave, a passageway that is near the natural entrance of the cavern. At nightfall, the bats leave the cave in gigantic swarms flying toward the Pecos and Black river valleys. There, they gorge themselves on moths and other night-flying insects. By the time they return, the bats have consumed thousands of insects that are harmful to the crops. Then the bats will sleep until they reemerge on the insects the following night.

After the ranger told the tourists about the caverns, and the bats that live in the caves, he said, "Well, I think we have kept you out in the heat long enough, so what do you say we go into the cavern where it is nice and cool. Remember, you are not to enter into any roped area to take pictures." With that, Rangers Bobby and Phillip guided them into the cavern, and if anybody had any questions, or wanted more information, they would be available. Then one by one, the visitors entered the cavern, and went from the scorching heat and bright outdoors into a cool cavern a mile down.

Marci and her family went from one cavern to the next, and when they came to the Blue, and Pink Rooms they were amazed at their size. The stalagmites looked as if they had been painted. It was so beautiful—yet so unreal. All this amazing and fascinating formations was so far down, and only those who went to visit the caverns saw what the rest of the world could only imagine what it is like. Further, into the cavern, Travis' family saw the King, and Queen Chambers that were even bigger than any Marci had seen so far. As the tourists went from one room to the next, everyone was especially carefully not to wonder to far from the trail. Some even went back to what they had seen earlier because they wanted to take more pictures. Then a tourist from another country did exactly what Ranger Bobby told them earlier not to do. He asked his friend to take his picture inside a roped area. As he took a step backward, he broke one of the stalagmites. Knowing he had destroyed something that could not be replaced, he immediately got out of the roped area. Both he and his friend were scared, as they knew they were in big trouble. Thinking no one saw them, they immediately walked back to one of the other chambers they had already been to. However, Marci saw what happened. She was so angry she told her father, and insisted on telling one of the rangers.

Ranger Phillip was also angry, but knew he had to remain calm. "He asked Marc, "If she could show him what it was the tourist broke. He also asked her, "If she remembered what the man was wearing." As Marci and the ranger were walking to the roped off area, she saw the man in the Blue Room, and pointed him out. Marci then showed the ranger where the tourist damaged the stalagmite. As soon as Ranger Phillip saw the damage, he called his partner. He described what the tourist was wearing and told him to detain the visitor.

Ranger Bobby caught up to the tourist, and asked if he had taken a picture inside one of the roped areas. At first, he denied it, but once he was told he was seen doing so, he admitted to what he had done, and they were escort outside the cavern. Marci was happy he admitted to destroying what had taken thousands of years to form, but she also thought he should be punished for what he had done. She didn't know what happened to the tourist, but she really did not care. He was careless and disobeyed the rules Having gone through the caverns a couple of times, Marci's family came out of the chilly cavern, and were greeted by the heat they left behind two or three hours earlier. This time no one complained about the heat because it felt so good. As they passed the Ranger's Station, Marci saw the tourist sitting in a chair looking extremely worried. All Marci could think was that she hoped they would be more careful next time they were taking pictures.

When Travis asked his family if they were hungry, Marci realized she had not eaten anything for five hours. Yet, no one thought of food while inside the cavern visiting this amazing wonder of the world. Suddenly the family was struck with hunger pangs, and they headed to the nearest restaurant. Travis and his family were settled in and New

Mexico was indeed their home. The family went on many outings, and explored other interesting sites, but their trip to White Sands, and Carlsbad Caverns would prove to be one the family would not soon forget.

Marci's Haircut

Even the sidewalks were too hot to walk on when Marci asked her mother if she could cut her hair. Marci told her mother she couldn't do anything with it, and it was sticking to the back of her neck. Marci and her mother discussed the pros, and cons of long and short hair, and after much discussion, Marie gave in to her daughter's request. Marie then asked Marci the one question she was dreading. "So Marci, where do you want to go get your haircut?"

Marci then broke out in a sweat when she told her mother she wanted Juanita to cut it. Marie hesitated, and told her daughter she did not think that was a good idea. Irritated, hot and not in the mood to argue with her mother, Marci said, "I think it is time I started to make my own decisions. Juanita knows exactly what she is doing. She always cuts her brothers', and sisters' hair."

Reluctantly Marie agreed, and told Marci, "You are absolutely right, I believe you are old enough to make your own decision, but all I ask is that you don't let her cut it too short."

Happy her mother was allowing her to make the final decision Marci called Juanita and asked if she would cut her hair. She wanted the same cut as what her younger sister Bess has because she wanted to comb it as she did. Juanita hesitated and told Marci she did not know how to cut hair other than on her dolls.

"Juanita, all I want is the same haircut like what your sister has," Marci replied.

"I don't know how it will come out, but I will try if that is what you want. So, when do you want me to do it?"

"Could you do it now? It is so hot, and my hair is sticking to the back of my neck because of the heat, it is driving me crazy, and I can't stand it. "

As soon as Juanita agreed to cut Marci's hair, she got on her bike and peddled to her friend's house as fast as she could. When Marci got there, she ran inside and saw Juanita had everything ready. It looked as if Juanita had done this many times. Again, Juanita told Marci this was the first time she cut anybody's hair. Marci didn't care, she just wanted to get rid of her long thick hair. Juanita told Marci to put her dad's shirt on so that she would not get her blouse full of hair. Then she had Marci sit on the chair next to the window.

"Okay Marci, I want you to close your eyes until I finish cutting it. When I am done, you can look in the full-length mirror, but not until I am done. You have a lot of hair, and as thick as it is, it might take me a while."

Ready for the transformation, Marci closed her eyes, and listened to the music on the radio. She knew once Juanita was done cutting her hair, she would look as pretty as her sister did. Then her mother could see she hadn't made a mistake by letting Juanita cut it.

Juanita started by parting and pinning Marci's hair in four sections, so far, so good. Little by little, Juanita started to cut Marci's hair. Snip, snip, snip went the scissors, and Marci could feel her beautiful copper hair fall to the floor. Marci knew she had a lot of hair, but did not realize how much until Juanita told her she was done. When Marci looked down, she saw the pile of hair on the floor. Juanita then handed Marci a mirror so she could see how she cut it in the back. Juanita told her it would no longer stick to her neck, and Marci would not have to worry about the heat. When Marci looked at the girl in the mirror, she was horrified, and thought she looked like a complete stranger. Marci looked like Caleb's twin, and all she had to do was to dress like him.

"Oh no, Juanita, what have you done?" Marci cried.

"I cut your hair like you asked me to. Marci, you look so cute; please don't cry," Juanita told Marci as she hugged her. Not cry, how could Marci not cry? She could not recognize the girl in the mirror. Who was the stranger that was looking back at her? Where was the beautiful haircut she was supposed to have that would make Marci look as pretty as her sister? Juanita tried her best to style Marci's hair, but there was nothing to style.

"I don't want anyone to see me until I take a shower, Marci said. Do you have a scarf I could borrow?"

When Marie saw Marci come home, she was surprised her daughter had a scarf on her head. Marie didn't know why her daughter was covering it up; all she wanted was to take a look at her hair.

"Marci let me see what your haircut looks like."

"Not yet mom, I want to take a shower and wash my hair before you see it".

Running into her bedroom, Marci took the scarf off her head and took a long look in the mirror. Marci thought, *maybe if I take a shower and style it myself it wouldn't look so bad.* Honestly, it would not have mattered how many showers Marci took. Her hair was so short she didn't know what to do with it. When she showered and got dressed, Marci heard her mother knock on her bedroom door. Marie asked if she could come in and Marci told her mother to wait a minute. Running to the dresser, she got the scarf and put it over her head. She then opened the door so her mother couldn't see her new look. Marie saw Marci still had a scarf on her head, so she asked her to remove it so she could see how Juanita cut it. Avoiding her mother's eyes, Marci then slipped the scarf from her head. Marci did not want to see the shocked look on the one person that asked her not to cut it too short. Marie could not help but gasp as she took one look at her daughter. Just as Juanita did, Marie told her daughter she looked cute. Marci knew what that meant, and when her mother left her bedroom, she closed the door, threw herself on the bed, and cried until she fell asleep.

As Marci was waking up, she heard Juanita tell her mother she had something for Marci's hair. Juanita went to Marci's bedroom and pulled a red bow out of her bag. She then asked Marci if she could clip it on her hair. "What hair," Marci asked. "I have none," but Juanita insisted Marci let her do what she came over to do. While Juanita was pinning the bow on her friend's head, Caleb walked in. He took one look at Marci, and at first, did not recognize her. Taking a second look, he started to laugh hysterically.

"Hey sis, did Shredder chew on your hair? You look like Minnie Mouse with that big red bow," he said. Marci knew she couldn't say anything because he was telling the truth. Not paying attention to her brother, Marci looked at herself in the mirror. She now understood why Caleb was laughing. He was right; she did look like Minnie Mouse with her one-inch hair sticking up, and her huge Dumbo ears protruding from the side of her head. However, Juanita told Marci she looked very pretty, as she heard her brother laugh. Marci was sure her mother was also laughing, but all she heard was her mother tell Caleb was to go outside and play.

What would her father have to say if this was their reaction? Not sure what to expect, Marci decided to prepare herself for what was to come. However, that never happened because all her father told her was, "Her hair was a bit short, but it would grow. No matter what you do to yourself, you will always be my little girl," he told her.

After that Marci would not go anywhere without her scarf. She had gotten so used to wearing it, that when she finally decided to take if off for good, her hair had actually grown. By now, it actually covered her ears, and she was able to start styling it. As she looked in the mirror, Marci swore never again would she let Juanita cut her hair.

Now that Marci was getting ready to celebrate her fifteenth birthday, she knew she had learned a valuable lesson the hard way. Her mother had been right all along, but she was stubborn, and wanted to feel grown-up. Marci now knew she was not old enough to make such important decisions. Months later, when Marci was able to laugh at herself, she wrote Juanita a poem.

Hair

Remember the day you sat me on a chair,
Looking in the mirror at my beautiful hair?
Cut my hair, I told my friend, Juanita.
Oh sure, my friend did reply,
As I gave a big sigh.
My eyes I did close,
And felt my hair fall down my nose.
I thought of the beautiful clothes,
To match the nail polish for my toes.
Your hair looks nice, my mother did say,
However, her smile gave her away.
I threw myself on my bed,
With the red bow on my head.
I cried myself to sleep,
But, had a dream of Little Bo Peep.
I heard the laughter of the sheep,
And called them un-lady like names that even
In my sleep, I had to bleep.
Minnie Mouse and her big red bow I did see,
In the mirror looking back at me.
My brother Caleb, how he did laugh;
Because my neck stuck out like a giraffe.
Now do you remember the day you sat me on a chair,
Looking in the mirror as I asked,
What have you done to my Hair?

Later on Juanita responded with her own poem:

In 'Haircut' Defense

As you recall It, a big red bow would not hide

The new hairstyle on you, my dear friend, I tried
It was a Gina Lola Lollobrigida hairstyle at a young age
Of thirteen or so, I wanted to create
The result was only Ginas' look that for my friend
I wanted to imitate.
The blame should be MOM's as she brought home
With her a pair of pinking shears
I was tempted by those scissors, and without fear
I thought of your beautiful copper colored hair.
What a wonderful look for you, such style, such flair
The result required an added touch
Therefore, the red bow was NOT a bit much
Yes, Caleb's sarcastic comments of my first
Haircut was a bitter pill to swallow.
Just thank God that I did not paint your hair pink or yellow
So why is it that recalling this memory still makes you shed tears?
How can I make it up to you?
No kidding is it I hear
Give up my pinking shears!

No matter how hot the day was, Marci never complained about her hair when she was around her mother or Juanita. The only thing they did was to laugh when the topic of hair came up because they thought of what Marci allowed Juanita do to her.

Marci had just gotten home from visiting Grandma when Emily called to ask if she wanted to go pick some red chili in Las Cruces. She was going to babysit her grandson, and she wanted to get some chili while she was there. Marci was given permission to go with Emily, and she went into her bedroom and threw a few things into an overnight bag.

Marci had not been to Las Cruces for many years and thought this would be a new experience. The scenery was the same going to Las Cruces as it was elsewhere in the state. There was the dry vegetation, the mesquite, and many times Marci saw the green lush alfalfa; wheat; hay; cornfields, and chili farms as far as the eye could see.

On the outskirts of Socorro, Marci thought Emily was driving past rest stops used to film a western movie. In the middle of nowhere are two wooden saloon structures on each side of the road. Marci could visualize actors hitching their horses to the posts while they went into the saloon to have a drink, and at high noon, a gunfight would ensue. In the background, mountains of every height, size, and shape added to what Marci was sure would be great pictures some of the tourists were taking. Overall, it was an interesting sight because it was different from any rest stop she had seen. Not having visited this part of the state for some time, Marci was still surprised to see the extremely parched desert alongside lush green pastures.

Polvedera (Dusty City)

As Emily continued driving, Marci saw the river they were about to cross-had a Spanish name. She knew the word "Rio," is river, but she did not know the other word. Emily told her it was the "Rio Salado, (Salty River)." Marci saw the river was dry, and was unable to hide her disappointment that so many rivers had no water. For every Spanish word that was on a sign, Emily told Marci what the Spanish word meant. When Emily told Marci "Rincón" meant corner, she thought, *where the heck did God put a corner in this vast open space?*

Again, Marci saw signs with names of the towns and recognized a town was named as that of her friend, Magdalene. Marci had not thought of her for some time and she now wondered how she was doing. Back in Virginia I used to have a friend whose name is Magdalene, she commented.

"Well then let me tell you what I know about the town of Magdalena," Emily replied. "My grandfather used to say the residents, and many visitors would look up at the mountain and see the profile of Saint Mary Magdalene. It is said; Mary Magdalene protected anyone who looked to her for refuge from the attacks of other Indian tribes. For the Indian tribes that lived there, this mountain was a sacred spot."

Hearing this, Marci said, "Wow, my friend, Magdalene was always looking out for others. Now I know why, and you know, she truly was a good, and caring friend. I think I will write to her when we get back, and let her know what I learned. Maybe she will answer my letter."

Once Emily drove through Socorro, it was nothing but desert, more farmland, and mountains. Not wanting to disrupt Emily's concentration, Marci listened to the radio and looked at the freshly paved road that loomed ahead of them. The more she focused on the freeway, the more it looked like a black cobra as it curved from side to side. It almost felt as if it was ready to devour everyone who went down its path.

Several miles down the road, they passed a sign pointing to Bosque del Apache. Marci recognized the word Apache and asked "Emily if the Apaches lived there." "No. Bosque del Apache is a National Wildlife Refuge for birds, snakes, animals and anything that needs a place to live. Many of the Sandhill Cranes and other birds use this refuge to rest when they are migrating as they fly south for the winter or north for the summer," she replied.

When they were about a mile from her son's house, Emily told Marci to look at the mountains to her right. "Those are the Sangre de Cristo Mountains. I think they are ugly because they are so jagged, and look so scary. Having lived in New Mexico all of my life, I have seen many mountains, but to me, these are the scariest, and like I said the ugliest." When Emily told Marci the name of the mountain she thought, *gosh, even the mountains have religious names. I would never have thought people would take the time to name them.*

As Emily and Marci arrived at their destination, her son, Estevan was also coming home from work. While Emily waited for her son to get down from his truck, her daughter-in-law, Frances opened the screen door as she held the baby. That evening, after everyone had eaten, and were relaxing, asked "her son if there were many chili pickers the week before." Marci had never heard of chili pickers, and wondered who they were so she asked, "What is a chili picker?" "Chili pickers are people who go to a farm and get permission from the farmer to pick the chili he planted," Estevan told her. "When the green or red chili is ready to be picked, many migrants are hired to pick it from the miles and miles of acres he planted."

Marci had never seen a farm with so many rows that it needed migrants to pick the chili, but she had never seen migrants either. All of this was new to her, and without realizing, she was thinking aloud Marci said, "I wonder how many line up before the farmer blows his whistle for them to get started." Emily looked at her son, and his wife and they started laughing. Marci apologized for interrupting their conversation, but since she had, she said, "You know, I didn't bring my canteen, do you think one of the migrants will share their water with us?" That only made them laugh even more, and as much as Emily tried telling Marci what they were laughing about, all she could say was, "Marci, you are so silly. You will see why we are laughing once we get to the chili farm."

The following morning, Marci got up to a bright and sunny day. Emily had been up for several hours, and had seen some of the neighbors placing items to sell at their yard sales. Not able to resist a yard sale, Emily asked Marci, "If she wanted to go with her and Frances back to the farm where they picked the chili."

"Of course Marci wanted to go," and she bought a few interesting items. By the time they returned, Estevan was up, and had the baby dressed and ready to go. Marci was so excited she forgot all about last night's conversation. All she wanted was to get out into the chili fields and see what takes place when migrants pick chili.

Once everyone had eaten breakfast, and were ready to go pick chili, Estevan drove from one farm to the next. When Marci saw the farm she was going to pick chili from, she was very disappointed. This farm had about six extra-long rows of chili, and a couple for vegetables. As Estevan was driving to the next farm, Marci saw a sign offering free rides on a horse and wagon, and asked if they could go. Emily knew the chili would be there, so she agreed they go for a ride. Besides, she didn't know if Marci would ever have another chance to get a horse and wagon ride down Main Street in Las Cruces. Because they were the only ones waiting for a tour, there was plenty of room in the wagon.

Making sure everyone was seated; the driver snapped the reins so the mules would pull the wagon. As he did this he said, "Come on Claudette, giddy up Clyde let's get this wagon moving." Claudette was a black mule whose face was half-black and half-white as if she was wearing a mask. The skin above her hooves were white that reached up to her knees making it seem she was wearing socks. Clyde was brown with long ears that stuck out to the side of his head. Other than that, his ears were so big, there was really nothing special about Clyde. As the mules pulled the wagon, the driver continued to talk to them, and as he pulled on the reins, Clyde and Claudette slowed their pace as they went through the older part of town. As they neared and circled the park, Marci heard a jazz band entertaining the crowd at a wine festival. Before leaving the park, the driver stopped long enough for the passengers he left earlier, to go back to their vehicles. Emily and her family did not get off the wagon as the baby had fallen asleep, and were enjoying the ride. This time there were more passengers, and little room to move. Marci moved closer to the mules as she was enjoying the clip, clopping sound their hooves made on the pavement. She also wanted to listen to what the driver said that made them obey.

As they were on their way to Estevan's car, Marci made a big mistake when she moved closer to the mules so she could hear the driver talk sweetly to them. Sitting behind Clyde, Marci saw the mules had a bag over their tail. Thinking the bag was to hold their tail in place, Marci soon realized that was not so. Clyde deposited a large amount of poop into his bag, and she smelled what went into it. She now knew why the mule's tail was draped over the bag as she got the full effect. How she wished they were closer to the parking lot so she could jump down. Not able to move because the wagon was full, Marci just sat, and held her hand over her mouth and nose. No one but Emily noticed what was going on because everyone was too busy talking, and enjoying the ride. However, when Emily saw what happened, she could not tell her son anything because she was laughing so hard. Yet, no one else seemed to be affected by the smell.

As the driver returned to the parking lot where the passengers left their cars, Marci could not wait to get down. She desperately needed to exhale, and get some fresh air to clear her nostrils from the smell that lingered. After their wagon ride, Estevan drove them to the chili farm and as they were on their way, Emily told her son and daughter-in-law why she was laughing while in the wagon. To say Marci was the butt of the joke is putting it mildly, but she joined in on the laughter, and added what she could.

By this time, they were at the chili farm, and sure enough, Marci saw row after row of the green chili hanging from the plants. *This*, she thought, *is surely the chili we are going to pick*. Seeing all of the green chili, Marci asked; "Hey guys, do you know who the first person was to have a chili garden?" Frances was the first to answer, and said," I do not know who the first person was to have a chili garden, but I know chili was first planted in the late 1500s with the Antonio Espejo and Juan de Onate expeditions." Having taken horticulture classes Estevan's wife also knew that landrace is a word used for anything that has been grown in one area for many years like the chili. Okay Marci, did you know that Hatch, New Mexico is known as the green chili capital of the world, and that New Mexico leads the country in producing chili? Marci did not know that and now it was her turn to learn something new about New Mexico.

As Estevan drove into the farm whose chili plants they had seen for miles on end, the conversation on how chili came to New Mexico ended. Driving up to the farm, Marci saw a woman sitting under a huge oak tree, and Estevan asked her if they could pick chili. She gave him permission and said there were quite a few chili pickers out there. The woman also told him there were gunnysacks down the road they could use.

Estevan drove down the dirt road, and Marci would now see what chili pickers and migrants looked like. Seeing there was no difference in appearance to what she looked like; Marci now understood why her remark and question last night made everyone laugh. No one was lined up waiting for the farmer to blow his whistle so they could pick the chili. Yet, no one had a water canteen; instead, some of the chili pickers were drinking soft drinks they bought at Sonic, Blake's, or any of the other fast food restaurants.

Within a couple of hours, Marci filled a gunnysack with chili, but as she was putting the sacks into the van, she realized how tired she was. Her back ached, and her fingers were sore, but she did not complain because she was happy. Excited because she did this all by herself, she now had something else to tell Vanessa. Having picked as much chili as they wanted, Estevan drove back to the farm where the sacks were placed on a scale and weighed. On their way back to Estevan's house, Marci relaxed, because she was very sore.

That evening after everyone had a chance to shower and relax, Estevan and Frances got ready for the party they were going to attend. As they were leaving, Emily told her son to be careful, have fun, and not to worry about coming home before the party ended. With that, Estevan and Frances were out the door ready to enjoy themselves and dance the night away.

Morning came too soon, and this time Marci stayed in bed listening to the baby, and his grandmother talk to each other. That was until the rest of the family got up, and Marci had no choice but to get out of bed. Dressed, and in the kitchen, Emily asked Marci if she wanted to go back to the farm they went too yesterday. Marci replied she would, and after they ate breakfast, they did just that. Today there would be no wagon ride, as all they were going to do was to pick more chili. This time, Marci walked to the middle of the row, and worked her way to the van. Within an hour, the three women managed to fill five sacks of chili.

When Emily saw how many bags were next to the van she laughed, and told her daughter-in-law it was time to go. Putting the sacks in the van, they took them to the farmer's daughter to be weighed.

As Emily went to pay, the farmer and his daughter were sitting under the big oak tree. Unloading the sacks to be weighed, the farmer asked Emily if she lived in town. She told him she lived two-hundred and five miles from Las Cruces, and were heading back home. When the farmer heard how far she traveled, he gave her a discount. The sacks of chili were re-loaded into the van, and Frances drove to her house.

For the third time, the chili was loaded into the van and after hugs, and kisses, Emily started the trip back home. Having gone a short distance, Emily stopped at a Dairy Queen and bought her and Marci an ice-cream cone. While they were enjoying their dessert, it started to rain, so Emily decided to leave before the weather got worse. Other drivers did not seem to have any problem driving, but she could barely see where she was going. Not wanting to take a chance on anything happening, Emily continued to drive at a slower speed. Marci was sure she had not dozed off, but she knew she was starting to see snow on the side of the road.

Not wanting to distract Emily from her driving, Marci thought, *I know I have been living here for a while, but how is it possible that one minute the sun is out, next it is raining and then it is snowing. What type of weather have we run into that it changes from one minute to the next?* Having driven through the bad weather, Emily was now able to increase her speed as the storm started to subside. Emily continued to drive in silence, as Marci looked out the window. She didn't know why she looked up to the sky, but when she did, she saw a perfect rainbow. Marci was glad she wasn't driving because this rainbow was so bright and beautiful. Not able to take her eyes off it, she said, "I wonder where the rainbow ends."

God has a way of answering our questions because no sooner had Marci asked the question when Emily slowed down. It wasn't raining, or snowing, but Emily was looking at something on the road that Marci obviously wasn't seeing. Curious to see what Emily was looking at, Marci focused her attention on the road ahead. To her amazement, she saw the vegetation on the side of the road had turned different colors. Some of the weeds were yellow; others green while some were pink. Marci didn't say anything, but she now knew where the rainbow ended. It was such a humbling and peaceful experience that Marci was in awe of what she was seeing. Emily continued driving, and as she did, Marci saw the vegetation was its natural color. She then asked Emily "If she thought anyone would believe her, if she told her friends she had seen where one rainbow ended. Or, would they brush it off as some do when they don't believe something?"

Emily replied, "They will believe you because this is the Land of Enchantment."

For the next few miles, they remained silent thinking of God's awesome gift. To those who had taken the time to admire what had just happened; it was inspiring. Yet, Marci wondered if they were the only ones who had seen the beauty of the rainbow close up on that gorgeous day. She then thought of her father's words, "How God displays his artwork for all to see, but so few take advantage of it." Having gone through that humbling, profound, and magnificent experience Emily drove a couple more miles and asked Marci "if she wanted to go to Polvedera?"

"What is Polvedera?" Marci asked.

"Polvedera is a small village also called Dusty City that on many occasions; my father would take me and my sisters to church. Later, he would buy us a Popsicle as a treat because we had behaved. I want to visit San Lorenzo because it always reminds me of him," Emily told Marci. She also wanted to see the church she went to visit when she was growing up. As they drove through Dusty City with its extremely run down homes, Marci wondered if the town was an indication of what the church looked like. If so, what a sad sight that would be. Arriving at the San Lorenzo Church, Emily stopped the van, and told Marci there was something she had to do before she went in.

"Do you see the big silver bell mounted on the cement block with an arch over it? Every time my dad brought us to visit San Lorenzo, we had to ring the bell to let those who heard it know we are sinners," she said.

Getting down from the van, Emily walked to the silver bell and pulled the rope. Her first try didn't do much, but on the second try, the bell rang loud and clear. Marci thought people were going to come out to see what the commotion was all about, but no one did. Seeing how easily Emily pulled on the rope, Marci tried to make the bell ring as clear as Emily did. When she pulled the rope, it was not an easy task. Yet, she wanted to let the people know she too was a sinner. Marci tugged at the rope, but the bell did not budge. Emily asked Marci if she wanted some help, but Marci was determined to do it on her own power. A couple more tries later, Marci finally made the bell ring, and it was the most pathetic ring she had ever heard. As she pulled the rope, she thought, *Okay, I know I haven't been the best daughter, and I know I could use a blessing. She knew God heard the bell*, but she wished she had let Emily help her. However, she did give it her best effort so she was happy. Having rung the bell, Emily and Marci went into the church.

As she walked in, Marci saw a statue of Saint Michael the Archangel and a notebook visitors sign in to document their visit. Emily signed her name and asked Marci if she wanted to let people know she had been here. "Who knows, one day your family might come here, and you can show them when you came to visit San Lorenzo." After they signed in, Marci looked around, and was surprised at how clean the residents kept the church. Both she and Emily walked up to the first pew, and knelt to say their prayers. While Emily said her prayers, Marci looked at the statues of the saints. As she looked to the south side of the church, she saw a short stocky woman standing in front of a small statue.

That day Marci did not do much praying because she was watching the woman, and looking around at the church's décor. Once Emily was done saying her prayers, she got up and walked to the altar. There, Marci saw the white linen was ironed and starched, and this made her think of

Grandma. On each side of the altar are statues of the Virgin Mary, the Sacred Heart of Jesus, and San Lorenzo surrounded by many candles left by those who visited.

Having said her prayers, Emily stood up, went to the statue of the Blessed Virgin Mary, knelt down, and prayed some more. She then walked to the statue where the woman had lit a candle. Not wanting to disturb her, Emily put some money into the donation box; got a match, and lit one of the votive candles.

The woman saw Emily was lighting a candle to San Lorenzo and asked her if she was coming or going. We are coming from Las Cruces where we were visiting my son, and are on our way home. Emily also told the woman, "My dad used to bring my sisters and me here on Sunday to attend Mass. Now every time I drive by I try to visit San Lorenzo in Dad's memory."

The elderly woman then told them "her name was Mrs. Chavez, and asked Emily if she knew the story of San Lorenzo's hands." Seeing the puzzled look on Emily's face, as she shook her head, the woman continued. "You were too young to remember when the church burned, but when I was a little girl the statues and part of the church burned. We didn't have the votive candles as we now have them. Before the church burned, people would bring their own candles; light them, and many left them next to the altar. One night the linen on the altar caught on fire, and destroyed the front part of the altar. The men in the village soon had the fire under control, but most of the statues were burned, and had to be replaced. San Lorenzo only needed minor repairs.

Years before the church burned, my mother gave me a doll. I loved her very much, and we were inseparable. That was until mom saw San Lorenzo no longer had his hands. Mother told me I was a very lucky little girl because San Lorenzo had chosen me to share my doll with him. I didn't understand what my mother was trying to tell me. Not until she told me, she was going to take my doll's hands from her. Because I was a child, I cried, and told my mother I did not want her to hurt my doll. Mother told me she would buy me another one, but I wanted the one I had. No matter how much I cried, my mother said we had to help San Lorenzo. Taking me by the hand, my mother and I walked to the church so I could see what San Lorenzo looked like without his hands. How he could no longer bless me, or anyone who came to ask him for his blessings. This time, I cried because as a child, mother and I had come to visit him, and ask him for favors. It seemed as if my prayers were always answered. When we went back home, I watched my mother as she carefully removed the hands from my doll. After she did this, we went back to the church and glued them onto San Lorenzo's wrists. See how mother left some of the material my doll had on her sleeve? She did that purposely. Mother told me people would not believe my story when I tell it, so I have the proof that I have not made it up. Guess this is why my mother in her infinite wisdom did what she had to do."

Emily told Mrs. Chavez, "I too would never have believed your story if you hadn't shown me the material under San Lorenzo's cape."

Once Mrs. Chavez told Emily and Marci, the story of San Lorenzo's hands, Emily thanked her, and we left to continue our journey home. The trip back home took less time than Marci thought it would. When they arrived, she helped Emily take the sacks of chili down from her van. When Emily took Marci home, she gave her a sack of chili for helping her. Having put her things away, and throwing her dirty clothes in the hamper, Marci told her mother everything that happened.

Tomé Hill

Juanita and Marci had not seen Grandma for a couple of days, and instead of riding their bikes, they decided to walk. Not only did they want to see how Grandma was doing, they also wanted to see if the baby chicks hatched. Nearing Grandma's house the girls could see her smoking outside on the front porch. After they got a glass of water, the girls sat on the porch steps across from Grandma. As Marci watched her take a puff of her cigarette, she asked her, "Grandma, when did you start to smoke." Grandma thought for a few minutes, and as she spoke, the cigarette moved up and down, and never fell off her lower lip. It seemed as if it was glued to Grandma's lower lip. Grandma said, "She could not remember how old she was, all she could remember was that she was very young." Marci then asked Grandma, "How old she was when she got married." "Boy Marci, you are nosey," Grandma replied, "but since you asked, I'll tell you what not even Juanita knows about me." Bring me a glass of ice water, and I will tell you how I met, and married my husband Patricio Gabaldon. After Marci brought grandma her glass of water, she took a drink, and told the girls what Marci wanted to know.

"My mother and father divorced when I was a little girl, and I came to live in Los Lunas. Father and I lived here for about a year, and every Saturday he used to take me to the dance. I was always too shy to dance because I was very awkward. During one of the dances, a friend of mine saw me sitting down, and took me out to dance. At that time, if a boy didn't ask you to dance; girls danced together. Anyway, my friend showed me the dance steps to several songs, and after that, I felt better when I was asked to dance. When the next dance started, Patricio Gabaldon came to ask me out to dance. Neither my friend nor I knew this young man, but he was very handsome; and he told us he had been watching us. Well, one dance led to another, and before I knew it, my father came and grabbed me by the arm. He also told Patricio he had better come with him. Not knowing what was going on, we did as we were told. I knew we hadn't done anything wrong, and I was embarrassed at what was happening. Then my father told me I was going to have to marry the boy I was dancing with because some girls had told him we had gone outside behind the trees, and that the young man had had his way with me. I tried to tell him that was not so, that all we did was dance, but Daddy believed the girls who made up the story. I was so scared because I really didn't know anyone here, and my mother lived in a different town several hundred miles away. The next day I was introduced to my soon to be mother-in-law, and I didn't know what I was doing there. My father told Patricio's mother what happened, and she too agreed we should get married to save my reputation. Because I was only thirteen years old, I had to lie, and say I was sixteen, or the justice of the peace would not marry us. That night Patricio went out to celebrate with his friends, and I asked my sister-in-law to hide me. I was very happy my husband was drunk because he went to bed and fell asleep. When he woke up, he asked his mother if she knew where I was. She replied she didn't know, but when Patricio found me, he took my hand in his, and told me we were now married, and he was my husband. My mother-in-law knew I was scared, and she talked to me as if she were my mother. She explained how I was now a married woman, and I would have to give up my childish ways. However, that never happened. My sister-in-law's and I would play with our dolls, and do everything a teenager would do. That is until I had to be a wife.

Months later, I wrote to my mother, and after several months passed, Patricio and I went to visit my family. When they met Patricio, they all loved him, and were very happy for us. I told my mother what happened, and at first, she was angry, but after she got to know Patricio, she thought he was good for me. A year later, I had my first child, Rafael, and even then, my sister-in-law's and I pretended he was a doll. We would dress him like we wanted, and when he was hungry we would feed him. My mother-in-law helped me raise my son because I really didn't know what I was doing. Of course, I was so grateful to her. I was never treated as an in-law, but more as her daughter.

When I married Patricio, one of the girls who accused me of doing something wrong, told my mother-in-law she wished that child was hers. She now regretted having lied to my father because all this time she wanted to marry Patricio and have his children. She asked my mother-in-law if she could hold the baby, but she was told to go have her own! Patricio and I were married for a couple of years when he came down with influenza and died. At that time, doctors didn't know how to treat this disease. Rafael was only nine months at that time and he never got to meet him. Some people survived but many died. After my husband died and was buried, we heard of a woman up north who died of the same thing. Her daughters also were not expected to live, so they left the grave open so the daughters could be buried with her mother. When the father was going to bury his daughters, he wanted to take a last look at his wife. When her coffin was opened, they saw the doctor had made a mistake, and his wife had been buried alive. A couple of years later I met my second husband. We got married, and I had five more children. So Marci, now that I have told you and Juanita how I met my husband, is there anything else you want to know?"

"Oh yes, grandma, my neighbor took me to Dusty City and we went to visit the church there. I want to know if you know anything about San Lorenzo, and if you prayed to him."

"Sure, I do," grandma replied. "The San Lorenzo Church in Polvedera has always had a special place in my heart, and that is why I named one of my sons Lorenzo. In my younger days, as the people made the annual Good Friday pilgrimage up the Tomé Hill, we used to hitch our horses to our buggies, and make the round-trip from here to Polvedera. We would stay for a couple of days with our friends, and together we would walk to the church to honor San Lorenzo.

My grandfather and uncle always told the family about the year the people of Polvedera worried about their crops. It did not matter what the people of Polvedera used to predict the weather; rain was not in sight. As some of us do today, we talk to God, but in those days, it must have been more meaningful. Anyway, one evening the farmers and their families gathered in their new church and prayed for rain. One by one, the families went up to the altar, and placed some of the seeds they were going to plant. They asked God to bless the seeds, and send rain so their crops would grow. As the days and weeks passed, the people knew God was testing their faith. The more they prayed the higher the temperature rose. The farmers planted the seeds but eventually everything started to dry up. When the farmers were about to give up, the rain came, and that year the farmers had the best crops. Grandpa said the residents of Polvedera would talk about the miracles that were happening throughout their village. They knew God was pleased their faith was so strong, and that they did not give up. Thankful for the rain and the best crops, the residents of Polvedera went to the church to honor their patron saint.

Many years later, another drought hit the little town of Polvedera, and again the crops were drying up. On one particular visit, Grandma and her family were taking a few supplies to their friends when they were told San Lorenzo's statue was missing. Residents from the village of Polvedera went in search of the statue for several days. While the men were out in search of San Lorenzo, the women and children prayed for his return. The search went on for a couple of weeks, until a couple of men found him in the bank of the Rio Grande. When the villagers heard the statue was found, those gathered at the church formed a procession to return San Lorenzo to his rightful place. Word spread throughout the small town of Polvedera, and someone went to get the priest. By the time the priest came down from Socorro to offer a Mass in thanksgiving for San Lorenzo's safe return, the residents were waiting for him. After the priest offered a mass of thanksgiving for the safe return of San Lorenzo, the residents of Polvedera went back to tend to their families, farmlands, and vineyards.

On a cloudy and stormy summer afternoon while residents were praying the rosary, they heard a big roar outside the church. Someone at the back of the church opened the door, and saw water roaring down the road. When he opened the door, he said, "Oh no," and the rest of the people went to see what was going on. Those who lived across from the church watched in horror as the raging river flooded many of their homes. The water was moving so fast it took everything in its path. On that day, Polvedera was hit hard. The people who were in the church knew, had they not been where they were, some of them would have been in their homes, or working in the fields near the river, and would have drowned. Within seconds, the floodwater reached the entrance of the church. When they closed the door, it prevented any water from going in. With no way out of the church, the residents had to wait until the water receded before they went out.

Hours later, someone carefully opened the door, and by that time, the water had subsided enough to where they could wade through the water and mud to their homes. Days later, the residents who drowned in the raging flood were pulled out of ditches, or out of the mud where they died. After the flood, families left their homes to higher grounds, and others moved to nearby towns. The families whose houses were destroyed never knocked the houses down because that was a reminder of San Lorenzo's miracle to them. That is why you see abandoned houses when you go visit San Lorenzo.

For the people who lived in San Marcial, the floodwaters destroyed the town, and they had no place to go. I remember grandpa telling us someone wrote a Spanish song about the San Marcial floods, and he would sing it. Sometimes he couldn't finish singing it, because he lost family and friends. I don't remember the exact words, but it went something to the effect that the town of San Marcial was flooded, and people cried because they lost their homes and loved ones. The last time San Marcial flooded some of our friends and relatives who lost their homes to the flood went to live with relatives. Some of them moved to Socorro, others went to live in Belen or Albuquerque. When my grandfather told the family these stories some of the younger relatives would not believe him, and he would get angry. I knew better than to doubt my grandfather because I believe these incidences are true miracles. For me, San Lorenzo has always been a special saint, and through him, I ask for forgiveness and receive strength. To this day, residents and their children continue to visit Saint Lorenzo for the many favors he continues to bestow upon those who pray to him."

Grandma then remembered Good Friday was coming up, and told Juanita she should take Marci up to the Tomé Hill. "This would do you girls some good. If you do, remember to lend a helping hand to anyone who needs it, Grandma told the girls. When my friends and I made the pilgrimage to Tomé, and we reached the top of the hill, we gave thanks to God for granting our petitions. We prayed the rosary, sang, and every now and then one of us would remember a passage from the

Bible, and we would quote it. Our greatest pleasure in walking was that every year there were more and more kids joining in the pilgrimage. You know, I don't think I ever heard any of the young kids use foul language. For some reason, the only thing on the pilgrims mind is to make it up the hill, and go back home. Somehow, everyone respects each other. How I wish that would happen on a daily basis. The last time I walked to the Tomé Hill, the path was hard to climb. Years later, I heard someone marked the trail with crosses to mark the path Jesus would have taken," she continued. Grandma said there were several stories as to why the crosses on the hill were put there. "Some said an airplane crashed, and three men died, so the family erected a memorial for them. Others said the crosses were erected because of a prayer granted to a soldier. Whatever the case, remember Good Friday is even holier than Christmas. Jesus was born on Christmas, but on Good Friday, He gave his life for us."

That year Juanita and Marci's families walked, and climbed the Tomé Hill, and what an experience it was. Police patrolled the main road leading to the Tomé Hill on vehicles, bikes, and horses to ensure those making the pilgrimage arrived safely at their destination. As people walked to the hill, they saw police giving tickets to those who were driving too fast. When Marci and Juanita reached the road leading up the hill, the police blocked the road to traffic except for those living in the area, or emergency vehicles.

The day of their pilgrimage, Marci saw many people carry crosses and statues to the top of the hill, but the most popular item carried along the way was a rosary. Reaching the top of the hill Marci heard people singing, and thanking God for helping them complete their pilgrimage. Having prayed their rosaries, many left them at the top of the hill with the rest left from previous years. Marci also left hers, as this was her way of giving thanks for everything she had. After Marci climbed the Tomé Hill, she now understood why people made the pilgrimage. Many years later, Marci learned the history of the Tomé Hill, and realized there were many similarities to the story grandma told her and Juanita.

El Cerro De Tomé (Tomé Hill) A Promise Kept—excerpt from People of God by Matt Baca, PhD.

Created by ancient volcanoes and rising more than 500 feet above the Rio Grande Valley, lies a dark basalt hill that is more than a mile in circumference. Every year on Good Friday, this hill is invaded by hundreds of people that, from a long distance, look like a long line of ants crawling up and down the hill. This hill is known as El Cerro De Tomé (Tomé Hill). Close to the hill is the historical village of Tomé (toe-meh) which is located on Highway 47 in Central New Mexico. In the late 18th century and early 19th century, the Penitente movement would use the hill as their place of worship.

While in Italy during World War II, Edwin Berry made a promise to God that if he would return home safely from the war he would erect three crosses (Calvario) on the summit of El Cerro de Tomé to honor Jesus Christ's passion. His crucifixion and the soldiers who died in World War II. In 1945, he returned home from the war and in 1947 began the hard and arduous task of construction. Like all great men with unusual ideas, he faced many difficulties including peoples' derision.

In 1947, Edwin Berry took it upon himself to erect three crosses at the summit of the hill. These crosses were built on site. Berry said he located the middle cross, Jesus' Cross, facing the Eucharist at the Tomé church in the valley below. He faced the cross of the good thief towards the cross of Jesus and placed the cross of the bad thief away from Jesus' cross. Construction of these 20-foot crosses was a logistic feat due to the fact that the hill is very high and rises at a very sharp angle. Construction materials had to be carried to the job site. Berry, with the help of a few workers and volunteers, manually accomplished this job by sheer tenacity. The steepness of the hill was a major obstacle. At that time, there were no mountain climbing vehicles. Animals such as horses and mules were not used because

of the steep incline. Water had to be hauled up by the bucket to mix cement for the foundation of the tall crosses.

For the first few years after 1947, the custom of climbing the hill on Good Friday involved only a few pilgrims. But today, people realize that Berry left them a huge legacy - a legacy of devotion to Christ's passion and the opportunity to connect people to people while on their pilgrimage to the Calvario.

Marci Who?

Even though everything was going smoothly at home, with her friends, and at school, Marci felt something was missing in her life. That was until she decided she was going to change the things she was doing. For some reason, Marci felt her life was not complete, and decided to search for the answer. First, she was going to stop hanging around with Juanita and her friends. Not that she was tired of them; she just wanted to see what it was like to hang out with Jan and her gang. Knowing they were always in trouble, and the rowdiest group in school, Marci wanted to get to know them. She wanted to be a bully. Marci didn't know why she was doing this; she just felt there was something lacking in her life. Once she made up her mind, Marci went to talk to Jan, and the girls that made fun of her when she moved to New Mexico. They were still the same girls, whose language was not what Marci was accustomed to, but she often wondered why they acted as they did.

True to her word, Marci joined Jan and her gang. Overnight Caleb and Marci's personalities changed, and it did not matter how many times Juanita tried to pull Marci away from Jan and her friends, she could not. The more Juanita tried to talk her friend out of joining the girls even the boys could not compete with, the more Marci wanted to be with them. From the minute Marci joined Jan's group, she started to use a lot of profanity when she spoke to others. Juanita tried talking to Marci, but she swore so much, Juanita left. Marci called Juanita every name in the book, and Juanita was finally fed up with Marci's bad attitude and language so she left her alone.

While Marci was waiting for her so-called new best friend, Juanita sat across from her, and asked her "what she thought she was doing."

"Juanita you wouldn't understand. You have always had brothers and sisters who you can argue, laugh, or just be angry at, and I only have Caleb, who has always been a pain in the butt! Just know this is something I have to do. I will be okay so stop worrying, and leave me alone, besides it's none of your damn business," Marci told her. Having heard all she wanted to hear Juanita got up, and walked away from her friend.

Marci's personality changed; she was obnoxious, no longer cared how she dressed, and every other word was one of obscenity. Now when she put her make-up on Juanita thought she looked like a clown. The makeup she now slapped on her face on a daily basis would have lasted the conservative Marci a couple of months if not more.

One evening while the family was eating dinner, Marci walked in with a cigarette in her mouth. Travis got up from the table so fast, his chair crashed to the floor. Seeing her father was angry, Marci laughed. "Hey, old man, what the hell, is wrong with you," she asked. Travis had had enough, and it was time he put a stop to his daughter's actions. As he was about to take the cigarette out of his daughter's mouth, he accidently slapped her. Never had he laid a hand on either one of his children, and Marie saw the shocked look on his face. To Marci, it was something else she thought was funny. She was so out of control that neither Travis nor Marie knew what to do. Caleb had never seen his father angry, and hurt as when he left the table. Not even, he could take Marci's attitude, and the sight of seeing his sister disrespect their father was too much for him. Caleb decided to excuse himself from the table, and not having finished his meal, Marci asked him, "If she could eat his food because she was starving. Hey brother, where do you think you're going? Sit your damn ass down and let's talk. Hey, do you remember when you made me smoke those cigarettes? Well I guess you should have had me smoke the whole pack as you threatened to do if I told

Mom and Dad. Do you remember that day? So now that I am smoking, do you want a drag from my cigarette?

Marie, too stunned at what was happening did not move an inch throughout the whole ordeal. Wiping the tears from her eyes she asked her daughter, "What has happened to my sweet little girl, and where did she go?

"Marie, you know how it is. This is how some of us want to show our parents we are grown up. I'm just doing what my friends do," Marci told her mother.

This time, it was Marci's turn to pick on her brother until he told her to leave him alone. Caleb was now the obedient, considerate, sweet, and mellow child Marci used to be.

For her elective class, Juanita chose to work as an office aide with the principal's secretary Marla Cox. Juanita knew Marla was going to grade her on how well she filed the paperwork in the student's files, how she answered the telephone; how accurate her messages were, and how she dealt with all of the confidential information. While Juanita was filing the notes for the day, she came across one the principal wrote on Marci. When she saw the comment he made, she was quite concerned. Juanita knew she had to keep this to herself, but it bothered her that her friend was getting herself into trouble. When she finished all of her work, Juanita asked Marla if she could make an appointment to talk to the principal.

"Is there something wrong?" Marla asked.

"Not with me, but with a friend, and I would like to ask the principal for some advice." "Well he is off the phone, so why don't you knock on the door and ask if he will talk to you."

Taking Marla's advice, Juanita knocked on the door as she was told to do. When the principal opened the door, he saw Juanita waiting to go into his office.

'Come in Juanita, he said. Is there something I can help you with? Are you having problems with your classes?"

"No," Juanita answered. "I wanted to ask you if you can tell me how I can help my friend."

"I will try to help you if you tell me what is going on," the principal replied.

After Juanita told him about the notes she saw regarding her friend Marci, he told her, "It was none of her concern. He could not discuss what notes she saw in any of the student files she had to file." Juanita then told the principal all about her friend Marci. How she changed just so she could experience what it would be like to have rowdy friends. She just happened to choose the rowdiest girls in the entire school. Yet Marci was still her friend, and she couldn't let her be suspended from school for something so silly. After she finished, the principal commended Juanita for being such a loyal friend. He told her he would call her into his office next time Marci was sent to see him.

Days later Marci, Jan and their gang were sent to the principal's office for various reasons. It was then that Marci realized how bad she had ruined her reputation. Yet whenever Marci was called into the office, Juanita was sure to be there. She was about the only one that was willing to stand up for Marci, and she knew the principal would listen to her. Soon Juanita lost count as to how many times she too was called to help her friend.

Not able to tolerate Marci's bad attitude, and foul language, Marie turned to Rosita and Emily for help. Their friendship had grown over the years, and Marie now sought help from the people who loved Marci as much as her family did. Knowing Travis and Marie were going through a difficult time with their daughter, Rafael also volunteered to help. Marie did not realize how stressed she was until she told Rafael and Rosita, how Marci changed and started to cry.

"I know Juanita has told you all about Marci and her bad attitude," Marie said, as she wiped the tears from her eyes. "Marci is not my little girl anymore, and I don't know her. Not only is she a stranger to her family, but her friends, and we need your help. Marci has taken up smoking, and acting different, it's horrible. Travis and I know how much you love Marci and this is why we are hoping you can help us get our little girl back. Throughout the years we have seen how disciplined your children are, and we know you can tell us what we should do."

"Oh is that all," Rafael said as he laughed and took a drink of his coffee.

Seeing the shocked look on their faces, Rafael told Marie and Travis not to worry. "Look, Marci is going through a stage she has almost no control over. It's as if she is testing the waters. She is challenging you to see how she can shock you. The more you respond to her actions the worse it is going to be. She is going to get so used to your crying it will become second nature to her. You can cry all you want, but let me tell you a little secret, she really wants to be her old self, but she doesn't know what to do. Next time she screams at you, picking on Caleb, or smoking her cigarette ignore her, but be prepared for outbursts that are more outrageous. One day when you least expect it, she is going to be in her room looking at herself in the mirror wondering what is going on. When she is in this mood, you need to wrap your arms around her, and hold her tenderly. Tell your daughter you love her no matter who she has become or what she has done. While she is crying and telling you how sorry she is, have her take a look at herself in the mirror. Let her see who she has become, and do not worry, she will come around, you will see. The more you make of it, the worse it is going to get. Pretty soon you are all going to laugh at how she was dressing, and how she looked like a clown with all that make-up on her face," Rafael told them.

"You mean we shouldn't take her to a psychiatrist?" Travis asked.

"Look Travis, if we had taken our children to a psychiatrist every time their personality changed we would be so deep in debt. You can take her to see Dr. Brewer, but all you are going to do is create a bill you don't need," Rosita told Travis.

Rafael and Rosita made so much sense, that Marie and Travis decided to do exactly what they advised them to do. The first couple of months were not as easy as Rafael and Rosita made it sound, but Travis and Marie knew they had to get their daughter back.

One morning while Travis and Marie were drinking their coffee, Marci walked out of her bedroom. Prepared for her to make insulting remarks, Marci surprised her parents. The first thing they saw was that she didn't have a lot of makeup on.

"Good morning, Mom and Dad, what's for breakfast? I'm famished." Marie and Travis could not believe what they heard, as they looked at each other. Then Marie asked her daughter "what she wanted to eat." "It doesn't matter, you know I like everything you cook." Marie was so happy to see their daughter come back, she made her a huge breakfast. "Mom, there is no possible way I can eat all this, do you think I can invite Juanita over?"

Before Marci called Juanita, she apologized to her mother and father for all she put them through. She promised never to do anything that would embarrass the family ever again. Hugging her parents, Marci saw her mother was ready to cry so she went to the phone and called her old friend to come over. When Marie saw Juanita coming up the walk she was happy to see Juanita had not given up on her. To hear the girls laughing, no one would ever have guessed they had parted ways for over six months, but that was the past and a bright future lay ahead of them. Marci was back, and everything happened as Rafael and Rosita told Marie and Travis it would. Even Caleb forgave his sister for the brat she was.

"So sis," Caleb said, "what are your ugly friends going to think now that you aren't hanging around them anymore?" "I truly don't give a shitty damn what they think. I don't need them as I need my family and true friends. So don't worry, I will take care of them," Marci said. To Marie and Travis, those were the most beautiful words they had heard Marci say for some time. They were happy to have their daughter back, and grateful for the advice Rafael and Rosita gave them. Marci and

Juanita had several encounters with Jan and her foul-mouthed girls, but they ignored them.

When Marci tried to apologize to her teachers, they found it hard to believe she had changed. Marci had been so rude, and cruel to them they could not easily forget what she did.

One day while Juanita was doing her filing, Marci, Jan, and her rowdy friends were called into the principal's office, and they did not know what to expect. They felt uncomfortable because they had not gotten into trouble for months, and no longer felt the need to have all the bad attention focused on them—even though it was.

"You are probably wondering why I have called you into my office, the principal said. Well I have been checking with your teachers, and they have told me you are doing your homework, and your grades are improving. I just want to tell you I am proud of you, as you have managed to stay out of trouble. You will be graduating soon and I want to wish you luck. Marci, you have a true friend, and if you ever make the mistake of losing her friendship, you have made a big mistake."

Marci hugged Juanita and thanked her for the many times she came to her rescue. Dismissed, and told to go back to their classrooms, the girls went their separate ways. The incident, with Jan and Marci soon passed, and when they saw each other in the hallways, cafeteria, or outdoors, all was good.

Childhood Reunion

Caleb and Marci were growing up and focusing on their education. However, Caleb's passion for basketball and baseball never wavered. He continued to invite his friends to the house, and Marci could not remember a weekend when the backyard was not full of sweaty, smelly boys. Of course, she was also starting to see boys differently. Caleb's friends were no longer the skinny boney, pimpled unruly boys they were in the past. His friends were maturing into handsome, well-built young men, and Marci did not mind watching them take their shirts off to play basketball. However, they were Caleb's friends, who had practically grown up in their house, and as far as Marci knew, none of the boys ever took a second look at her. To them, she was Caleb's older sister.

Marci's seventeenth birthday party was coming up in a couple of weeks, and her mother was tying up loose ends. Everything was going along just fine until Travis asked Marie if she had given Marci her gift. "Mom, what gift is daddy talking about that you haven't given me?" Marci asked. "The only thing I want is to spend my birthday with my family and friends."

Marie told Marci she was going to give it to her at her party, but since her father spoiled the surprise, she might as well let her open it. Going to the cupboard, Travis and Marie surprised Marci with an early graduation gift.

"Open it little one," Travis said as Marie gave her daughter their gift. Marci was having a hard time unwrapping it because Marie made sure she put enough scotch tape on it. Not able to un-wrap the box fast enough Marci got the scissors and cut the wrapping on the box.

"Sit down Marci, and open the box. Your gift is inside, and we are hoping it will fit you," Marie told her daughter.

Marci's hands were shaking so much she could barely open the green emerald jewelry box. Thinking it was a necklace she hugged her parents before she looked at the contents inside the box.

"Little one, you don't even know what is inside. Open the jewelry box," her father told her.

Marci finally opened the box, but did not see a necklace inside. Instead, Marci saw a round trip ticket to Virginia. Her parents were sending her to visit the friends she left behind seven years ago. Marci jumped all around the room and could not stop crying. There was no way she could ever thank her parents for the early graduation gift.

Marci and her friends had a lot of fun at her party, but all she could think of was that she was going to visit her friends in Virginia. Marci was so excited she could not wait to call Vanessa and tell her she would see her soon.

The week before Marci was to leave New Mexico, she went shopping for souvenirs. The day of her departure, Marci was to leave, she got up earlier than normal. After she got dressed, Marci went to tell Juanita she was going to Virginia. Marci should have known Juanita was still sleeping, but in her excitement, she forgot to check her clock. Rafael was the only one awake and once again, Marci was sitting in his kitchen drinking a cup of coffee. Disappointed Juanita did not wake up as Marci was hoping she would, she asked Rafael to tell her good-bye, and she would see her in a month.

When Marci arrived in Virginia, Vanessa and her parents were waiting for her at the airport. Marci had changed so much no one recognized her. Vanessa had also changed; she was taller, her hair was no longer blonde, and she now wore glasses. Vanessa finally recognized her friend and ran to greet her. The girls screamed, cried, and laughed as old friends do when they have not seen each other for a long time. Other passengers who were waiting for a relative or friend, and those lined up ready to board the airplane turned to see the reunion between friends.

Everything was great as Marci and her old friends were reunited. Anne, Cecilia, and Magdalena couldn't believe Marci was back. They had all changed, but had remained friends throughout the years. Their features might have changed, but they were still the friends Marci left seven years ago. They went shopping at the mall, went to the movies, the beach, and did anything they wanted. They even went to visit their fifth grade geography teacher, who by this time had retired. When Vanessa took Marci and the other girls to Ms. Andersen's house, Marci thanked her for everything she had done for her, and gave her the souvenir she bought her. Her teacher was happy to see Marci, and told her there were many times she thought of her. I see New Mexico has been good to you. There were times I would ask Vanessa what happened to you, and she would tell me how you were doing. I pretty much kept up with what was happening to you through Vanessa. Now I can see the scared little girl, who left Virginia, is just fine. "I can't tell you how pleased I am that you thought of me," Ms. Andersen told Marci.

Before Marci and Vanessa realized it, their visit lasted longer than they planned. Marci was glad she went to visit her former teacher because it made her very happy. Marci promised Ms. Andersen she would write, and Vanessa told her she would visit her more often.

The girls also went to see the house Marci used to live in. When Marci saw it, she could not believe how small it was. She could not imagine why she cried and wanted to stay behind. About to leave, Marci saw the girl who had grown up where she lived, and went to talk to her. The following day, Vanessa, Magdalene, Anne, Cecilia and Marci went for a swim at the beach. There, she saw Sandy and her friends who were still the bullies she left behind seven years ago. She had actually thought if she was to see Sandy, she would talk to them, but all that changed when Sandy started to bad mouth Marci.

Later they went to see Beth at Carvel's Ice Cream Parlor. At first, Beth Perine did not recognize Marci, but when she did, she could not believe Marci was actually there. To celebrate her homecoming Beth treated the girls to a double helping of everything on their banana splits. The same toppings they had the day Marci told her she was moving to Mexico. Having taken care of her customers, Beth went to join the girls at their old booth. There was so much Marci had to tell Beth that she talked non-stop. Marci told Beth everything that happened to her. How her skin dried, and she thought she was going to turn into a reptile, how she thought an Indian god was going to sacrifice her to their god, and so much more. Marci had Beth and her friends laughing so hard their sides hurt. Everyone was having such a good time no one noticed how quickly time had gone by, and before Marci left, she gave Beth the souvenir she bought her. She also told Beth she would visit her before she went back home.

The days passed by quickly, but Marci soon longed to be with her father out in the desert. Not only did she want to hear her father call her, "Little one," she also wanted to see the sunrise, the sunset, and the stars. Strangely enough, Marci needed to feel the hot sun on her face and body. A month was a long time to be away from home, and Marci had two weeks left before her vacation ended. She loved the time she spent with Vanessa, and her friends, but she was getting homesick. Oddly enough, Marci even missed Caleb and was ready to get back to her family and New Mexico. Her parents were right when seven years ago they said everything was rushed in the city.

By now, Marci was used to the slow-paced country life, and by the end of the third week, she was exhausted. The end of the month was almost here, and it was time for her to go back to New Mexico. The ten-year-old girl no longer existed, and the life she left behind so many years ago was no longer for her. Marci was happy she had a chance to visit Vanessa, Cecilia, Anne, and Magdalene, but she no longer wanted to live in the city. Her home was now thousands of miles from Virginia. If she did not know it then, she now knew New Mexico, The Land of Enchantment, was indeed the home she wanted to return to and never leave. The day Marci left Virginia she was happy to board the airplane, and this time when she said good-bye to her friends she did not cry. Instead, when she saw them disappear into the distance, Marci focused on how soon she would be home. Six hours is an excruciating amount of time when someone is eager to get home, but for Marci it was all worth the wait.

When the airplane landed in Texas, she had a two-hour layover so Marci walked around the terminal. Finally, it was time for her to board the airplane back home, and she did that with so much enthusiasm, she almost tripped going up the boarding ramp. All Marci wanted was to go home and see her parents, Cleopatra, and yes, she wanted to see Caleb and Shredder. Imagine that! When Marci felt the airplane taxi off the runway, her heart was beating so fast she could hardly catch her breath.

Then she, along with the other passengers heard the pilot over the intercom, "Ladies, and gentlemen we will arrive in Albuquerque, New Mexico in about a half hour. The staff and I thank you for flying Frontier Airlines, and we hope you will book your next flight with us."

Now when Marci looked out the window, she saw hundreds, and thousands of jewels in the desert. As the sun had set, the lights from the houses, streetlights, and the buildings shone brightly. Marci now knew this was God's way of telling her she was home. Even though her hands were shaking, Marci got her camera, and took a picture of what she saw below so she could remember her homecoming, and put it in her album. When the airplane taxied down the runway, Marci thought, *home, I am home*, and this time she smiled, and her heart skipped a happy beat.

When Marci departed from the airplane and entered the terminal, Juanita along with Marci's family was waiting for her. Happy as she was to see her family Marci was extremely happy to see the friend she knew would always be by her side no matter what happened.

Having unpacked, Marci went to help her mother prepare dinner. While the family was eating, and sharing what happened during the day, Caleb told Marci how much he missed her. He was so sincere Marci got up and hugged him. When it was Marci's turn, all she had to say was that she was happy to be home, but was very tired. Tomorrow was another day, and she would tell them all about her trip. Before going to bed, Marci called Vanessa and thanked her for all she did to make her visit so much fun.

The following morning, Marci woke up earlier than she normally did. Knowing Juanita was still sleeping, she decided to wait before she called her. In the meantime, she decided to surprise her family by preparing breakfast. Marci now answered all of their questions, and told them she had a wonderful time, and that she saw many of her friends, Beth, and Ms. Andersen, but she was ready to get home.

Breakfast was over, and Caleb went to visit his friends while Travis had some errands to run. This left Marie and Marci alone to catch up on what had taken place while she was gone. Marci told her mother she went to see their old house, and remembered the day her mother tried to comfort her when they were moving to New Mexico.

"Mom, do you remember when you told me one day I would look back on the day we moved, and we would laugh?" As Marie nodded, Marci asked her mother if she had ever told her how she had planned to stay in Virginia."

When Marie told her she had not, Marci ran to her bedroom and took her diary from her desk. Now, more than ever, Marci wanted her mother to read how she reacted when told they were moving from the city to the country. How at ten years of age, Marci planned on staying back and asking the new owners to adopt her. How at that tender age, Marci thought she could get a job so she could help her new parents with her expenses. Most of all, Marci wanted her mother to read how scared she was because she thought her father was moving his family to a Third World Country.

Marie read what her daughter had written, and when she finished, she lovingly and tenderly embraced her daughter. Until now, Marci had not realized how badly she needed her mother to hold her. Suddenly she started to cry, and did not know why. All Marci knew was that she felt good now that she was able to tell her mother how she truly felt. Marie continued to hug her daughter and told Marci she was sorry she had gone through such a traumatic time all by herself.

"Honey, Daddy, and I thought you were happy we were moving from Virginia. You sure fooled us because until today I did not know how scared you were about the move," Marie told her.

"Mom, I was scared because I thought we were going to live in a foreign country, and I was losing all my friends."

Marci could not finish telling her mother what she was going through because she was crying. Then, Marci started to laugh uncontrollably. Marie could not figure what was going on, but she was patient and waited for her daughter to tell her. Going into the den, they sat down, and talked about everything they could possibly bring up. Marci felt so good now that she was able to laugh at herself. Marci then told her mother how lucky she and Caleb were to have such loving and wonderful parents. After their conversation, Marci then asked her mother if she could pitch the tents in the backyard. She wanted to catch up with the latest things her friends had done while she was gone. She also wanted her friends to look at the stars, and listen to the crickets chirping in the night. With that, she and her mother planned what they would do when Marci's friends came to camp overnight.

Later that day, Marci went into her room and took her encyclopedias down so she could read all about the solar system. Never thinking she would enjoy reading about the stars, she was surprised to learn the handle on the big dipper is a cluster of five stars. Marci kept reading because she wanted to impress her friends as to how much she knew about the stars that sparkled like diamonds above them. As she continued reading, she also learned the smallest cluster of stars is Scorpio, her mother's zodiac sign, and the largest is Virgo. However, for Marci the most interesting part was when she read how at one time there were thirteen constellations, but one was dropped to even the number of months in the calendar in 1582. By the time she finished reading about the solar system, Marci knew she could surprise her friends with her wealth of knowledge. If everything was just right, Marci and her friends might also see a shooting star, but Marci was hoping for too much. She was just happy to be home.

When Marci's friends arrived, they spread their sleeping bags out on the grass. That evening when Marci's friends came over to spend the night, and as Marci planned, she pointed to the stars. She surprised her friends with what she learned about the sparkling diamonds in the sky above them. Her friends also added to what they knew, and tonight, Marci realized how important true friends are, and even though they did not see any shooting stars, Marci and her friends had a great time. Marci thought of Vanessa and her friends in Virginia and felt bad for them. They did not realize what they were missing by ignoring the beauty of their surroundings. Her friends were still interested in what was showing at the theatre, who bought the dress on the display window at the mall, or who had the cutest bikini, and how much money they could spend.

In New Mexico, Marci did not have to worry about any of that because her friends did not judge her by what she was wearing. Besides, she had her beautiful acre of land right outside her door.

Grandma

Marci stayed by Juanita's side when her grandmother died at ninety-three. Knowing what she had gone through when she was depressed, and thought no one was there for her, Marci tried to help Juanita cope with the loss of her grandmother. Marci reminded Juanita how generous Grandma was, how she was one of the greatest storytellers; how much she loved teaching the children their prayers, going to church, and how she believed faith in God, and family are the foundation for a happy life. She also reminded Juanita how they had to sweep the patio at Grandma's house, for the queen and her family, how Grandma got angry at Juanita when she cut Marci's hair, and she called her a mule.How they ate Grandma's rice pudding, her enchiladas, how Marci learned to make tortillas, and how they had to go into the chicken coop to gather the eggs in the morning. Juanita, do you remember how comfortable and warm Grandma's house was in the winter? Marci asked her friend.

As they reminisced about the things, they did with Grandma, Juanita and Marci felt less saddened by the passing of their beloved Grandmother. Even though Juanita's Grandma was not Marci's Grandmother, she loved her just the same. She knew she was going to miss the Grandmother who came into her life when she moved to New Mexico. Grandma was a special person who influenced Marci's life in more ways than she could ever imagine. Marci, just as Juanita, knew that she was not sure what she was going to do without her beloved grandmother.

A wake was something Marci hoped she would never have to experience ever again because this scared her. Marci could not go into

Juanita's house by herself while Grandma was lying in a casket in the living room. Every time Marci looked at Grandma, she looked like she was breathing, and would get up at any minute.

The day Grandma's casket was lowered into the ground was too much for Juanita and Marci. That was when they knew they would never see Grandma ever again. Holding on to each other they cried as their Grandmother was laid to rest.

Going back home, Juanita asked Marci, to tell her about her grandmother. "I know I have never asked you about her, so what was she like?" "The only thing I know is that I was named after my grandmother to my mother's side of the family. My real name is Marcella, but I do not like that name, and I asked my mother if I could shorten it to Marci. She almost allowed me to shorten it legally, but Daddy stopped her. I have gone by Marci for as long as I can remember, and I'm asking you not to call me by my given name," Marci told her friend. Marci did not talk much about her grandmother because there was nothing to tell.

Back home, Juanita and Marci had many stories to share about Grandma with the cousins from Albuquerque, and what the stories meant to them. The cousins were saddened that they did not have the memories Marci, who was not part of the family, had. On the other hand, Marci felt extremely fortunate to have the fond memories the cousins from Albuquerque could never take away from her.

Days led to months and Marci, Juanita and her friends were now going to pep rallies, basketball, and football games to watch Caleb and his friends. For as much as Marci, Caleb and their friends were involved in extracurricular activities, they always made sure they helped each other. Of course, it was not all studying. They also went out on dates, dances, and most of all, made sure they went to their final homecoming football game. This was the ultimate game as the two rival teams meet. The rivalry between Los Lunas and Belen was so bad; the local police patrolled the grounds to make sure no fights broke out. This was the game of the year, and the majority of the Los Lunas residents attended. Residents from the Los Lunas and Belen area came out in force to see the Tigers beat the Belen Eagles by a sizeable margin. After that, the whole town celebrated and the kids went home to get ready for their homecoming dance.

Marci and Caleb were now thinking very seriously about which university they wanted to attend. Marci and Juanita knew they had to apply for scholarships to pay for their schooling. However, Caleb and Ernest did not have to worry about scholarships because they were awarded a full athletic scholarship to the university in Nevada. All they had to do was to keep their grades up, and for Caleb, that was not a problem. Must have been all the comic books he read when he was younger that helped him.

One day as Marci was preparing for her final school assembly she thought back to her freshman year in high school. She thought how scared she was when she, along with other ninth graders were initiated into high school. She remembered the heavy history, math, and English books she had to carry for the upper classmate who sat in the back of the classroom. She also thought how along with other ninth graders, she had to sweep the sidewalk with a toothbrush and go to school wearing pajamas. It was so embarrassing, but she was not the only freshman being initiated, and went along with all of the activities. The final initiation activity for the ninth graders was to go up the 700-foot tall El Cerro de Los Lunas hill. There, they were to repaint the rocks arranged in double LLs. The best thing about this was that the students were excused from their classes. Approved by the National Honor Society, and the principal, the upper classmates and the freshmen started their hike up the hill. This would end the activities they had to do, and were now released from bowing to the upper classmates. Marci remembered how much fun it was and every time she looked up at the LL hill, she knew that at one time she was part of the team who painted the rocks. Never in her wildest dreams would she have imagined doing something like that in Virginia. Of course, this never happened at her old school because the place where she lived did not have any hills like the El Cerro de Los Lunas.

Marci's senior year was one of her most memorable. Once she graduated from high school, she and Juanita would soon be on their way to college. Juanita knew she could not afford to move away from home, and did not know if she really wanted to. On the other hand, Marci knew she wanted to get away from her past mistakes and start fresh. She knew she was going to miss not only her classmates, but some of her teachers as well. She knew she was going to be alone, but it was time she moved out of her parent's home and started a life of her own.

The week of graduation was extremely hectic for Marci and Juanita as they studied for their final exams. All this ended too soon, and Marci and Juanita were now standing in line, ready to receive their diploma. Waiting for her name to be announced, Marci wondered what was going to happen to her, and if she was ready for college. However, she did not have time to think, as the graduates ahead of her were moving forward. Soon, her name was announced, and as she was about to receive her diploma, she heard Caleb and his friends cheer for her.

The ceremony was over, and the graduates along with their parents were congratulating one another. Even Jan and some of her friends came to congratulate Marci and Juanita, and they did the same. Juanita and Marci laughed, cried, and today, went their separate ways. Each one was going to celebrate their accomplishment separately. Juanita would celebrate her graduation at home where Rosita planned a special meal for her. Along with her family, Marci was going to the Luna Mansion, and later they would go to the Sandia Tramway.

College Years

The weeks after graduation, Marci was busy getting ready to leave home. As for Juanita, she was going to enjoy the summer before she started her college career in the fall, and she and Juanita spent as much time together as they could. Marci knew it was going to be exceptionally hard to leave her parents, and her best friend. However, she had to do what she had her heart set on doing. Now that it was time to leave, she was not sure she had made the right decision.

When it came time for Marci to leave for Eastern Highlands University, she was a nervous wreck. The only thing Marci was happy about was that she decided to have her family drive her there. This meant a lot to her, as she knew it would be some time before she would be going home. When she decided to go to college, Marci knew she wanted to be as far away as she could. Knowing she wanted to be independent, she sent her application to Eastern Highlands in Las Vegas that was several hundred miles away from home.

The day before Marci went off to college, she went to tell Doctor Brewer goodbye, as she did Juanita, Ralph, Rosita, Emily, and some of her teachers. On the following day as Marci's family was taking her to the university, she was happy to hear her parents tell her how proud they were of her and who she had become. "Little one," Dad said, "It seems like it was just yesterday I held you in my arms, and we were bringing you home from the hospital.

Now you are a young woman going off to college and we will miss you. Caleb will also be leaving us soon, and your mother and I don't know what we are going to do without you."

"Yeah sis, even I will miss you, but I now get to have Mom and Dad all to myself," Caleb remarked. They laughed, even though Marci knew that was true.

The trip was a pleasant one, and it did not take as long as Marci thought it would. However, the two-hundred mile trip to Las Vegas, New Mexico was enough time for Marci to realize just how much she was going to miss her family. As Travis drove up to the dorm and seeing the university made her even more nervous, and the butterflies in Marci's stomach started to act up.

Caleb exclaimed, "Wow, look at this place, it is so big!"

When her father stopped the car, Marci helped her father, and Caleb remove her suitcases from the trunk. Entering the dorm, Marci saw her roommate had left her a note telling her she would be back later, and to make herself at home. Yet, it helped that the room was very cheerful, and that made Marci feel somewhat better. Travis and Caleb put Marci's suitcases on the bed, while Marie was busy putting a family picture on the dresser.

Wanting to extend their stay, Marci asked her family if they wanted to take the tour around the campus. When Marci applied to the university, she did not realize it was so big, and wondered how she was going to get from one class to the next. Travis knew his little girl was scared, so he told her she would find shortcuts like those he did. That helped a little, but Marci did not feel as confident as did her father. The tour was over, and Marci and her family went back to her dorm. Now came the part Marci was dreading. It seemed as if they had just arrived, and now it was time for them to head back home. When Marci said good-bye to her family, it was a sad and lonely feeling. Today there was no one she could turn to because there was no friend who could comfort her.

By the time, Marci unpacked her suitcases; her roommate came in just long enough to say "Hi," and was off to meet a friend. Marci was glad because she was extremely tired, and slept until her roommate Jeanette Rich woke her up the following morning. Marci could not get used to all the noise around her, and she longed for her home in the country. Jeanette was an energetic, fun loving girl from Texas who liked to talk. She talked so much there were times Marci would go to the library to do her homework just to get away from Jeanette. Yet, Marci enjoyed having Jeanette as her roommate, because she was funny, and made Marci's time away from home tolerable. When Marci was not studying, she would join Jeanette at the gym, and watch her practice for their next volleyball game.

One day Marci was going to the lunchroom when she saw two of her high school classmates. Overjoyed to see someone she knew she practically ran to where Jan and Elaine were sitting. The girls were also excited at seeing someone they knew, and the three decided to meet at the library to study. Unfortunately, that did not work out as they planned because Jan and Elaine had to change their class schedule, and the trio soon drifted apart. Marci was grateful she did not see them again as they might have told Jeanette about her rowdy days. Marci had grown up and felt good about her life. Now that she was in college, her classes were more difficult than she thought, but Jeanette and Marci helped each other as much as they could. When the girls were homesick for their families, they put their homework aside and shared childhood memories. No matter how much they cried, or how many times they held on to their family pictures, Marci and Jeanette were there for each other. When Marci was down, Jeanette would drag her away from their dorm, and they would go to the movies, or just walk around the campus. Marci soon realized what a true friend Jeanette was turning out to be. Marci knew she could not have wished for a better roommate, and through Jeanette, Marci met many friends, but none measured up to her roommate.

Marci could not go home as often as she wanted because she did not want to take time off from her studies. Besides, money was tight, and she did not want to burden her family. Marci knew they would go for her, or send her the bus fare if she asked them too, but it was her decision to go to a university away from home. The only time Marci went home for more than a weekend was for Christmas break when the university closed down.

Marci was so involved with her studies she completely forgot Caleb would be graduating. However, that was several years away, or so she thought. When she received Caleb's graduation invitation, she was shocked. Graduation for both Caleb and Marci was but a couple of months away, and she knew how quickly that day would come. No matter what she had to do to go home, Marci knew it would all be worth it.

Luckily, for Marci, her semester was over two weeks before Caleb graduated. Not wanting to call her parents to pick her up, Marci decided to take the Greyhound bus home and surprise everyone. Once again, Marci was with her family preparing to celebrate a big event in their lives.

On a mild May afternoon, Marci went to visit Rafael and Rosita, even though she knew Juanita wasn't there, she really went to have a cup of coffee with Rafael. She never forgot what was not supposed to be good for her could taste so good. Like the many other times, Rafael and Marci laughed as they enjoyed their coffee. This time Marci asked Rafael to add two teaspoons of sugar, and a bit of milk to hers unlike her first cup of coffee.

Graduation for Caleb, Ernest and Isidro was here and Marci's eyes welded up with tears because she was so proud of her brother. When Caleb Bennett walked up the stage to receive his diploma, he saw his mother wiping her eyes, and saw the proud smile on his father's face. He also saw his sister clapping and shouting to show him she too was proud of him.

Graduation ceremony was over, and instead of going out to eat at the Luna Mansion, Travis's family had planned a barbeque for Caleb, Ernest, and Isidro at their house. The celebration lasted late into the night with other graduates and neighbors coming and going. At the same time, Marci and Juanita along with other friends had time to catch up on what was happening in their lives.

The two months Marci spent with her family flew by. This time when Marie, Travis and Caleb took her to the bus depot, Caleb was not going back home. He too would be leaving, and would go back during the Christmas break. Marci's little brother had grown up and Marci was saddened she was not around to see it happen. Caleb was no longer the little brother Marci left behind a couple of years ago. He had grown up, and even though she hated to admit it, he was actually very mature as were Ernest, Isidro, and the rest of Caleb's friends.

No matter how difficult her classes were, Marci managed to stay on the dean's list. Calls home were a weekly routine for Marci. Not that she needed her father, or her mother's help with her homework, she just needed to hear their voices. "Caleb just finished talking to your mother," Travis would tell his daughter. That was how it went for the years Marci and Caleb were away from home.

Marci's final year at college was extremely hectic. By this time, all she wanted was to complete her master's degree, and go work in a small town where she could meet people on a personal basis. Marci knew once this happened, she could enjoy her time back home with her parents. That was until she got a job, and found a place to live.

Everything was going as Marci had hoped it would. Her classes were getting easier, and she would soon be home. Toward the end of her senior year, Marci received a call from her neighbor. Emily's voice was raspy and muffled and Marci was having a hard time trying to understand what she was saying. All Marci heard Emily say was that her parents were in an automobile accident. Between sobs, Emily told Marci, she needed to get home immediately. A friend of hers who worked at the police department called her because she didn't know how to get in touch with Marci. Emily told Marci, "She was not sure how bad her parents were injured, but to get home as soon as she could and that she had also called Caleb, and he was going to catch a flight home.

Marci could not remember if she finished her conversation with Emily, or if she hung up. She just remembered asking Jeanette to take her to the bus station. Jeanette offered to drive Marci home, but Marci told her she would be okay. "Besides, you have your volleyball tournament, and you have been practicing so hard for it," Marci replied.

When Caleb heard about the accident, he, Ernest and Isidro bought a ticket to New Mexico. Because it was standby, they were not sure what time they would get home. An elderly couple heard the boys talking and when they heard what was going on, they told the boys they would let them take their place. They were in no hurry to get to their destination as they were on vacation. Because of their generosity, Caleb, Ernest and Isidro would be in Albuquerque in an hour. Having thanked the couple, all five went to talk to the flight attendant at the counter. There, the exchange took place, and the elderly couple told Caleb they would say a prayer for his parents.

In the meantime, Marci caught the next Greyhound bus out. Sitting, at the back of the bus, the words parents and accident continued to resonate in her mind. No matter how hard she tried to think of something else she could not. Four agonizing hours later, the bus finally arrived at the bus depot in Albuquerque, and Marci called a taxi to take her to the hospital. The driver was a very nice man, but Marci was in no mood to carry a conversation with anyone.

"Where to young lady," the taxi driver Roberto asked Marci.

"To the Presbyterian Hospital, and could you please hurry," Marci replied.

Thinking one of her friends was having a baby, the taxi driver asked, "If Marci was going to visit a friend?"

"No, my parents were in a car accident, and I don't know the extent of their injuries. All I know is that they are in critical condition. My neighbor called me to come home immediately." I'm very sorry miss. I know a shortcut and I'll get you there in no time."

Having said that, the driver stepped on the gas and rushed Marci to the hospital. When Marci got down, and was reaching into her purse to pay; the driver left.

Marci stopped at the information desk to ask the woman if she could direct her to the Intensive Care Unit. "Take the elevator to the fourth floor, and the floor nurse will help you," she replied. Getting off the elevator, Marci went to the nurses' station, but no one was there. When a nurse came out from one of the patient's room, Marci asked her, "If she could tell her what room her mother and father were in?"

"What is your mother's name," the nurse asked?

Marci could have sworn she had given the nurse her mother's name, but in her frame of mind, she was not thinking clearly. As soon as Marci gave the nurse her mother's name, the nurse looked at the chart and led Marci to her mother's room.

"Your father is across the hall," the nurse said and left as another patient was paging her. When Marci entered her mother's room, she saw Caleb, Ernest and Isidro sitting next to her. Neither heard Marci as she walked in, but Marci heard Caleb talk to his mother as he held her hand in his. When Ernest and Isidro saw Marci approach the bed, they stood up so she could sit next to her mother. As she did, Caleb looked up and saw Marci standing at the foot of the bed. Placing his mother's hand on the bed as gently as if she were a child, he stood up and hugged his sister for comfort. They held on to each other for a few minutes, and Marci then sat on the chair Caleb was sitting on. Marci could not believe this was her mother lying in the hospital bed because she did not recognize this stranger.

Knowing her father was alone across the hall, Marci did not know what to do. How could she stay with her mother when her father was all alone? Yet, how could she leave her mother to be with her father? Neither Caleb nor Marci knew what to do for the people lying on the beds. They looked like strangers with tubes and wires all over their body keeping them alive. Marci spent time with her mother, and later she and Caleb went to their father's room. Ernest told them "He, and Isidro would stay with Marie while they spent time with their father."

Agreeing to leave them with their mother, Marci and Caleb entered the room across the hall. When Marci saw her father, he too was attached to machines that were keeping him alive. Marci held on to Caleb, as they knew what the outcome of the accident was going to be.

"Caleb, we can't leave our parents alone. We can go from one room to the other, but we can't leave them all by themselves. Let me stay with Dad for a few minutes, and then I will stay with Mom," Marci told her brother.

Left alone with her father, Marci kissed him. Then she begged, and bargained with God to bring her parents back. Knowing no amount of pleas was going to help, she talked to her father so he would know she was there. Marci was trying hard to be brave, but Daddy's little girl was heartbroken. She didn't know what to do—so she cried. Marci stayed with her father for several hours before she told him she would be back. Getting up from the chair, and leaving her father alone, she walked into her mother's room. Caleb looked like a little boy hurt, confused, and wondering when his mother was going to wake up. They knew it was not going to make a difference as to who was, or was not with Marie or Travis. In their hearts, they knew their parents were aware of their presence.

Ernest and Isidro were like sons to Travis and Marie, and they too were heartbroken at what they saw and feared. Both Ernest and Isidro volunteered to stay with either parent, but Marci told him, "If you want to help us, you need to go back to school so that you can tell Caleb what is going on."

As much as Ernest and Isidro wanted to stay, they knew Marci was right in what she was asking them to do. Before he left, Ernest told Marci he would call and check on them. Ernest told Caleb, "Not to worry. He would tell his professors what happened to his parents. He would also take notes, and let him know what was going on in class."

That afternoon when a nurse came to check on Marie, Marci asked her, "If it was possible to have her parents in the same room." Marci told her it would make it easier for Caleb and her to take care of them." The nurse told her, "It was hospital policy to separate male and female patients, and what she was requesting was not possible."

Marci cried, and asked, "If she could talk to the supervisor to ask if something could be done. These were her parents, and it was extremely hard for her and her brother to be separated." The nurse apologized and told Marci "she was very sorry, but she could not break the rules." Knowing she was right, Caleb and Marci took turns going from one room to the next.

Exhausted, Marci fell asleep while she was in her father's room. In her state of exhaustion, she heard her father calling her. However, when she opened her eyes, Marci's father had not woken up. Seeing how the machines were keeping her parents alive, she wondered how this could have happened. She also wondered what she and Caleb were going to do if their parents did not make it.

"I cannot think like this," Marci said. "We have to be brave and let the doctors do what they have to do. She then pulled the chair closer to her father's bed, and talked to him about her classes. She hoped he could hear her and wake up, but she knew better. Because it was a one sided conversation Marci leaned back on her chair. As she did, her stomach rumbled, and she realized just how tired and hungry she was, but she did not want to leave.

Marci always thought her parents would live a long life, and would die of natural causes, but now, it didn't seem as that was going to happen. As Marci rested her head on her father's bed, she closed her eyes and held his hand.

When Emily went to visit, she tried opening the door as quietly as she could, but Marci woke up, and saw she was still holding on to her father's hand. Placing it on the bed, Marci got up and hugged her neighbor. Emily comforted her, and once she sat down, she told Marci the priest had given Travis and Marie their last rites. Marci started to cry, but Emily told her that was a normal procedure. Marci knew almost nothing about the accident until Emily came to visit Travis. She told Marci, "All I know is that your parents were on their way to a movie when a driver crossed the medium, and slammed head on into their car. So far, no one has been charged, and the police are still investigating the accident."

Marci listened as Emily told her about the accident, but Emily had no information that would help them cope with the chance their parent's might not survive. Now, all Marci wanted to know was if the driver of the other car survived the accident. Emily told Marci, "The driver was being treated for lacerations, and injuries he sustained in the accident." That did not make her feel any better. Marci knew if there was a consolation, it was that the driver would have to live with what he did for the rest of his life.

As Marci listened to what Emily had to say, she thought she had seen her father move his hand. Then she realized it was a reaction to the medication. After Emily left, Marci spent a few hours with Caleb, and both were grateful Emily had come to be with them. Marci thought about going to see the man who did this too her parents, but what was she going to tell him? She wished it were he instead of them.

Tired as she was, she decided to take a nap, but no sooner had she closed her eyes than the telephone startled her. Marci panicked because she did not want to answer it, but she was not at home where she could ignore it. When she picked it up, a nurse told her the man whose car crashed into her parent's car was being released. He wanted to visit her parents before his sister picked him up if it was all right with both Marci and her brother.

"Visit my parents! What the hell was he going to do, sit next to them and ask them how they are doing?"

"Sure," Marci said, "Tell him he can come and visit them. I want him to see what he has taken away from my brother and me."

Marci was extremely angry by the time the nurse hung up. She was finally going to get a chance to tell the monster that hurt her parents what she thought of him. Caleb walked in on Marci while she was talking to herself, and she told him about the phone call. Both Caleb and Marci were furious, and ready to give this person a piece of their mind. Again, as in the past, things never happen the way they should.

When the nurse came into Marie's room, she told Marci and Caleb, "The man would not be coming. His sister came to pick him up earlier than he expected, and she was in a big hurry," she said.

"The coward, how dare he ask to see our parents, and then leave the hospital," Caleb said. "The nurse replied, God knows what has to happen, so maybe it was for the best he went home."

By this time, Caleb and Marci were living at the hospital, and during that time, they got to know the doctors and nurses. Everyone was very helpful in answering their questions about their parents, and tried to make them comfortable. They understood what a difficult time this was for them, and gave Marci and Caleb words of comfort to help them. They were Marci and Caleb's angels, in human form—so wonderful and caring. No matter how cheerful they tried to be, the look on their faces told Marci and Caleb different. Marci was afraid to ask any questions because she did not want to hear what she already knew. Many times Marci and Caleb thought they had seen their mother, and father's hands and feet twitch. Days such as these, their hopes rose, and sank as they prayed for a miracle. By this time, Marci had read every magazine in the visitor's area and done as many crossword puzzles as she could.

Every day was the same as the last, and they soon lost track of what day it was. It helped that Juanita, Rafael, Rosita, Emily, Sal and Dr. Brewer would come to help Marci and Caleb as much as they could. Sometimes no one could be with Caleb and Marci, but they understood.

Marci hardly left the hospital because like Caleb, she wanted to be there should her mother or father wake up and ask for her. One evening as Father Gene was sitting with Marci; the doctor came in. He sat next to her, and said, "Marci, there is nothing you or Caleb can do. Your parents are being taken care of and, if there is a change in their condition, we will call you. If you do not take care of yourself, I will be admitting both you and your brother into the hospital."

"Doctor, what if my mom, or dad wake up, and I am not here? I know you are doing everything you can, but what if I don't get to tell them good-bye?"

The priest then told Marci, "I have watched you when you are with your father and mother, and I know you have told them good-bye many times over. It is not easy to let someone you love go, but maybe that is what they want to hear you say. I've heard you ask God to help your parents, well, maybe it's time you ask him to help you."

Marci didn't know how many times she heard the same thing from the nurses, and their friends—this time she listened. She was scared to leave, but she knew everyone was right. For the first time in many weeks both Marci and Caleb went home.

The house felt big, cold, and empty and it was a lonely place without their parents waiting for them. When they looked out the dining room window, Marci started to cry as she stared at the garden that was left unattended. Caleb comforted Marci as best he could, but he knew she had to cry just as he had to. While Marci and Caleb were taking care of their parents, Emily, Rosita, and Juanita cleaned the house, and took care of their animals. Juanita was left to clean the refrigerator while Rosita and Emily went to the store to buy groceries. Marci and Caleb knew they could go eat with them any time they wanted company, but for now, they wanted to be alone. As Marci walked aimlessly about the house, the telephone rang. Immediately, she thought it was the doctor calling them to go back. Instead, it was her friend, Jeanette, from the university checking on her.

Marci was extremely happy to hear from her friend, and for the first time she was able to tell someone how she felt. She told Jeanette everything that happened to her parents, and once she got off the phone, Marci felt better and decided to go outdoors. Knowing she was going to stay outside for a while, she made herself a sandwich, got a coke, water, and put them in a bag. Before she went outside, she asked Caleb if he wanted a sandwich, but he was not hungry.

After Marci went outdoors, Caleb decided to go for Shredder and Cleopatra, at Rosita and Rafael's house. They were kind enough to take them to their house and made sure they were fed and had water to drink. After Marci sat down on the grass, she put her hand on the ground. It felt warm and the healing power of the desert came over her. She could not remember how long she sat outside, but she suddenly felt someone standing next to her. So absorbed was she in her thoughts Marci did not hear Caleb as he walked toward her with Cleopatra and Shredder.

Shredder ran around chasing a lizard and Cleopatra purred as Marci held her. As Marci and Caleb shared memories of their parents, they heard themselves laughing. Neither one had done that for so long it gave them the strength they needed to continue. Marci felt God's healing power come over her as she and her brother sat outside. Caleb stayed with his sister for a while, and then decided he would go to bed. That night as she sat outside, and looked at the stars, she asked God to help her make the right decision as she thought about what the doctor told her. Then she thought of Vanessa, and she decided to go inside where she wrote her a lengthy letter. She knew she could call her, but as she put her feelings down on paper, she was able to release the hurt she was feeling.

The following day Caleb and Marci returned to the hospital refreshed and prepared to face the inevitable. Marci was sitting with her father when the nurse came into the room, and told her someone wanted to visit her parents.

"Who is it?" Marci asked.

"It's the man whose car hit your parents," the nurse replied.

"Is he sure, he wants to see them? Has the coward returned, to say he is sorry?"

"I'm not sure, but I can tell him to leave if that is what you want," the nurse replied.

By this time, Marci had calmed down, and figured she could say what she had too without losing her temper, and raising her voice. All she had to do was let him see what he had done.

"Sure, tell him he can come in," Marci told the nurse.

Caleb and Marci talked about the possibility of this happening, and agreed they were okay with the visit. Realizing she was not prepared to face this man, she went to get Caleb. Marci also knew she wasn't sure what she was going to do, or say, no matter who was, or wasn't with her. Thinking it would help her calm down, she went to the window, and looked out at the parking lot. It might help her find the words she needed to talk to this man. Caleb joined Marci, as he knew she needed to have him nearby.

As she heard the door open, Marci could not turn around to face the man who walked in. For as much as she wanted to see who it was, she was having a hard time turning away from the window. Caleb was also dreading meeting this man, but he managed to turn around, and said, "Marci, you need to turn around." Taking a deep breath, and asking God to help them, Marci turned around. Now she was ready to tell this person what she thought of him, but that too did not happen.

A teenager on crutches, not more than seventeen years of age was standing by her father's bed. As he stood there, he looked so sad and remorseful, and Marci did not know what to do. She thought it would be someone who was the same age as that of her father, maybe older. It never crossed their mind it could be a teenager—he was so young.

"Thank you for allowing me to visit your parents," the young man said.

"My name is Neil, and I came to tell you how very sorry I am that I caused your family all this pain."

However, neither Marci nor Caleb could say, or do anything, other than for Caleb to stand behind his sister, and for Marci to tell Neil her name. Neil asked them, "If they wanted to know what happened on that horrible night." This was what both Marci and Caleb had been waiting for, but now that they had the chance, they didn't want to know. Marci then invited Neil to sit with her father, and if he wanted to, they could go next door to their mother's room. Neil was in a lot of pain, and again asked Marci if she wanted to hear what happened.

"Yes, please tell us. Maybe then we can accept all of this," Marci told Neil, and so, he re-lived the events of that evening. As Neil was telling Marci and Caleb the events of the tragic night, tears were rolling down their faces.

"It was the night of our senior prom, and my cousin and I were on our way to pick up our dates. Earlier in the day, it rained, and we were about a mile from our destination when my car went through a puddle in the road and hydroplaned. I remember seeing a car coming at me, and hard as I tried, I could not do anything to prevent what I knew was going to happen. I slammed into your parent's car and my car flipped over. When I came too, the paramedic told me my cousin was dead. He said he died instantly from massive head and internal injuries. Today when we buried my cousin, I went to the scene of the accident and placed a marker with his name on it. Pieces of shattered glass from the window were on the side of the road, and I found the corsage he was going to give his date. The hardest thing for me was when I went to give her the corsage, but it was something I had to do. In order for me to live a normal life, I knew I had to come and talk to you. I need to ask you for your forgiveness. In a split second, my life changed because of something I did. It was my fault, and even though I don't know what you are going through, I have to deal with what I did to you, and to my cousin, Felix. I don't think I will ever drive a car again, but, if I do, I promise I will be more careful."

When Neil told Marci and Caleb his cousin, Felix died; they were unable to say anything. Both were in shock. Felix was a couple years younger than Caleb was, and was the one who challenged Caleb to a basketball game for Thanksgiving. Caleb couldn't get over the fact his friend was dead; he was so young. As Marci got up to hug Neil, she looked into his eyes, and told him they forgave him. How could she not? How could she look into the face of a young man who had his whole life ahead of him, and let him carry such a heavy burden? It was something he had no control over, and together they would all deal with the tragedy that brought them together.

"I am happy you had the courage to come see how our parents are doing. We don't know if they will survive, but whatever you do, please don't blame yourself," Marci told him.

"Not only are you carrying the burden of having your cousin die while you were driving; you need to know you were not responsible for what happened to our parents, or your cousin. We are hoping you will stop blaming yourself for anything that happened because it was not something you could prevent."

Marci, Caleb, and Neil cried for the loss of their loved ones and again, Marci told him she would keep him in her prayers. Caleb then walked him to the elevator and once again told him how sorry he was that Felix was dead. He also thanked him for coming to help him and his sister come to terms with the accident.

Looking outside the window, Marci was extremely thankful she did not lash out at Neil as she had intended. When Caleb came back, they talked about the teenager, and what a burden he was carrying.

"I'm glad you were here to meet him," Marci told Caleb, "he broke my heart."

Caleb then asked Marci if she wanted something to eat, and they went down to the cafeteria.

That night when the nurse asked Marci if she was going home, Marci told her she was. No longer did she feel guilty at leaving her parents because she knew they were in excellent hands. Besides, what could she do for them that the doctors had not already done? It had been an extremely emotional day, and she needed to do some thinking.

Several more weeks passed, and Caleb and Marci were told they had to make a decision as to how long they wanted to keep their parents on the life support machines. It was not an easy decision for Marci and Caleb to give the doctors permission to remove their parents from the machines that were keeping them alive. Both Marci and Caleb were glad Father Gene was there because as soon as the machines were unplugged, their parents died. Marci and Caleb thanked the doctors for all they had done for their parents. They also thanked Father Gene as he gave them the courage to make the decision.

On an overcast summer day, Marci and Caleb went to scatter their parent's ashes in the desert they so loved. Rafael, Rosita, Emily, Ernest, Juanita, Sal, Dr. Brewer, nurses, and doctors along with many of their friends and neighbors came to pay their final respects. The receptionist along with other employees from the Extension Office who knew Marie as a friend were there. Marci was surprise to see Neil there, and when she saw him, she asked him to join her and Caleb as they were going to conclude the services out in the desert.

As Marci was scattering her father's ashes, a gently breeze came along and carried his ashes over the desert where he felt so at home. Marci thought, *now my father will forever see God display his artwork even if few take the time to admire His handiwork.*

Caleb was about to scatter his mother's ashes, when the breeze subsided, and for a few minutes, her ashes fell at his feet. Suddenly, the breeze started up, and Marci now knew her father had come to take their mother by the hand, and in a second, they were gone. Travis and Marie's ashes were scattered on Marci's acre of land where they belonged.

For Marci, this was where she would come visit them. Marci now knew her parents were in a better place than staying in the hospital attached to machines. That evening, Neil, Caleb, and Marci sat outside on the porch and got to know each other. With so much in common, they soon became close friends and kept in touch.

Weeks after Travis and Marie died; Marci received a letter from Vanessa and Ms. Andersen. Along with those came sympathy cards from Beth, Magdalene, Anne and Cecilia. Having read the letters and cards, Marci held on to them and cried.

Marci and Caleb were still in mourning, and were lost without their parents. It was hard to accept the fact they were gone, and would never be there for them to come home to. Had it not been for their neighbors and friends, Marci and Caleb would never have resumed their normal lives.

Today was especially hard for Caleb and Marci because it was Caleb's birthday. However, Rosita did not forget, and she baked him a beautiful cake. After they celebrated Caleb's birthday, he, and Marci went home. While they were watching TV in the den, Caleb told Marci he wanted to go back to college. He also told her she should live in the house, and Marci agreed. The only thing Caleb asked Marci was to take care of Shredder.

Finals at UNLV were a month away, and Ernest called Caleb to tell him "he had to get back as the professor could not send Caleb the exam." This was exactly the incentive Caleb needed to get back to a normal routine. The night before Caleb returned to college, he and Marci talked about their parents into the early hours of the morning.

As Marci sat up in her bed, she wondered what she was going to do now that she was going to be by herself. Caleb, on the other hand, thought how much he hated to leave his sister, but he knew he did not want to stay home without his parents there. No matter how much they needed their rest, neither one could fall asleep.

On the afternoon Marci took Caleb to the airport, he told her, "He did not know when he would be back." Trying to hold back the tears that filled his eyes he said, "Marci, I don't think I can come back to Los Lunas. I think I would be better off if I complete my education, and find me a place to live in Las Vegas. There are too many memories here, but I will call you every week to see how you are doing." Having said that, Caleb hugged his sister, said good-bye, and boarded the airplane.

Marci now felt a loneliness she had never known before. Her parents were gone, and this time Marci did not have anyone to turn to. She knew she could talk to her friends or neighbors, but she did not want to burden them with her problems. Juanita was busy with her studies and Jeanette returned to her hometown in Texas. Marci was lonely, and it was the most horrible feeling. It was something no one should have to face alone. If Marci thought she was lonely when she was growing up, or when she went to the university, nothing compared to what she was experiencing now. Wanting to return to the university, Marci realized she could not get herself to leave her home. Her time with her parents was cut short, and she felt she needed to be where she could be closer to them.

Museum of Natural History

The day after Caleb left, Marci was up at dawn, and went out to get the morning paper. As she was drinking her coffee, the mail carrier knocked on her door. She needed to sign for a letter from the insurance company. Along with that letter, Marci also received a letter from the university she attended. The letter was from the Registrar's Office at Eastern Highlands letting her know she passed all of her classes, and her degree would be mailed in a couple of months. Setting the mail aside, she continued reading the newspaper and drank her coffee. As she turned to the classified section, a job announcement caught her attention. A position for an Assistant Curator was needed at the Museum of Natural History. Marci knew she could do the job; all she needed was to get an application and fill it out. She continued to read the requirements, and when she came to the deadline, she panicked because that was but a few hours away.

For the time she had been home, Marci had not thought of looking for a job but she knew she was the perfect person for this job. Marci called the number listed, and asked if she could speak to the personnel manager. The woman who answered the telephone told Marci, Bernadette was out to lunch, but would be back in an hour.

"I don't want to lose the opportunity to get an interview," Marci told the receptionist.

"Would you like Bernadette to return your call?"

Marci told her she would like that; gave the receptionist her number and hung up. Not wanting to miss the phone call, Marci decided to work on her résumé. It didn't take Marci long to get everything together, and once she was done with her résumé, she took a shower and waited for Bernadette to return her call. It was midafternoon, and Marci was still waiting for Bernadette to return her call. Getting restless, she thought it was silly for her to wait for the telephone to ring. Marci then decided to go outside to enjoy the day, and started to water her mother's flowers. No sooner had she gone out of the house than the telephone rang.

Running to turn the water off she heard the answering machine go on, and by the time she ran into the kitchen, the answering machine's light was blinking. Pressing the button to listen to the message, Marci was angry she decided to go outdoors instead of waiting for Bernadette's call.

"Hello Marci, this is Bernadette. I am sorry I missed your call, but could you please call me at my direct number as soon as you get my message." Having written her number on a piece of paper Marci sat down and returned the call. Marci tried calling a couple of times, but the line was busy. On the fourth try, Bernadette finally answered.

"Hi, Bernadette," this is Marci.

"Oh hi Marci, I got your message regarding the Assistant Curator's position. I realize this is short notice, but could you bring your résumé, and stay for an interview? Our director is going out of state for a couple of days, and would like to interview as many applicants before he leaves." Marci told Bernadette she would be there in an hour. With that, their conversation ended, and Marci ran upstairs to change her clothes. Anxious to get her résumé to Bernadette on time, Marci took shortcuts that would get her there sooner. When she arrived at the museum, she had no idea it was so big. Entering the building, she went to the restroom to make sure she looked presentable. Satisfied with how she looked; she went to ask the security guard if he could direct her to the Personnel Office. Pointing to the office at the far end of the building, he told her to ask for Bernadette.

Walking into the receptionist area, Marci told the receptionist she was there for an interview. Marci was told to have a seat, and she waited for Bernadette to come out. A bit nervous, Marci sat down and picked up a magazine to keep her occupied. Later, Bernadette walked out of the Director's Office, and approached Marci. She told her, "The interview had to be re-scheduled because the director had to take his daughter to the doctor." Marci had no choice but to agree to return the following day.

"What was she going to say, No, I can't come back tomorrow, I'm sorry his daughter is sick, but I came for an interview, and I want it now?"

Sure, I understand," Marci replied as Bernadette took her résumé, and rescheduled her interview for 10 a.m. the following day. "I will call you if your appointment has to be changed, if not, just come in."

Marci smiled, and walked out of the museum, but on her way home, she could not help but think this was a bad sign. She was certain this was their way of preparing her for what was to come. Feeling as if she had been tossed aside like a wet mop, Marci decided to go to a movie, but when she got there, none of the movies appealed to her, so she went to buy a dress for tomorrow's interview. That is if there truly will be one, but she could not take the chance that would not happen.

Now that her parents were no longer there to help her, she was on her own, and needed to start supporting herself. It was late in the evening when Marci got home, so she decided to go to bed, as she was tired. Going upstairs, she saw the light on the answering machine blinking. Not wanting to listen to the messages, she continued going upstairs. Before she reached the top, she decided to listen to her calls. It could be that her appointment had been re-scheduled for a second time. The first two calls were from credit card companies offering her a great deal if she applied for their card. Marci listened, and along with a call from Caleb, and Jeanette there was a call from the director at the museum.

"Hello Marci, this is Emilio from the Museum of Natural History. I have gone over your résumé very carefully, and I am confident you are the person I am looking to hire. I don't know if you will get my message before tomorrow, but if you want the job, it is yours. Please report to work tomorrow at seven-thirty in the morning, and Bernadette will introduce you to the staff. If she tells me you did not show up, I will understand."

"What, and give up the chance to work at a place I have studied for all of my life? Of course, I will be there!" Marci shouted, and with that, she went to bed.

The next morning, Marci arrived early for her first day at work, and this time Bernadette showed her around the office. She introduced Marci to Elaine Garcia and Jeremiah Castillo who were always the first to report to work. Elaine was a middle-aged woman with hair even redder than Marci's, and that was saying a lot. On the top of Elaine's head, she had a number two pencil sticking out of her ear. As Elaine turned her chair, Marci saw she also had another pencil holding the hair that was twisted into a bun.

First impressions are often so wrong! When Bernadette introduced Jeremiah to Marci, she thought he was still in high school. When Marci asked him what grade he was in, Jeremiah laughed. To her amazement, and shock, he told her he was married and had four kids. At thirty-five, he and his wife moved to Albuquerque from Nebraska to work at the museum.

After Marci met, the other employees she was going to work with, Bernadette took Marci to her office. Marci then asked Bernadette, "how Emilio could hire her without a personal interview."

"That is how Emilio does it. He likes to hire people even if he does not actually interview them. So far, he has not been wrong. Jeremiah was another employee he hired, and he has been with us for five years. Elaine has been here about as long as I have."

"So is his daughter feeling better?" Marci asked.

"No. He had to cancel his trip to Florida for a later date because his wife also got sick." As if to change the subject, Bernadette said, "If you want to get started, I'll show you which files have to be reviewed, and filed."

With that, Bernadette took Marci into the file room where she was to get the files in the blue in-basket. Grabbing a couple of files, Marci went into her office and started her first day at work. Bernadette then told her, "If she needed anything to let her know and she would get it."

Jeremiah Castillo had slipped away and was coming back from lunch when Elaine looked at her watch. Seeing it was past her lunch hour, she decided to go out and get something to eat. Knowing Marci had not taken a break, she invited her to go eat with her. By the end of their lunch break, it was as if the two had known each other forever.

Elaine was glad she got up late, and did not have time to prepare her lunch, as this gave her a chance to get to know Marci. The day had been very hectic and getting away from the office was just what the two needed.

Emilio was in and out of his office, but never went to see what Marci looked like, if she liked her job, or to ask if she needed anything. When Marci thought she would never see who Emilio was, he came in to introduce himself. Marci would never have known that the tall, slender man who walked into her office was her boss. When Emilio came into Marci's office, he was carrying files that also needed to be reviewed. Marci thinking he was an employee from another department, told him, "To place them in the basket, and she would get to them as soon as she could. The man then said, "Hi Marci, my name is Emilio."

Marci dropped the file she was working on, and stood up from her chair. Embarrassed, she apologized. Emilio told her, "That was not necessary. How was she to know who he was when up until this moment, they had not meet?"

Not realizing Emilio was monitoring her work, he told her she should not try to do everything all at once. He did add she was doing a great job as he had checked a dozen, or so of the files she worked on. However, he did not want her working the late hours she was working. Marci told Emilio, "She loved her job and she wanted to make sure she did her share. To her, it did not matter how many files she had to work on as she enjoyed every minute. Besides, since her parents died, she only had the animals to go home too." After Emilio placed the files in the basket, he asked Marci "if she wanted to take a ride to one of the ruins Henry, one of the archeologists had uncovered."

Marci was delighted Emilio wanted her to see the ruin a seventy-year-old man discovered. The site is about twenty miles from here. "If you want to go, we need to leave before Henry calls it a day. He has been working long hours, and I'm hoping he will be there when we arrive."

On the way to the site, Marci enjoyed talking to Emilio, and by the time they arrived there, they had gotten to know each other better. Marci now felt like they were sharing the same interests, and felt even better about her job.

Arriving at the site, Emilio parked the truck and both he and Marci got down. As she did, she froze where she stood and could not move. Marci looked at the man who stood up to shake Emilio's hand, and knew he would one day be her husband. Never had Marci felt this way about the men, she dated in the past. For some reason, Henry McCoy was different. Who would have thought she would meet the man of her dreams while she was examining bones out in the desert.

Henry was a handsome man about thirty-two-years old, with a full head of thick black wavy hair, whose tanned skin accentuated his beautiful smile, and sparkling white teeth. As soon as Henry shook Emilio's hand, he knelt on the ground to show him what he uncovered. But before Henry could show Emilio what he uncovered, Emilio introduced Marci to Henry, but he had not seen Marci as she was standing behind Emilio. Getting up to shake her hand, he apologized for not seeing her. He told Marci he wasn't trying to be rude, he was excited about their discovery. He then invited her to look at the remains he had uncovered, but all she could focus on was his gorgeous body.

Marci had met many men in the past, but Henry was different. From the minute Henry shook her hand, all she knew was that she wanted to get to know him better. Yet, all he wanted was to show her the bones his crew excavated. Knowing she had to focus on the findings, Marci asked him if he had contacted any of the local agencies. What was the matter with her, of course he had. Henry thought Marci was a bit cocky, and he knew she was nervous, so he thought he would tease her, and see how much she knew about the profession she chose. There was no hesitation on Marci's part as she answered his questions to his satisfaction. Henry did not want to let Marci off that easy, so he asked her, "If she brought her tools". Marcy said "I did. Not knowing what tools I would need I just brought my bag."

"You carry that around with you at all times." "Yes, better to be over prepared than having to borrow," Marci replied.

Not sure where Henry was going with his questions, Marci knew Henry was testing her, but she did not mind. If this was his way of getting to know her, she would answer any question he asked. Yet she got a bit upset, and told Henry, "Let me tell you, I know as much, maybe more than you do. If you want to know what I have done, just ask Emilio. He would not have hired me if he did not think I was capable of doing my job."

"Wow! So it is true when people say redheads have a temper," Henry said in a teasing way.

Now to answer your question, Yes, after we discovered more bones we knew we had to contact the authorities. They are sending someone to examine the ruin to make sure we are not trespassing on sacred land. We think the bones we excavated have been here more than five-hundred years. One or two skeletons may not tell us how these people lived, but several here and there can."

Kneeling next to Henry, Marci could smell his cologne. He looked so masculine and smelled so manly. Marci so wanted to wipe the sweat beads off his back. She knew she had to concentrate on the skeleton that was on the ground, and not the one that still had flesh on it—the one that was kneeling next to her. Henry and his crew could not do anything until the authorities came to examine the ruins. In the meantime, Henry invited Marci to sit in his truck while Emilio went to talk to the other men.

"We can at least get out of the scorching heat," Henry told her. "So what brings you here?"

"Emilio invited me, and because this is what I have done in the past I figured I'd take him up on it," Marci replied.

"Guess I take after my father in that I love the outdoors."

Within two hours, a representative from the tribal agency showed up. When it was determined not to be sacred land, Henry and his crew continued where they left off with their excavation. After the men made a detailed recording, and they took pictures of their findings, Henry then had his crew place the bones in boxes where they would be taken to the museum. With utmost care, and respect the crew placed the bones in boxes and labeled them. At the museum, the bones would go through extensive examination to estimate their exact age, at the time of their death.

As Emilio was driving Marci back to the office they talked about the skeletal remains, Henry uncovered. Emilio then asked Marci, "So what do you think of Henry?" Marci told him, "She thought he was very intelligent, and a nice guy. He knows exactly what he is doing, and is not intimidated by a woman who is smarter than he is. However, he gave me plenty of tips that I did not learn in college, and I would like to try them out," Marci replied.

Emilio laughed and said, "You know, he isn't married." When Marci heard Henry wasn't married, she knew Emilio saw how she reacted, and didn't know what to say.

After their first meeting, Henry and Marci met on more than one occasion to discuss the remains he discovered out in the desert. Having worked with Henry for several months, Marci wondered when Henry was going to ask her out on a date—but that was the furthest thing from his mind. Marci had never known what it was like to feel what she was feeling for Henry. Every day was pure torture when the man of her dreams was around, but she had to concentrate on the reports she was working on. Marci worked at home late into the night, writing, revising and making sure she had everything she needed. Knowing Emilio was waiting for the report, Marci felt good about the information she had gathered. Now all she had to do was to put it all together.

The next time Marci saw Henry, he told her he was going to be gone for a month or so, and wondered if she needed help with her portion of the report. Then he asked Marci the question she had waited for from the day she met him. Marci didn't know what she was thinking as all she wanted to say was, "Yes." Instead, she said, "Uh let me check my calendar. My friends and I scheduled a girl's night out, and I'm not sure what Friday, or Saturday it is."

Henry pretended he did not hear Marci turn him down. Sly as he was, he asked Marci, "If she wanted to go to a movie, and later go have a beer and a pizza." This time, Marci accepted, and the conversation changed to what movie they would go to, and which pizza place was their favorite.

Friday, Marci told Bernadette she was going to work on her report at home. She was almost done, and would have a rough draft for Emilio on Tuesday, or Wednesday. Pouring herself a cup of coffee, Marci got a couple of chocolate chip cookies out of the cookie jar, and started to work on her report. Concentrating on her work, Marci did not notice how quickly time had come and gone. Almost six hours passed, and other than the cup of coffee and the cookies, Marci had not eaten anything. She had worked on her report, and needed but a few more graphs to add when Henry called her to tell her he would pick her up around seven.

She had even forgotten she was going to go out with the man of her dreams. Because Henry had only seen her in her uniform or wearing jeans on Fridays, tonight she wanted to select a dress that would flatter her figure. Once she was dressed, she waited for Henry. However, he made her wait, and Marci walked up and down anxiously awaiting the man of her dreams. When Henry took one look at Marci, he could not take his eyes off her, and told her how beautiful she looked. "You should dress up more often," he told her as he sized her up and down several times. She too thought he was well worth the wait as he was wearing Levis that showed what a great butt he had, and a blue shirt. Holding a bouquet of flowers, he gave Marci a kiss on her cheek. Marci could not imagine how much better the night could be, but other than the kiss on her cheek, it was everything she thought it would be.

That night they went to the movies, and after that, they went to have their pizza and beer where Henry's friends came to talk to him. However, when some of the girls came and gave him a kiss on the lips, Marci was furious. Of course, she could not let him know how angry she was so she just smiled. When Henry took Marci home, she invited him in. I want you to read my report, she said. With a sarcastic tone, Henry asked, "Is that all?"

Kicking her shoes off she said, "I'll be right back." Now it was Marci's turn to ignore his remark. Henry followed her as she went to her study to get her computer. Not finding it where she normally put it, Marci went to the den only to find the sliding door was open. Marci knew she did not leave the door open, and went to tell Henry. Suddenly the mood changed from what might have been a romantic evening to one of a more urgent nature.

Henry told Marci to stay where she was, and to call the police while he checked the rest of the house. Not finding anyone in the house, Henry went into the den to wait for the police to arrive. Having done all they could, Henry told Marci, "they needed the report, and if there was any way, she could remember what she had done?" As she fought back the tears Marci replied, "There's was so much information in that report, and there is no way I can remember everything."

"What could anyone possibly want with it?"

"It's okay Marci we can still recover the information," Henry told her. He then asked her "if she happen to save any of her notes." "I have some notes in my trashcan. Maybe I have enough to put together and turn it in to Emilio. I will explain what happened, and pray he does not fire me," Marci said as she started to cry. Henry put his arms around her and tried to comfort her as he told her, "He won't fire you. Emilio likes you and I will talk to Emilio."

Henry waited until the police made their report. Being that nothing other than her computer, and her briefcase were taken they left. Once Henry knew Marci was going to be okay, he left so she could start working on their report. Again, she searched high and low, but no briefcase. Not knowing what to do, she finally called Emilio. Explaining what happened, he told her, "To calm down, and to retrace her steps from the time she left to the time she got home." "Emilio, I have already done that, I even called the police," Marci said.

"Don't panic, I'm sure you have notes all over the house and at work; I know you. You never throw any of your notes until everything is completed. Stay home and call Henry to see if he can be of some help. In the meantime, I'll have Elaine take you one of the extra laptops so that you can work on the report."

Taking Emilio's advice Marci dug into her trash basket, and was able to come up with most of the information. She also called Henry to see if he could take her the notes he had given her so she could complete the report.

Once again, Henry teased Marci and asked her, "If she was inviting him for breakfast. Is this like a date," he asked, but when he heard Marci's frantic voice, Henry came over. After they ate the bagels he bought, they worked nonstop. By the time either one realized it, time to eat lunch had past, and Marci still had a lot to do. Marci and Henry managed to get the information she needed for her report, and when she called Emilio, he was extremely pleased. Tired, Henry went home and left Marci to finish the information she had in her previous report. Marci stayed up until she was satisfied with the report and then went to bed.

No sooner had she closed her eyes than the alarm rang louder than at any other time. Marci got but a couple of hours sleep. Yet, she thought some sleep was better than not getting any at all. Anxious to turn her report in to Emilio, Marci showered, dressed, ate, and went to work. Had Marci not been so focused on getting to work, and looked in her rear view mirror, she would have seen the car that was about to rear-end her vehicle. By the time she realized what happened, the impact pushed her car into a telephone pole. Lucky for her, a customer at one of the local restaurants saw what happened and called the police. After the paramedics checked Marci for injuries, and asked her a few questions, she was transported to the hospital. Still thinking of her work, Marci asked, "If she could take her briefcase with her."

Everyone at work knew about the accident, and when Emilio arrived, Bernadette told him what happened. Emilio rushed to the hospital where he heard the doctor tell Marci she had no serious injuries, and all the tests were normal. She did tell Marci, "She had a bump on her forehead as big as her fist. She was to go to her doctor within three days, or go back if she still felt bad." About to leave, Marci told Emilio "The report he was waiting for was in her briefcase on the chair."

"I don't want you to be home by yourself so I will call Elaine and ask her to take you home. I know she will want to stay with you until you feel better." Emilio told her.

Satisfied Marci was going to be all right, Emilio knew he had to call Henry to tell him what happened. After Elaine took Marci home, she was afraid to leave her by herself. Elaine did not let Marci go to sleep because she did not know if she would wake up. Elaine did not trust what the doctor told her friend, so she kept Marci awake for a couple of hours. When she felt it was all right to let Marci sleep, she helped her to her old bedroom. Marci slept for a while, and when she woke up, Elaine had made her chicken soup. Marci ate a little bit, and told Elaine to go home because she would be fine. She had Shredder and Cleopatra to protect her. Elaine hesitated, but she knew Marci could take care of herself.

Bernadette called Marci every day to check on her progress, and told her not to go to work until she was feeling better. In the meantime,

Emilio had a chance to read Marci's report and was extremely impressed, and pleased that she had done such a wonderful job.

Henry was out of the country when Marci had her accident, but she was the first one he went to see once the airplane landed. The best thing that happened to her was that she and Henry stared to date on a regular basis. Henry was back and after the information was documented, and the skeletons were examined, they got a decent burial where no one could exhume them.

When Caleb heard about Marci's accident, he was angry she took so long to tell him about it. The thought of losing his sister was more than he could take, and all he could do was to let Marci know how upset he was. However, once Caleb settled down, Marci told him all about Henry McCoy and his mood changed. She told Caleb how she met Henry and they talked, and laughed for several hours. Caleb was also happy to hear she found someone who wanted to spend the rest of his life with her. "He sounds like he is a great guy, and I hope he makes you as happy as you deserve to be," Caleb said. Caleb was also happy Marci now had someone to share her life with other than Cleopatra and Shredder. He hated the thought of his sister living alone in Mom and Dad's house, but she was happy.

Henry and Marci dated for a couple of years, and at the end of the second year, Henry proposed. When Marci called Caleb to tell him the good news, she asked her brother if he would take her father's place and walk her down the aisle. "If you had not asked me, I would have been hurt and very disappointed. It will be my honor to escort you down the aisle. I know I can't take Dad's place, but I will do my best," Caleb replied. "Marci, if it is ok with you, I would like to buy your wedding gown that is if you haven't already bought one." Marci was speechless, and once she was able to speak, she thanked her brother for his offer.

Henry on the other hand asked Emilio if he would be his best man as he was the one who brought Marci and him together. Emilio was surprised, but pleased Henry thought enough of their friendship to ask him. That evening when Henry went to pick Marci up from work, he told her, "Now that I have selected who the best man is going to be, we can take our time in planning our wedding. Time is on our side, and we can relax."

Marci was about to reply when, Emilio happened to go into her office and heard what Henry said. "Henry, you do not realize how quickly your wedding day will be here. If I were you, I would listen to Marci if she wants to start planning her wedding tonight," he said.

The next day, Marci called Elaine and Rosita to tell them she was getting married. She knew Juanita had married Ernest, but did not have her phone number. So, when Marci called Rosita, she immediately told Marci she would call Juanita to give her the news.

"I'm sure Juanita will call you tonight after she gets this message, and I would also like to bake your wedding cake if you will let me," Rosita told Marci.

"But, you have so much to do," Marci replied.

"Oh, don't be silly, I will be hurt if you have someone else bake it. Besides, that will be our wedding gift to you, and Henry."

Having called her friends, and neighbors, Marci called Elaine and asked her, "If she wanted to go to lunch tomorrow." Agreeing to meet her at the Frontier Restaurant, Marci told her she would be there by eleven-thirty. Thinking Elaine would be waiting for her at the restaurant, Marci had to wait another twenty minutes before she arrived. When Marci saw Elaine walk into the restaurant, she placed their order, and by the time Elaine sat down, their food was ready. Midway into their lunch, Marci told Elaine, "She was getting married, and asked her if she would be her maid of honor." Elaine was so excited and had more questions than Marci had answers. Immediately, Elaine went into her role as maid of honor, and asked Marci, "If she had thought which florist, she was going to order her flowers from, and where she was having her reception."

"Gosh Elaine, I just got engaged. It's not as if this will happen tomorrow. I still have a year before I get married."

"Yes, I know that Marci, but before you know it, the year will be up, and we have a lot to do."

Emilio had just told Henry a year was not that far away, and Elaine was now reminding Marci of the same thing. Emilio and Elaine were right, and the year did go by faster than either one realized. Within a couple of months, Marci had her wedding gown. The bridesmaids had their dresses. The parents of the ring bearer, and flower girl accepted the invitation to have their children participate in the wedding. Rosita was baking the cake. The flowers were ordered. The band was paid for the hall was reserved, and the food was going to be catered. By this time, Marci and Henry could not think of anything else they had to do.

A month before the wedding, Caleb called Marci and told her he wanted to spend some time with her. When Marci told Henry her brother was going to come home, he was extremely nervous. He knew how close Marci and her brother were, and this made him a bit uneasy. Seeing how Henry reacted, Marci could not resist teasing Henry, as she had never seen her fiancé so nervous.

The day Caleb flew in, both Marci and Henry went to pick him up from the airport. Marci was happy to have her brother back home, and by the time they arrived home, Henry and Caleb formed a family bond that would grow as time went on. Seeing and hearing them get along, Marci knew this brother-in-law relationship was going to be one she was going to enjoy. When Shredder heard Caleb's voice he howled, barked, and jumped because his master was home. Caleb was just as happy to see Shredder, and once again, the two were reunited.

The week Marci was to get married was a big blur as she rushed around tying up last minute details. In a couple of days, she would marry the man she wanted to spend the rest of her life with, and there was still so much to do. Marci was so happy she could not believe it was really happening.

The week of their wedding, it rained for several days. However, on their wedding day, the weather was just perfect, and everything was going along just as planned. On this, her wedding day, Marci was nervous, as any bride can be. She had butterflies in her stomach and could not eat a thing. Henry was just as nervous, but he managed to eat breakfast with Caleb at a local restaurant.

Marci's wedding day was here, and as she entered the church, she saw her friends waiting for her to make her grand entrance. When Caleb came to escort her down the aisle, she had to look twice. Caleb looked like their father dressed in his tuxedo, and Marci could not help but cry. She so wished her parents could have been there, but she knew they were there in spirit. Henry and Marci's wedding was everything they wanted it to be, and everyone had a wonderful time.

Caleb was now taking care of Marci's house as he decided to stay while she and Henry went on their honeymoon. Shredder could not be happier as he and Caleb lounged around, played ball and took long walks. One afternoon as Caleb and Shredder were walking around the block, Caleb saw how Shredder had aged. "Shredder, I don't look forward to the day I have to leave you, but I know sis is taking care of you, and Henry is a great guy. I will miss you, and I know you are a good dog." Wagging his tail, Shredder sat staring at Caleb as if he understood every word his former master was telling him.

Arriving home after their honeymoon trip to Australia, Marci, and Henry started their lives as Mr. and Mrs. Henry McCoy. It was difficult for Marci to get used to having a husband around, but she adjusted to married life in no time. Marci and Henry were extremely happy, and as newlyweds, they loved every minute they spent together. She now had someone to talk to, and she no longer ate alone. Even Cleopatra and Shredder were adjusting to having Henry around, and enjoyed the leftover dinners given to them.

Henry showered Marci with flowers, candy, handwritten notes, or beautiful cards letting her know how much he loved her. Marci could not be happier, and it got better and better as the days went by. Henry and Marci loved to explore, and Shredder looked forward to the weekends when he could run free in the desert. Shredder was living the life of a spoiled dog, and while his owners were at work, he protected their home, as any good watchdog should.

Stepping outdoors, for her daily run, Marci felt the cold breeze on her face. Getting her sweater from the hall closet Marci and Shredder went for their morning run. The season was changing, and Marci thought of her father, as she looked at her surroundings. As she looked around, she saw some of the leaves falling to the ground, while the breeze blew others here and there. While some of the neighbors were trying to rake the leaves, the gentle breeze swirled them around. Along with the change of weather, flu season was here, and employees were now getting sick with the flu. To avoid others getting sick, employees were asked to stay home to avoid spreading the flu to other departments.

Bernadette was out for a week, and when she returned, she was still coughing and sneezing. Being around Bernadette, Elaine and Jeremiah started to cough, and in a couple of days, they too called in sick. Marci was grateful she hadn't caught the bug that was going around, and tried to do more than her share of the work. By the end of the month, almost everyone was back at work and feeling better.

One evening as Marci was preparing supper, she felt sick to her stomach. A few of the employees were still calling in that they weren't feeling well, and had not gotten over the flu. "Again, they were told to stay home so as not to spread the germs to those who were still vulnerable to the bug."

When dinner was over, Marci went to rest on the couch, and fell asleep. Henry tried to wake her, but her body ached, and she was too sick to move, so he carried her upstairs. After a week, Marci didn't know why she wasn't getting over the flu, and why it continued to linger. Dizzy and losing her balance, Marci blamed it on her previous accident as she continued to feel poorly.

Deciding to go to the doctor for whatever was ailing her she scheduled her appointment as early in the morning as she could. On the day of her appointment, Marci left before she started to feel worse.

However, she was not the only one who thought of scheduling an early appointment, and by the time she arrived, the doctor's lobby was full. One by one, the patients were taken into the examination room, and then it was Marci's turn. Having examined her, the doctor told her, "She did have the flu, but there was something else going on. He wanted to run more tests before he could confirm what he suspected." Marci was scared because all she was expecting to hear was that she had the flu. Yet, Doctor Brewer wanted her to take some blood tests. She knew there were certain diseases that ran on both sides of her family, and she was scared he was going to tell her she had cancer.

"Doctor Brewer what do you think it is?" she asked.

"I want to be sure, before I tell you, but don't worry it's not anything that is contagious. Now go get the blood work done, and after that, go home and rest."

Marci would much rather have waited in the office, but not knowing what was going on, she did as Dr. Brewer told her to. She was to return the following week when he would tell her what the results of the test were.

Wednesday morning, Marci was the first patient Doctor Brewer called into his office. After she sat on the examining table, Doctor Brewer told her she did have the flu, but he also told her she was pregnant. Not prepared to hear she was going to have a baby, Marci started to cry. Doctor Brewer asked, "If there was a reason why she was upset at the news because he thought she would be happy.

"Oh Doctor Brewer, you just don't understand. I don't know how I am going to tell my husband—he thinks I have the flu."

Concerned about Marci's welfare and that her husband was an abusive man, Doctor Brewer asked, "Is there a problem at home?"

"Oh no, it's not what you think. My husband and I are very happy; I am just trying to think how I should tell him about the baby. We have talked about having children, and now that I am pregnant, I have no idea what I am going to do."

Dr. Brewer was relieved to hear Marci's only concern was how she was going to break the good news to her husband. Happy his suspicion was wrong he congratulated her, and wrote a prescription for prenatal vitamin pills. He told Marci, "There was nothing she had to be afraid of because both she and Henry were going to be fine."

As Marci was driving home, she kept thinking how she was going to tell Henry the wonderful news, and passed the pharmacy. Going around the block one more time, she took her prescription to get it filled. As she waited for her prescription, Marci walked around the aisles, and passed the greeting card section. "Aha," Marci said," Now I know how I will tell Henry we are going to have a baby." But she didn't think she could keep the wonderful news to herself. So on that evening Marci prepared Henry's favorite dinner. When he asked for a second helping, he saw the card his wife placed under his plate. Anxious for Henry to read the card, she took her time serving her husband another portion of pork chops smothered with mushroom gravy.

Wondering what Marci was up too he opened the card. The time was here, and Henry read the poem. At first, he didn't get the full meaning of it until he read it a second time. As Henry looked up, he saw Marci's grin, and asked Marci, "If she was pregnant." Nodding her head, he pushed his chair away from the table. He was so excited he forgot about everything else. Now all that mattered was that his wife was in a delicate condition, and he had to take care of her. What a romantic evening that turned out to be.

When Marci told her friends at the office she was expecting, they were just as excited for her. Bernadette made sure Marci did not get tired, so she took some of the reports away from her, and had Elaine help her. Marci told Bernadette, "She was grateful, but she didn't have to distribute her work to others. I am pregnant, not injured like the last time. If I get tired I will rest," Marci told Bernadette. With that, Bernadette left Marci to work at her pace.

Not knowing if Marci was hungry, Elaine asked, "If she wanted to go out to eat, or get something from the cafeteria."Not only was Marci up to going out for lunch, she told, Elaine, "She was famished."

After they were seated at the restaurant, Marci told Elaine, "She had to go to the restroom. When the waitress comes, get me some tea with a couple of slices of lemon." As Marci returned to their table, she saw Elaine had a grin from ear to ear, and knew something happened that was out of the norm. However, with Elaine, anything could happen. As Marci was about to sit down, she asked her friend, "Why the silly grin."

"Well you won't believe it," Elaine said.

"Knowing you, I will believe anything," Marci replied.

"Okay. When you went to the restroom, I was going to get my purse and I saw three women sit on the booth in front of us. Two were elderly, and the other was about our age. When I lifted my eyes off the menu, one of them was looking at me. I smiled at her, and she smiled back which was nice. She had a very nice smile, and looked familiar. I didn't have my glasses on, so I couldn't place where I had seen her. When I got the menu to see what I wanted to order, I reached for my water, and I saw the woman was doing the same thing. Everything I did she did and it was starting to annoy me. Then the woman who was sitting behind us left, and I realized I was looking in the mirror. I knew I couldn't get up and ask her what her problem was because the person I was going to tell off was me."

When Marci stopped laughing, she asked Elaine, "How did you not know that was you?" "You know how people say there is a twin for everyone in this world? Well I thought I was seeing mine. When we sat down, the door to the other dining area was closed, and I was looking at the menu to see what I wanted to eat. Guess someone opened the door, and left it open. When I looked up, I thought I was seeing another woman, but I was actually looking at myself. The woman was wearing a hat that, in the mirror seemed as if I had it on my head. Can you imagine? No wonder the woman looked familiar, it was me," Elaine said as she laughed.

All Marci could say was, "Elaine you are so silly."

Then in a low, but serious tone, Elaine said, "Marci, I have to tell you something that happened to me when I went for my yearly exam. I don't think I can face anyone if they know what happened to me. So, you have to promise me you won't tell anyone."

"Elaine, whatever it is, I give you my solemn promise I will never tell anyone." Marci couldn't imagine what her friend was going to tell her, but she was ready to listen and give her friend a shoulder to cry on if she needed one.

Leaning forward on her chair, so she could tell Marci what happened to her in the doctor's office, the server came to take their order. After she left, Elaine again made Marci promise she wouldn't say a word. Elaine took a deep breath and said, "Marci, you know I have told you how much I hate going to a doctor, right? Well last week I went for my annual checkup, and when the nurse took me into the examination room, I was as nervous as I could be. She gave me a gown and told me to remove my clothes. When she left, I developed a bad case of the butterflies because I remembered the same thing happened with another doctor, but I was unable to stop it. About to get off the exam table, the door opened and a handsome, young doctor came in, and he asked me if I was ready. I told him I was, and as he was going to start his exam, he told me to relax. Not realizing how nervous I was, I relaxed a little too much and I let go of some mean smelling gas. The poor doctor got the full effect of my gas bomb. When he stood up, he was shaking his head back and forth like a dog that has been sprayed by a skunk,—I guess in a way he was. His eyes bugged out, and he coughed as he excused himself. After he walked out, his nurse came in, and she had a silly grin on her face. The minute I saw her, I knew the doctor told her what happened. The nurse told me to get dressed, and the doctor would be in shortly to give me the results of my examination. When he returned, he told me everything was fine, and would see me next year.

Marci, you just don't know how embarrassed I was. Believe me when I tell you I will never go back to him. Next time I have to see a doctor I will make sure I go out of town."

While Elaine was telling Marci what happened, Marci was laughing so hard she almost choked on her food, and could not say anything. She knew there was nothing she could do to help her friend because this never happened to her. Yet, Marci was relieved it was not what she was afraid it was going to be.

Able to compose herself, Marci asked Elaine, "What happened to get her stomach so upset?"

"Earlier in the day, I ate a pizza with extra peperoni, and, you know how I love pizzas. Anyway, when I placed my order, I told the server to put extra peperoni. Obviously, I was not thinking of what I had to do the remainder of the day. Embarrassed to tell the handsome, young doctor I had an upset stomach, and needed to go to the restroom I told him I was ready. That is when it happened. Well I tell you Marci, I will never eat a peperoni pizza no matter what type of exam I have to go for," Elaine said.

Even if Elaine had been in the next room, and had whispered, everyone within a short distance would have heard anything, and everything Elaine said. That is how it was on this day. The two elderly women sitting at the table next to them overheard what Elaine told Marci. They too could not stop laughing, and before they left, they told Elaine, "They had never enjoyed their lunch as much as they did today. However, she was not to worry, they wouldn't tell anyone."

That evening when Marci went home, Henry asked her how her day went. All Marci could say was, "That it was extremely relaxing, and she and Elaine had a wonderful day."

The next nine months, Henry and Marci remodeled Caleb's old bedroom to get it ready for the baby. Concerned Marci might over exert herself by doing too much, Henry told her to relax and take it easy. Not knowing if they were going to have a boy or girl, they left the room the same color as when Caleb was living there. Once the baby was born, they would paint it either blue or pink.

When Marci started to go into labor, Henry was out of the office, but Marci managed to call him. By the time he got back, he was a nervous wreck. Henry managed to compose himself, and drove his wife to the hospital where she gave birth to a handsome and healthy baby boy. Their first child was here, and the new parents were ready to take him home to start their life as a family.

Growing Family

On the day the baby went home, he was introduced to Cleopatra. When she saw him, she hissed and walked away. Shredder on the other hand could not get enough of the baby and licked him all over. Now Shredder knew he had someone he could take care of, and who in turn would be his new master. When the baby was a couple of months, Henry and Marci talked about who would be their son's godparents. Not giving Henry, a chance to tell her who the godfather was going to be Marci called Caleb, and asked him, "If he would do them the honor of baptizing their son." Caleb was surprised Marci would even consider asking him. However, he was extremely excited, and promised, he would be the best godfather any boy ever had. The only thing I ask, "Is that I choose his name," Caleb said. Marci agreed, and with that, she handed Henry the phone so he could talk to his brother-in-law. Walking into the nursery where the baby was sleeping, Marci heard Henry laughing at whatever Caleb was telling him. The sound of a man's laughter sounded so good, as it reminded Marci of her father. While she was in the nursery, Marci tried every name she could think of to see if it would fit her son, but was not satisfied with any of them. What to call her son was now a big concern for her. Before Caleb hung up, he told Henry, "He would call them when he got permission from his parish to baptize the baby."

Having talked to Caleb, Henry called his sister, Christina, and asked her if she would be the baby's godmother. Christina was just as happy as was Caleb, and they now had their son's godparents.

Later on in the week, Caleb called Marci to tell "her the classes he had to attend would not be held for another couple of months. Seems he missed registering for the classes by a week, and there wouldn't be any more classes for five months." That meant her baby boy would have to remain nameless until the parents, and his godfather completed their classes. Marci told her brother, "They too had to go through the same classes because they had never been sponsors for anyone."

But how could her baby boy go that long without a name? Knowing there was nothing she could do, she told Caleb to keep in touch. Once they completed the classes there would be no problem baptizing any baby. Christina on the other hand had been through the classes, and did not have to repeat them.

Several months passed and Caleb called his sister to tell her he completed his classes, and was ready to baptize his godson. At last, her baby boy was going to have a name, and Marci was anxious to hear what it was going to be.

The following day, when the rectory opened, Marci called to tell the priest "her brother had completed the classes, and they were ready to have their baby baptized." The date for the baptismal was set, and Marci called Christina and Caleb to give them the information they needed. Later that evening, Marci and Henry discussed what they were going to do to celebrate this joyous occasion. Marci knew better than to ask her husband how he wanted to celebrate the occasion because he would do whatever she decided. All Henry wanted, was for his son to have a name, other than "Daddy, or Mamma's big boy."

Caleb flew in on Monday, the week his godson was going to be baptized, and Marci sent Henry to pick him up. This time when Caleb entered the house, he noticed Marci had wild flowers in every room of the house, and it reminded him of his mother. Caleb was happy he no longer saw the house as having sad memories of his parents; it now had a family who called it their home. When Caleb saw Shredder lick his godson's face, he was happy his dog found another master. Not sure, this was what Marci or Henry allowed Shredder to do, he chased him away.

"Henry told Caleb not to worry, as that was how the baby got his face washed after he ate," and he laughed. Caleb could not believe his sister would allow this, and he looked at Marci to see if this was true. Marci lifted her eyebrows, and turned her back on him. She could not believe Henry would tell Caleb something like that, and that Caleb would be gullible enough to believe it. Henry could not believe his brother-in-law took him serious, and told him, he was joking. Giving Henry a jab on his shoulder, Caleb went to get him and Henry a beer. While the men were having a good time, Marci called Christina to see if she wanted to come over for dinner. She told Christina, "Caleb had flown in so he could spend some time with them."

The conversation at the dinner table was all about the baby, and Christina told Marci she bought the baby's outfit. She then apologized because she had done this without asking Caleb if he wanted to go shopping. Caleb told Christina he was happy she had done that, as he did not like to go shopping. He then offered to reimburse her, but Christina told Caleb not to worry about it. Now the only thing they had to discuss was what they were going to do to celebrate this great occasion.

Sunday was here, and Caleb and Christina would now baptize their godson. To Henry and Marci it did not matter their son was the oldest baby to receive the first sacrament of the church. All they wanted was for him to have a name they could put on his birth certificate.

Father Gene went from one baby to the next and when he got to Caleb and Christina, he asked, "Godparents, what name do you give this child?" Looking at Marci, Caleb said, "His name is Travis after his grandfather, and Christina said, "I give him the name Caleb after his godfather." Marci was so happy she could not hold back the tears. Of all the names, she imagined Caleb would give their son; Marci never thought it would be that of their father. Looking at her son, Marci thought of everything she was going to tell him about his namesake. Caleb was just as surprised when he heard Christina had chosen Caleb as his middle name.

Throughout the ceremony, Travis behaved like the little angel he was, and after the baptism, Henry and Marci took Caleb, Christina and Travis out to celebrate. Caleb stayed with Marci and Henry until the end of the month, and was extremely happy everything was going well for his sister and her husband. On the day Caleb was leaving, Marci's house was full of laughter and love just as he remembered it when their parents were alive.

Both Christina and Caleb were great godparents. Christina would visit her precious godson as often as she could, and Travis would eventually get to know his godfather. True to his word, Caleb was indeed an exceptional godfather. He called as often as he could, and Travis soon recognized his voice. Henry's baby boy was an extremely good baby, but some of the neighbors said he would change, as he grew older. Yet, Travis was everything Marci and Henry wanted in a child. Even the babysitter did not mind taking care of him. All Travis did was sleep, as all infants need to do. When he discovered his feet, Travis was fascinated by them, and would wiggle his toes so his mother would play with them. Now every time Henry learned something new, it was an exciting time for his parents.

The day Travis said his first word was a day for celebration. Henry however, was a little upset his son's first word was, "Mamma," but he soon got over it. The day Travis actually said, "Dada," Marci's macho husband cried, and Henry knew he had the smartest child anyone could have. If they thought Travis first word was exciting, the day he took his first steps, Henry got his camera to take pictures of his every movement. While Henry took pictures, Marci clapped, and danced around her son. Several pictures were going to be framed and placed on the mantle for all to see and the rest would go into his baby book. That was not to say a copy would also be sent to his godfather, godmother and half of the neighborhood.

From one day to the next, Travis did one extraordinary feat after another. To say Marci had a few pictures to send Caleb was a slight exaggeration. Travis was growing up too fast and Marci felt she had to capture every minute of his life. When Travis called his godfather by his name, Marci heard Caleb scream for joy, and this too was something she would write in his baby book. Now every day was more exciting than the day before for Henry and Marci.

Two years later Marci once again surprised Henry with news she was expecting. This time they went out to eat at a nice fancy restaurant. Marci wanted everything to go as smoothly with this pregnancy as it had with Travis. Again, Marci started her prenatal exams with the same doctor she went to when she had Travis. She trusted Doctor Brewer, and did not want another doctor delivering her baby. On one of Marci's visits to her doctor, she felt extremely weak. When she heard the nurse call her name, Marci got up, and started to walk toward the door. Feeling woozy, she felt, her knees buckle, and felt, someone catch her. Doctor Brewer caught Marci and took her into the examination room.

Soon as Marci smelled the ammonia, she opened her eyes. Feeling better, she listened to her doctor who told her everything was fine. Throughout her pregnancy, Marci visited her doctor on a regular basis, and there were more questions with this pregnancy than the first. Her emotions were all over the chart, and she didn't know what to do. She cried for no reason, was moody, and had different cravings than with Travis. Doctor Brewer listened to Marci, and explained how every pregnancy is different. "You have nothing to worry about, these are normal reactions every mother goes through," he told her.

On her final appointment, Marci had so much energy she went to the supermarket to buy groceries. Everything was going even better than she thought, and she wanted to prepare a nice dinner for her family. While Travis slept, Marci had a chance to prepare the dinner she planned for her family. Everything went as smoothly as she hoped it would, and Marci was happy everything turned out so well. That evening after Caleb gave his son a bath and tucked him into bed, he and Marci sat out in the patio enjoying the cool evening breeze. As with Travis, they waited until Marci gave birth to find out what they were going to have.

Then on December 15, their little bundle of joy was born. She was a beautiful and healthy baby, and as with Travis, Henry and Marci were ready to take her home. When Marci held her baby girl in her arms, she knew she was special. She was the image of her father, and had her grandmother's smile. Her little girl had black curly hair that curled naturally around her little round face, and when Marci touched her face, the baby opened her eyes. The minute Travis saw her; he fell in love with his little angel. Here she was but a few minutes old, and she already had her father wrapped tightly around her little finger. Once again, Henry and Marci were proud parents of a beautiful baby girl. When other parents went to see their babies, Henry and Marci knew their little angel was the only one that captured everyone's attention. She was everything Marci and Henry had prayed for and they would now complete her nursery with all the frilly things Marci wanted for her daughter. Henry and Marci were anxious to take their baby home so they could spoil her as they did Travis.

The day Henry brought Marci, and the baby home, Travis was with his godmother. When Christina brought Travis home, Marci thought he had grown overnight. Next to Travis, the baby looked so small and fragile. Travis on the other hand, looked like a little boy instead of Marci's baby. The first time Travis saw his sister he cried for his mother's attention.

Yet when Shredder saw her, he liked her, as he did when Travis was born. When Henry put the baby down in her basinet, Marci went to take a nap as she was tired, and needed her rest. This was what Travis was waiting for and he ran to Marci. Henry knew his wife was tired so he took his son into the den. The minute Henry picked Travis up; he screamed at the top of his lungs and cried for his mother to hold him.

Not wanting her son to think she was abandoning him, Marci went to get him. When Travis saw his mother was up, he ran to her and expected she give him her full attention. While Marci was talking to Travis about his sister, Henry went to check on her. Coming out of the nursery, Marci saw Henry was holding the baby, and asked him, "Why did you pick her up?"

" I couldn't help it; she looked so tiny in her basinet. Besides, she opened her eyes, and I knew she wanted me to pick her up," Henry replied. Seeing his father was holding the baby, Travis jumped off his mother's lap, and demanded his father's attention.

At two-years of age, Travis could not understand why this baby was not going away. Thinking this was the perfect time for Travis to get to know his baby sister, Marci knew she had to do something to help him understand what was going on. She told Henry to bring the baby so Travis could hold her. Travis pushed his sister away, and did not want anything to do with her, but his baby sister won him over. Soon after Travis accepted his baby sister, Marci put both kids to bed so she could take a nap. Marci was sure she had not been asleep for more than fifteen minutes when she heard the baby cry, so she got up to feed her. Going into the kitchen, Marci knew she left Travis asleep on her bed, but when she got back, he was in the crib talking to his sister. Marci tiptoed away from the door so she could get Henry. "Honey, you have to see this," she told her husband.

When he and Marci looked into the baby's bedroom, they saw Travis had crawled in the crib, and was asleep next to her. Henry went to get his camera so he could take a picture of this moment. He wanted to send Caleb, and Christina a picture of their godson taking care of his baby sister. Hours later, Travis woke up hungry, and crawled out of the crib. Having fed Travis, Marci took him outdoors to sit with her on the porch swing. When Travis heard his sister crying, he said, "Mamma, baby cry". Jumping off his mother's lap, Travis ran to the door so he could go inside. From that day forward, there was no turning back for Travis, and he ran every time his sister needed him. Now anytime Marci went to the baby's bedroom, Travis was at her heels. He knew he had to help his mother take care of his sister. Times like this Marci could not help but see how much her baby boy had grown up. As the weeks passed, both Travis and the baby bonded like Caleb and Marci did as children.

When it came time for Henry and Marci to choose the baby's godmother, Marci knew exactly whom she wanted. However, Henry also had someone in mind. After some discussion, Henry came up with a brilliant idea; why not let the baby choose her godmother? Marci would write the name of the godmothers they wanted, and Henry would put the baby on the carpet next to the pieces of paper. Henry and Marci knew it would not matter who their little girl picked because Juanita, Emily, Bernadette, and Elaine would be terrific godmothers.

Knowing their six-month-old daughter would pick the godmother she wanted, Henry and Marci were excited to find out who it was going to be. Sitting next to their daughter, they watched as she tried to get the pieces of paper. The baby finally selected one, and as she was about to put it in her mouth she dropped it. She then picked another piece of paper, and this time she held on to it. Marci tried to take it away from her so she could see who her godmother was going to be. The baby's chubby wet fingers were holding it tightly, and it was not easy to pry it from her.

For someone to be so small, she had a strong grip. However, given the choice of her bottle and a wet paper, she chose the bottle. Before Marci had a chance to open the slip of paper that had the godmother's name on it, Henry took it from her. As he opened it, he looked at his little girl and smiled. "Come on Henry," Marci said, "Who did she choose?" "Well I can't see who it is. The paper is all wet, and the name is not that clear," Henry replied. Knowing he could see the name on the paper, Marci grabbed it from his hand and saw the baby selected Juanita to be her godmother.

The following day Marci called Juanita to ask her if she wanted to go out for lunch. Juanita was not feeling well, and asked, "If she could take a rain check". "Sure," Marci replied, "just let me know when you want to go." With that, Juanita hung up, and Henry told Marci "to go over and give her the good news."

"No, she's not feeling well. I am just going to wait and see if she calls me tomorrow. If she doesn't, then I will take the kids with me and I will ask her", Marci told her husband.

Now all Marci could do was wait to see if Juanita would call back—but that did not happen.

A week later, Juanita returned the call, and told Marci she wanted to take her up on her offer. On that day, Henry and Marci had plans to meet for lunch, but Marci called him and cancelled their luncheon date. "Juanita is taking me up on my lunch offer and I don't think I can wait another day to give her the good news," Marci told Henry.

"Honey, do you want me to come along," Henry asked.

"No, I want to do this by myself. I want to see Juanita's reaction when I tell her the baby picked her name. I'm running late so I'll talk to you tonight," and with that Marci hung up, put the kids in the car and drove to the restaurant.

By the time they arrived, Juanita was waiting for Marci, and the kids. When they finished eating, and before Marci ordered dessert, she told Juanita she had something to ask her.

"What is it?" Juanita asked.

"Well, the baby, Henry, Travis, and I would like to know if you and Ernest would do us the honor and be our daughter's godparents." Juanita was so happy she didn't know what to say other than, "Yes, yes, yes, of course, I am so honored you would ask me. Can I hold the baby," Juanita asked. Marci then handed her baby girl over to her godmother so they could get to know each other. However, Marci was not prepared for Juanita to ask, "If she could take the baby home," but how could she refuse Juanita's first request.

"Was this why you wanted us to have lunch last week?" Juanita asked. Marci nodded her head and Juanita said, "Marci, you should have told me. I wouldn't have minded if you had asked me over the phone."

"No, I couldn't do that because it was too important, and I wanted to see your reaction. Besides, I wanted you to have this. When Juanita opened the small white box, she saw a slip of paper with her name in it."

"What's this," Juanita asked. Marci then told Juanita how the baby picked her to be her godmother. Juanita laughed and knew her goddaughter was one smart little girl. By the time Marci got home, Henry was waiting to hear all about her luncheon with Juanita. When he didn't see his little girl, he asked, "Where's my angel girl?"

"Juanita took her, and she will be home later tonight. Let me put Travis to bed as it has been a long day for him, and I will tell you all about it," Marci replied.

Later that evening, Juanita and Ernest took the baby home to her parents. After putting her to bed, Henry, and Marci spent several hours enjoying a glass of wine with good friends.

While Juanita and Ernest were visiting, Marci asked Juanita if she had any names in mind for the baby. Certain her good friend would tell her the names she chose for her daughter, Marci was surprised when Juanita responded, Marci, you will just have to wait until we baptize her. "But Juanita, what am I going to call her? I can't call her my angel girl, until she gets baptized."

"Who said you can't, your dad called you, little one, even when you were grown up." Smiling, Marci agreed to call her baby, "Her little angel until she had a name of her own."

Marci thought if she continued to ask Juanita what name she had chosen for their baby, she would tell her. However, Juanita kept telling Marci she had not thought of a name for her godchild. Not paying attention to the conversation between the women, Henry asked Juanita what name she was going to give the baby.

"Gosh Henry, I just finished telling Marci, I don't know, but when I do I will let you know," Juanita replied. This was Marci's last chance to get Juanita to tell her so she said, "Juanita, you know we want our daughter to have a special name, and I know you will do just that. All I'm asking is that you tell me what it is." Of course, Juanita did not give in. She just laughed and told "Henry and Marci they would have to wait."

The following day Juanita stopped by on her way to the store, and told Marci, "she had a name for the baby. I just had to see your expression when I tell you what it is," Juanita told her. "Juanita that is wonderful, what is it?" Marci asked. "Please don't make me wait until she is baptized. Tell me what name you chose for her, this way I can get her used to hearing it."

"Okay, I guess I've made you suffer long enough. Yesterday I was at the florist selecting a bouquet of flowers for my mother, when I thought of a name for my goddaughter, and I know it will be the perfect name for her."

"Oh, please let me guess what it is," Marci replied joyfully.

"Is it Rose, Daisy, or could it be Dahlia, or maybe Amaryllis?"

Juanita laughed, and said, "Sorry Marci, it isn't any of those names, of course they would be beautiful names for her, but what do you think of Venus Fly Trap?" Juanita asked.

"Juanita, you have to be joking!" Marci exclaimed.

"Yes and your reaction was priceless. I wish I had a camera where I could have taken your picture because I will never be able to explain it to Ernest."

"Marci, you know it wouldn't be fair if I told you and not Henry. You will just have to wait a couple more weeks until she is baptized. All I will tell you is that it came to me last night when I was in my car. Deejay Carlos G. played a song and I thought it would be the perfect name for my goddaughter. Once she is baptized, I will tell you all about it. Oh, heck Marci, I'll tell you what, as soon as I think of her name I will tell you," Juanita said as she walked out the door.

The week before the baby was to be baptized Juanita took her shopping for her baptismal dress. "Marci asked to tag along," but again, Juanita told her, "That was for her, Ernest and their goddaughter to do."

Saturday, Juanita went to Marci's house so she could take the baby home. Juanita told "Marci it was up to the godmother to keep the baby overnight, and get her ready for her big day. You will see her when we arrive at the church. Just remember you can't hold her until I hand her over to you and Henry," Juanita told Marci. "Come on, Juanita, you're not serious," Marci said, but she knew better, Juanita was serious.

Sunday morning, Juanita walked into church with her six-month-old godchild covered in a white satin blanket. When Juanita uncovered the baby for Marci, Henry, and Caleb to see, tears rolled down Marci's face. The baby looked so beautiful in her white ruffled satin dress. Marci's baby girl looked like a porcelain doll with her black hair combed in soft ringlets around her face. This time, Marci was happy her daughter was older than the other babies. They were pretty, but Marci's little angel was beautiful.

After the priest gave the sermon, the godparents along with the babies were called to the baptismal fount so they could get baptized. As each baby was given a name, the priest moved on to the next baby. Then it was Juanita's turn to tell everyone what name she was giving her godchild. "Godparents, what name do you give this child," the priest asked. Juanita looked at Marci and replied, "Tammy Marie."

As if she had given her godmother her approval, the baby opened her eyes. When Marci heard the name Juanita gave her daughter, she looked at her brother Caleb and tears rolled down her cheeks. Her mother's name was Marie and her mother-in-law's name was Tammy. Marci knew Juanita could not have chosen a more fitting name than that one. Henry not wanting to miss a single thing was taking pictures and did not hear what name his little angel was given. All he wanted was to make sure he had plenty pictures of his daughter's baptism.

Now that the babies were baptized and Mass was over, Marci wanted to get her baby back in her arms. Instead of going out to a restaurant, Marci prepared a dinner at her house to celebrate Tammy Marie's baptism. While they were eating, Henry asked Juanita what she had named the baby. When he heard the baby's name, he too was very pleased. Marci then asked Juanita to tell her where she bought the baby's dress, and how she came to choosing her goddaughter's name.

"When my mother and I went shopping for Tammy's dress, I didn't like any of them. Mom then told me why not make her dress—so I did. As for her name, well do you remember when I told you I was in the car, and turned the radio on? Well a male listener called in to request a song for his wife who was having their baby. He asked the deejay if he could play as many songs that had girl's names. They couldn't think of a name for their baby, and that might help them. Well, deejay Carlos G played Ruby, Oh Donna, Daisy Lou, Maryann, and Sheila. I didn't like the name Ruby because as the song went, her boyfriend was going to steal her away. Donna, left her boyfriend brokenhearted, Sheila's boyfriend begged her to be his. I used to know a girl whose name was Daisy, and she was a bully. So, when I heard him play the song, Tammy, I said, that's it! When I heard the name, I knew that was what I wanted to name my goddaughter. The only thing I did not know was what her middle name should be. Ernest suggested Marie. He said he liked Marie, and after I thought about it, I remembered your mother's name was Marie," Juanita told Marci."

Besides, you know how the song goes, Tammy, Tammy, Tammy my love. I heard that, and I thought one day some young man is going to come along, and is going to fall madly in love with her. In the meantime, she is my precious godchild.

"Juanita you are crazy, but I do love her name. I was a little worried when you joked about naming her Venus Fly Trap," Marci told her friend. Marci looked at her baby girl and this time she had a name and it fit her perfectly.

When Travis hit the terrible twos, Marci was not prepared for it, and she now knew why they called it terrible. From one day to the next, Travis turned into a monster. He threw tantrums, learned how to use the "NO" word at the top of his lungs, and was unbearable. Marci hated to admit it, but her neighbors were right. The first couple of tantrums, Travis had Marci's undivided attention. She asked her neighbors and her doctor what she should do.

Some told her Travis would outgrow this stage, or to walk away from him, and leave him alone. Yet, others told her to spank him. "Spank him! How could she spank her baby boy, much less leave him alone in his crib until he fell asleep exhausted from crying."

How Marci wished her mother was alive to help her. However, by the time Travis threw his third tantrum, he learned Marci was not going to put up with his behavior. Travis learned how to open doors to the cabinets in the kitchen, bathrooms, and the laundry room where Marci had her detergents and cleaning supplies.

No sooner had Henry installed locks on the cabinets than Travis discovered the electrical outlets. Both Henry and Marci now had to be on their toes, and make sure everything was high enough so their two-year son old would not get hurt.

One evening when Henry got home, he found Travis, Tammy, and Marci asleep. There was no way he would wake her, as he knew how tired Marci had been lately. When Travis heard his father's voice, he woke up, and insisted his father pick him up. Henry played with Travis until he thought it was time to prepare dinner. Putting Travis down on the floor to play with his toys, Henry started to peel potatoes. As he was doing this, Travis ran into the bedroom and woke his mother up. He then ran under the table, and continued to play with his toys.

Tammy was sleeping, and this gave Marci time to help Henry prepare dinner. "I was going to make us hamburgers and fries so why don't you just sit and keep me company," Henry told his wife. Marci was so tired; she did exactly what her husband told her to do.

Thinking this would be a good time to play with her son, she looked under the table to see what he was doing. Travis was very content playing with his toys so Marci went to check on Tammy. When she got back, Travis was not where she left him.

"Honey, do you know where Travis went to?

"Isn't he under the table? He was there a few minutes ago. I wasn't watching him, as I was preparing the hamburgers" Henry replied.

Travis was a smart two year old, and Marci knew he could open the cabinets, so she went looking for him. Knowing the mischief Travis could get into, Marci went to find him before he hurt himself. She looked in the bedrooms, bathrooms, and anywhere she thought Travis could hide, but she could not find him. Not sure where her son had taken off to, she ran into the kitchen and told Henry "she didn't know where Travis had gone." "Stay here with the baby, while I look outside." Sure enough, Travis opened the back door, and was outside with Shredder.

Travis, now taller, and smart enough to open doors was going wherever he wanted. Relieved at finding his son, Henry picked him up, and took him back into the house where Marci could watch him. No sooner had Henry brought Travis indoors, than Tammy started to cry. Poor baby, how could she tell her mother or father she had an earache? All she could do was tug at her ear until it turned red. Now it was she, who kept Henry and Marci awake at night. No matter how hard Henry tried to sleep, he heard his little angel crying. Henry knew he had to get some sleep so he spent a couple of nights in the den. Along with Tammy suffering from earaches, she was also teething.

Travis never had an earache when he was a baby, so Marci didn't know what to do for her baby girl. The following morning she called Juanita to see if she could give her some advice. Juanita came over to help, but she could not do anything for her goddaughter.

"Let me call my mom," Juanita told Marci. "I'm sure she has a remedy for earaches." Sure enough, when Juanita finished talking to her mother, she had a remedy they could use that could help Tammy.

"Okay, Marci, this is what I was told we have to do; we need to get some cod liver oil; warm it up and put a couple of drops into Tammy's ear. We need to make sure it's not hot to where it will burn her, so we need to try it out first. "Mom said Tammy might fall asleep, so not to worry." Not having any cod liver oil in the cupboard, Marci went to the store, and followed Rosita's advice. It was as if a miracle happened.

Tammy stopped crying and fell asleep. For as much as Rosita's advice helped, within a couple of days, Tammy was again tugging at her ear. Marci could not stand to see her baby in pain, so she finally took her to the doctor. When Doctor Brewer examined Tammy, he told Marci, "Her baby had a lot of wax building up in her ears." He asked, "If she had done anything to relieve the pain," Marci told him, "She put drops of cod liver oil in her ear.

"That was a good thing to do as it loosened some of the earwax. I will prescribe medication you can put in her ears before she goes to bed. When you give her a bath, be sure to protect her ear canals. You can go to any pharmacy and buy a little bit of sheep's wool, or just put some cotton in her ear. If you put Vaseline on the outside of the cotton, this will protect her ears so water will not get into them. The sheep's wool doesn't need any Vaseline."

To Henry and Marci's relief the medication and the sheep's wool worked on Tammy's ears. When Travis saw Tammy was getting all of the attention, he too decided to cry for no reason. Marci didn't know which one to take care of first. She knew she had to take care of Tammy's needs, but Travis continued screaming at the top of his lungs. Exhausted, and at the end of her wits, Marci did the one thing she thought she would never do. For the first time in Travis' life Marci spanked him. This was such a shock to her son that he stopped crying. Marci couldn't let Travis know her heart was breaking, and see the tears roll down her checks, so she walked away. She couldn't let him know she wanted to pick him up, and tell him, "She was sorry."

Travis able to climb out of his crib went looking for his mother. Tears running down his rosy fat cheeks, and tugging at her skirts, Travis said, "Mommy, I sorry." Marci knelt next to her son, and hugged him. "Honey, mommy loves you, but you aren't a baby anymore, and I need you to help me with your sister. Do you think you can do that?" Travis nodded his head, and ran into Tammy's bedroom. When that episode was over, Travis was a different little boy. Now Marci could not ask for a better helper than her son.

Peace being restored, Henry and Marci were getting a good night's sleep. Tammy and Travis were growing so fast, and after her bout with her earache, and teething she hardly ever got sick. When she did, it was something Marci could handle. A couple of months later, both Travis and Tammy came down with the chickenpox.

Once again, Marci asked Rosita and Emily for their help. "Both Rosita and Emily told her to rub them with Corn Starch, or to go to the pharmacy and buy some Calamine Lotion. Either one would help with the itch and would help them sleep."

"Rosita told her chickenpox were contagious while the kids had fever, but once the scabs started to fall off they were okay."

Marci did everything Rosita and Emily told her to do, and thought it could be worse, as she dealt with the childhood diseases her children were going through. The only thing she did not know was how she was going to sit across her children, and eat while the scabs were hanging on. But, that too was part of raising children. After the kids got over the chickenpox, Marci was happy because she had lost ten pounds. She was now a veteran mother who could tell any new mother what to expect if they were to ask her.

One evening Henry asked Marci, "If she wanted to go out to dinner and a movie. The kids were fine," and Henry knew the babysitter had always been willing to take care of the kids on Saturday nights.

Mid-week Marci called the babysitter to ask if she would stay with the kids. Knowing her mother could not continue to make excuses for her, Kathleen decided to be honest with Marci. She told her, "She would babysit Tammy, but not Travis. I can't take his screaming because I don't know what to do. You know I love the kids, but Travis doesn't listen."

Marci told her, "He no longer did that, and she would be surprised at how much he changed."

"Okay, I'll babysit this one time, but if Travis acts up I will call you to come home. Is that okay with you?" Marci told her that was a fair arrangement, and with that, they hung up.

Saturday evening when the neighbor girl came to babysit, Travis ran to her, and took her into his sister's bedroom. He was so proud of her he wanted everyone to see her. Surprised at how much Travis had changed, Kathleen told Marci and Henry, "To enjoy their night out."

Not sure how Travis was going to react, Marci told her son, "Daddy and Mommy will be back soon. Help Kathleen take care of your sister, and be a good boy."

While they were enjoying their dinner, Henry and Marci did not realize how much they needed a night out. They decided if Travis behaved, they would do this on a monthly basis. For now, Marci was worried as to how the babysitter was doing, so she asked Henry, "If he would take her home."

Unlocking the door, Henry told Marci, to check on the sitter, as he did not want to scare her if she was sleeping. Walking into the den, Marci saw Travis had fallen asleep on Kathleen's lap. When Kathleen heard Marci and Henry open the door, she said, "You're home early".

"Yes, I was worried Travis might be giving you a hard time, so I asked Henry to bring me home."

"Oh, you should have called me; Travis was such a good boy, and very helpful. He helped take care of Tammy, and after I put her to bed, we watched a movie, and ate popcorn. I am sorry you cut your night short. I would have told you if I was having a hard time."

We should have," Marci said, "But we didn't want to take a chance."

While Marci took Travis to bed, Henry walked Kathleen home. As they were walking, she told Travis, "He could count on her to babysit anytime they need a sitter."

Tammy was now learning to talk, and would imitate her brother. "Mama and Dada" were the most beautiful words Marci heard come out of her daughter's mouth. However, once she learned to talk there was no stopping her. She was a little chatterbox repeating everything anyone said. Tammy was also learning how to crawl, and was now putting everything she found in her mouth. Like Travis, Tammy would share Cleopatra's food, and when Marci couldn't find her, she knew where to look.

Travis and Tammy were growing so fast, and Juanita was always asking if she could take her goddaughter to her house. Every time Juanita took Tammy for a couple of days, she seemed to grow right before Marci's eyes. The day Tammy Marie took her first step she was with her godmother. Running to the telephone, Juanita called Marci to let her know what her baby had done. Juanita was so excited Marci was having a hard time trying to understand what she was trying to tell her.

"Marci you should have been here to see Tammy. I put her down so I could get a glass of water, and when I turned around, she was walking toward the coffee table."

"How many steps did she take?" Marci asked.

"Two, three, I really don't know because I was busy, but she took two more when I turned around to give her the bottle. I took a couple of Polaroid pictures of the baby walking by herself and I will give you one."

Marci felt sad her baby did not start to walk at home, but sometimes godmothers need to share the joys of their godchildren as they grow up.

From the day she was born, Tammy was a very good girl, and not even the terrible twos changed her personality. The day finally came when the children were no longer taking the bottle, and Marci no longer had to buy diapers. As any parent, Marci and Henry were glad those days were behind them. Now they could visit their friends without having to pack diapers, bottles, and formulas. No matter what their children did, Henry and Marci loved every minute of their role as parents.

As Travis and Tammy grew up, it was up to Henry and Marci to share their New Mexico traditions with their children. Together, they would put the brown paper bags with the candle in it to welcome Jesus on Christmas. Travis and Henry would light the candles, and put Luminarias to honor their parents, and grandparents. To honor Grandma, Marci would decorate their traditional tree, and gather the tumbleweeds for the tumbleweed snowman. She wanted to be the one to have a tumbleweed snowman for those who had never seen one. Marci wanted the children to talk about the thorny white snowman to her friends, as did Marci when she was ten years old.

As in the past when Marie was alive, Marci's house would be where Joseph and Mary would come to ask for lodging. They would now be the ones who would provide refreshments to the residents who participated in *Las Posadas* for Christmas. As a family, they would climb the Tomé hill, and join the rest of those who made the pilgrimage. They too would leave their rosaries up on the hill on Good Friday, and she would tell them the story of the three crosses. Now it would be up to Marci and Henry to take their children exploring, and experience all the wonderful things they did with their parents.

Travis grew up faster than his parents would have liked, and by this time he was celebrating his sixth birthday, and time for Marci to enroll her son in school. On the day Marci left her baby boy in the hands of his elementary teacher, Ms. Lucero, she had no idea how difficult it was going to be. Travis was now in the first grade, and Marci lingered around, looking into the classroom to make sure her son was all right.

Marci did not leave until Ms. Lucero told her "to go home, and come back at two-thirty when class let out."

On her way home, Marci cried as she went to pick Tammy from Juanita. How dare the teacher tell her to leave! Marci could not believe this teacher was that cruel. This was Travis's first day at school, and the way he looked at his mother, she knew her son was wondering why she had left him with a stranger.

Juanita saw Marci come up the driveway, and by the time she entered the house, Juanita had a strong cup of coffee waiting for her. "I knew it was going to be a rough day for you, so I baked cookies for Travis to eat when you bring him home."

Knowing Marci was holding back on her emotions, Juanita told her friend to let it all out, and cry as much as she wanted. Once Marci stopped crying, she was able to enjoy the coffee and cookies.

"Why don't you leave Tammy with me until you go for Travis? You know how much I love babysitting my godchild. When you get home, you and Travis can have a couple of minutes together. Then he can tell you all about his day while he eats his cookies," Juanita told Marci. Marci agreed to leave the baby with Juanita because she thought time would go by faster. When she got home it was a different story, and it seemed as if the clock had no hands, as time suddenly stood still. The more Marci looked at the clock the slower time passed.

Finally, it was time for her to bring her son home where she could take care of him. Thinking she would be the first parent to pick her child up, Marci was surprised she was almost the last one. Her little boy looked tired as he ran to his mother. Before Marci could ask his teacher how Travis behaved, Ms. Lucero told her, "he had a very full day, and was ready to go home." "How could this teacher be so cold?" Did she actually think Marci was not concerned as to what her child learned today, and how he behaved?

Marci got to know Travis teacher and she learned many things about her. Marci learned Gloria was a single parent who was diagnosed with cancer. Fortunately, the doctors caught it in time, and Gloria was now in remission. Left with a child to take care of, she now had to work so she could take care of her son. Her husband left when their son was a couple of months old, and was told his wife had cancer.

"He told Gloria he could not cope with the thought of having to come home, and find his son no longer had a mother."

The coward of a husband abandoned his wife and son when they needed him the most. Travis loved his teacher, and once Marci got used to that, she felt better. Marci no longer hung around, nor did she cry when she left Travis. Once her son started going to school it seemed as if he grew up faster than they wanted him to. He talked about his friends what they did in the classroom, and what he did for recess. But most of all, Travis told his mother his teacher told him, "He was a good boy." When Travis showed his father what he made at school, Henry praised him, and told him "how proud he was of his little man."

The day Travis gave his father his handprint made out of plaster of Paris; Henry took it to his office and put it on his desk so he could brag about his son. Grateful she still had her daughter to go home too, Marci spent as much time with Tammy before she too started going to school.

Caleb continued to check on his godson as often as he could. Of course, he could not forget about his niece. He also talked to Marci and Henry, but Travis and Tammy were his main concern. On the day Travis answered the telephone, he told his godfather what he did at school, and how he played with Shredder. Hearing his godson tell him everything he was doing was too much for Caleb. Deciding he would surprise Travis, Caleb took time off from work; called the airlines, and purchased a ticket to New Mexico.

The day Caleb called for someone to pick him up at the airport Henry thought he was joking. Convincing Henry he was in Albuquerque, Marci dressed Travis so he could go with his father. Neither Henry nor Marci told Travis where he was going; all they told him was that "it was a surprise." Arriving at the airport, Travis asked his father, "If they were going to get Uncle Emilio?" "No, it's a better surprise," his father told him. When Travis saw his Uncle Caleb coming into the terminal, he ran to him. Excited at having his godfather home, to the minute they got home, Travis did not stop talking.

While Henry parked the car, Marci ran outdoors to greet her brother whom she had not seen for a while. "Caleb I am so glad to see you. How long are you going to stay? I hope it is more than just a weekend trip."

"Well I thought I'd stay for two months that is if you can stand me for that long. Wednesday, after I talked to Travis I realized I had to spend more time with him, and Tammy. I want to take Travis to school, and meet his teachers. I also want to take them exploring, and show my godson and his sister what our parents showed us when we went on road trips. I knew I could not let my godson grow up without telling him about his grandparents. I also wanted to tell him what I did when I was growing up.

"Caleb you are crazy, but you are welcome to stay as long as you want," Marci told him.

Henry was happy his brother-in-law wanted to spend time with his family. He knew Caleb was going to make a huge difference in the kid's lives, and decided he too would take time off from work to spend time with his brother-in-law as well. After the kids were in bed, Henry now had a chance to catch Caleb up on everything that had taken place since his last visit two years ago.

Saturday morning, while the men and the kids were sleeping, Marci decided to visit Rafael and Rosita. She had a craving for Rafael's coffee, and had some pictures of the kids she wanted to give them. Besides, she wanted to let them know, Caleb was in town, and would be visiting them soon.

When Rafael and Rosita saw her, they were pleasantly surprised, and the three shared a good cup of coffee, homemade chocolate chip cookies, and good conversation. Caleb had so much he wanted to do that he woke the kids and Henry. When he saw Marci's note he took Henry and the kids out for breakfast. Later he asked Travis, "If he wanted to climb the hill by the school." Uncle Caleb wanted the kids to see what their mother did when she attended high school. Then Travis would have something to share for show-and-tell. Tomorrow, he would treat Travis and Tammy to a movie: Monday, he wanted to take his godson to school because Caleb wanted to meet his teacher. However, today was Sunday, and after they went to church, the family would go to the Albuquerque Zoo. But for now, the family was going home to change from their church clothes, and eat breakfast.

Inside the zoo gates, they saw the lions, tigers, giraffes, monkeys and the other animals. Caleb made Travis and Tammy laugh when he acted like one of the monkeys. Later he pretended to be a tiger as he growled at Marci. Henry had never enjoyed going to the zoo, as much as he did that Sunday. After they saw the animals, the kids were hungry, so Marci asked Henry to get the picnic basket from the car.

Sitting on the grass, they ate the sandwiches Marci prepared earlier. Once they were done eating, they went around the zoo one more time before they headed home. Exhausted as Travis and Tammy were, they fell asleep as soon as they were in the car. Getting home, Henry woke up. Henry thinking the kids were too tired to stay up was surprised when Travis asked his Uncle Caleb, "If he wanted to play basketball." Caleb was happy his godson liked basketball, and showed him a few moves he used when he played basketball. A few minutes later, when Henry joined them, they played for a couple of minutes, when the men realize Travis had sat down to watch them play.

Tomorrow was the beginning of a new week, and Caleb wanted to take his godson to school so he could meet his teacher. After he met her, Caleb was pleased that his godson had such a caring teacher. Having taken Travis to school, Henry then took his brother-in-law to an excavation site they were working on. Impressed at what he saw, Caleb asked Henry more questions than Marci did when she met him.

All this time they would joke about what he did, but to watch Henry in action was quite an experience for Caleb.

For the time Caleb was visiting the family, they went exploring the desert, or went to visit other small towns. Then it was time for Caleb to go back home, but he promised he would come back. Before Caleb finished packing his suitcase, Travis gave his Uncle Caleb a picture he drew for him. When Caleb looked at what his godson drew, he saw three boys playing basketball. Caleb praised his godson on his drawing ability, and told him he was going to frame it and hang it in his office at Elko High School, so his students could see it.

The family then took Caleb to the airport, and after Caleb hugged and kissed his godson, and niece good-bye, he told Marci and Henry he would be back. Watching Caleb leave the airport terminal, and board the airplane, Travis and his family went home.

Until the family got home, they did not realize how quiet the house would be now that Caleb was gone. With nothing to do, Marci took Travis and Tammy to visit Rosita while Henry went outdoors to work in his shed. By the time Marci and the kids got home, Henry was taking a nap in the den.

Monday morning, Marci woke up with so much energy she decided to bake chocolate chip cookies for Travis's class. About an hour later, Marci was on her way to her son's classroom. Looking into the classroom, Travis teacher was sitting on the floor with the children reading them a story. When Marci opened the door, the kids along with their teacher looked up to see who was coming in. Marci told Gloria, she baked cookies for the children's snack. As Marci placed the chocolate chip cookies on the counter, she saw how tired Gloria looked. Marci then asked her, "If she could take the children exploring. I know how hard you teachers work, and I thought it might be fun to help. You can relax while the children and I are out looking for rocks and insects."

By the time Marci brought the children back, she was extremely thirsty as it was hot outside. Knowing the children would be ready for their snack, Gloria was ready for them. She then gave the children a couple of cookies with a glass of juice, and later she had the children take a nap. Marci thoroughly enjoyed the snack she shared with Gloria and the children. Gloria thanked Marci and told her, "How much she appreciated what she had done to help her." While you and the children were exploring, I was watching. You are so good with them, and they like you. I saw how they listen to you, and how much fun you had with them, so why didn't you go into the teaching profession? You would be so good at it," Gloria told Marci.

"Thanks Gloria, but no thanks," Marci replied. "I'm glad I can help, but I couldn't do this every day. I'll leave that up to you."

After that when Marci took Travis to school and saw Gloria looking tired, she would stay for a little while. Spring, summer, and fall had come and gone, and winter was almost here. That meant Christmas was near, and this year, Gloria decided to do something different from her traditional Christmas play. She wanted the children to show their parents how the animals might celebrate Christmas if they were to celebrate it. When Travis came home, he had a note pinned to his jacket.

Dear Parents,

This year I would like to show the children how animals might celebrate Christmas. I would like my children to be different animals so I need costumes for them. I am in need of two squirrels, two rabbits, two deer, two skunks; two mice, two porcupines, and two bear cub costumes. I will be the mama bear, but if anybody wants to be the adult bear, I'll gladly let you play that role. As of yet, I have not assigned what animal each child will be.

A few weeks later Travis got home from school, and had another note pinned to his jacket. Marci now knew her son was going be one of the bear cubs. Once she read the note, Marci started to panic, as there was no way she could make the costume and immediately called Rosita. She asked her, "If she would help make Travis' costume."

"Rosita told Marci she would make all of the costumes if the parents got her the patterns and the material."

When the parents heard this, they were happy to buy the materials Rosita needed. Marci, along with other mothers did not know how to sew that well. This year Gloria would be able to enjoy the Christmas program as someone else volunteered to be the adult bear.

The night of the Christmas program, the baby animals came out two by two followed by a big brown bear. As the small animals came out, they had acorns, nuts, Piñon, honeycombs, corn, and other savory snacks any forest animal would enjoy. When the lights were turned up, the parents saw more animals under the tree waiting for their cue. Everything went smoothly until the children were to hand out the candy canes. No matter how loud the mother bear called for her cubs, only one cub came forward. Travis did not answer, and no one knew where the little bear was, so mama bear started to look for him.

As the children moved away from the tree, the parents saw the other bear cup curled up under the Christmas tree. Marci then nudged Henry to get him. Travis did not wake up, and the skunks along with the bear cub went into the audience to distribute the candy. The parents laughed as the bear cub slept through the entire program. Tammy also went to sleep, and like her brother, slept through the entire Christmas play. Once the candy was distributed, and the parents had their children, everyone sang a Christmas carol. This would be the last day of school, and the beginning of the two-week Christmas break.

Now that Travis and Tammy were learning and understanding what was happening, Marci would teach them what she learned when she was younger. For Henry's family, this was going to be the beginning of many beautiful memories for their family. This too would be the beginning of Marci's Christmas traditions.

Marci, Juanita, and Tammy spent many hours together until Marci registered her daughter for school. If she thought it was hard to let go of Travis, it was many more times as painful to leave her baby girl. Tammy was not like Travis who cried on his first day at school. Instead, she went straight to the dollhouse where other little girls were playing. This time, instead of Ms. Lucero having to send Marci away, she now had a harder time sending Juanita home. Today there was no one baking cookies for Marci and Juanita to eat while they cried. Instead of going home, Juanita and Marci went to Manny's Donut Shop. They wanted a strong cup of coffee as they shared their thoughts at leaving Tammy at school.

Drinking their second cup of coffee, and having eaten six chocolate donuts, they decided to go home. Marci took Juanita home, and today both would go to an empty house. This time Marci was truly alone as Henry was at work, and both Travis and Tammy were now in school. Once school let out, Juanita was going to go for Tammy, and Henry would bring Travis home, which left Marci with more time alone.

Travis was involved in every sport he could join; however, Tammy wanted no part of sports. All she wanted was to dance. Now that the children were in school, Henry and Marci's schedules changed. The first month was probably the hardest for them. Marci and Henry never thought they would be spending so much time away from home. If they weren't at a PTA meeting, they were at one of the sports fields, or at the dance studio. Yet, they enjoyed seeing how their children were growing up. The day Tammy put her tutu on for her dance recital; she pranced around the house, as she wanted her family to see her twirl on her toes. But, she especially wanted her daddy to dance with her. He, of course, enjoyed every minute he had to dance with his little angel. The night of her recital, Tammy danced to her heart's content. She, along with the other little girls danced as if they were butterflies fluttering all over the dance floor. They were so excited their parents were there to watch them; they soon forgot to follow the teacher's instructions. Nonetheless, that made it even more entertaining because the little girls were dancing for their families.

One night after the children were in bed, Henry and Marci were looking at their children's baby books. They saw how quickly the years had come and gone. First, second, third and fourth grades all seemed to have merged into one. Their children were growing up and the one thing Marci hated to admit was how quickly they would leave them. It seemed every time she turned around another year had come and gone. Tammy on the other hand, was taking after both her father and mother. She loved flowers, music, and the outdoors, and she excelled at spelling, and won many trophies at the spelling bee. Tammy also liked to have her friends over for slumber parties as often as she could. Henry and Marci enjoyed every minute of their children's childhood, including Tammy's normal teenage years that were nothing like her mothers.

When Tammy asked her mother if she could cut her hair, Marci thought her daughter was going to make the same mistake she made, and have one of her friends cut it. Instead, Tammy said, "She wanted to go to the beauty shop." With a sigh of relief, Marci scheduled an appointment for the weekend so she and her daughter could get their haircut and styled. Travis and Tammy were growing up, and Marci admired many of Travis' characteristics that reminded her of her brother. However, his sarcastic attitude had to change as it got him into many bad situations. It was the end of the school year, and the entire school filled the gymnasium to honor those who were retiring. This was the year Ms. Lucero decided to retire and when it was her turn to go up for her award, she was surprised by the entire school, as they presented her with a special gift. Not only was Gloria honored for her dedication to her students she was also selected as the *Outstanding Educator of the Year*. The principal talked about Gloria's patience, and the important role she played in the lives of her students and their families. After some of the students spoke as to how Ms. Lucero helped them, the principal presented her with a plaque engraved in gold lettering. It read, "In Recognition of Your Devotion to Our Students." Lastly, Ms. Lucero was presented with a check for five thousand dollars. The only stipulation was that she was to spend it on her, and her son. Of course, no one could really tell Ms. Lucero what she was to do with it; that was entirely up to her.The assembly was an emotional one for Ms. Lucero, and she thanked everyone, especially her colleagues, Marci, and friends for their support. The assembly was over, and students young and old, along with their parents came to thank Gloria for being there when they needed her help and guidance. By this time, Tammy was a restless sophomore in college who wanted to explore the world. She wanted to get a job where she could excavate, and learn all about fossils and ancient ruins, just as her parents did. On the other hand, Travis completed his junior year at the university, and was not sure he wanted to continue.

Mid-week Travis called his mother, and told her he was bringing a special friend for dinner. Bringing friends over was not unusual for Marci and she assumed he was bringing a classmate. Travis and his friends had big appetites, and Marci made sure there was plenty for all. She made an enchilada casserole, Spanish rice with tomatoes and onions, sopapillas, and cooked a fresh pot of beans. When Travis and his special friend arrived, Henry and Marci were surprised their son brought his girlfriend, Lora. They were dating, and Marci did not consider Lora, Travis' friend. "I wish you had told me you were bringing Lora. Then I would have prepared a special dinner," Marci told her son.

"Yeah Mom, but we wanted to surprise you and Dad. Besides, you know how much Lora loves your cooking," Travis replied. As Marci and Lora were setting the table, Marci noticed Lora was not her usual talkative self. She was nervous about something, but Marci didn't know what was going on. The table was set, and Marci went into the den to let the men know they should come eat before the food got cold.

As they were eating, Marci said, "Are you going to tell us what your surprise is?" Again, Marci saw how nervous Travis and Lora were, and wondered what was going on. Looking at each other, Marci and Henry waited in anticipation of what the kids had to tell them. Not able to keep her thoughts to herself, Marci said, "Okay Travis, Lora, I can't stand it anymore, what are you two up to? What is it that you are going to tell us that has Lora practically jumping out of her skin?"

By this time, Travis had pushed his chair away from the table, and was standing behind his girlfriend. "Well Mom, Dad, you know Lora and I have been dating for some time, right?" Well, tonight we came to let you know we are engaged."

Marci and Henry were speechless, but once they were able to say something, they were excited at the news. Marci and Henry knew Travis and Lora were dating, but did not realize it was this serious. Henry also told his parents not only were they engaged; but they were getting married in three months. When Henry heard this, he almost choked on his food as he exclaimed, "What!"

"I know you are surprised, and it is sudden, but Lora accepted a job in Florida, and I also went for an interview with an engineering firm, and am waiting for a phone call. Even if I don't get the job I applied for we are still moving. If I don't get it, I will think about going back to college to finish my engineering degree," Travis told his parents.

Happy as they were for them, Henry and Marci could not believe their son was serious about marriage. Once that was over, the only thing they could talk about was how quickly the wedding would be here.

Marci then asked her son when "he was going to tell his godfather."

"Oh mom, he knows, and he is very happy for us."

"When did you tell him?" Marci asked.

"It's okay. Uncle Caleb knows everything, and he told me if I need anything, I am to let him know."

"Oh heck, it doesn't matter who you told, tell us what we can do to help you get ready for your wedding," Henry told his son. Now that the news was out in the open, Lora relaxed, and the family continued eating their supper. Lora was now able to enjoy the dinner her soon to be mother-in-law prepared for them. "I would really like it if you would come meet my parents," Lora told Henry and Marci. "I am sure they would like to meet you." "That would be great," Henry told his future daughter-in-law.

That evening, Tammy called home and Marci told her, "Travis was getting married." Tammy was not surprised, and immediately told her mother, "She was happy for him. She also told her not to expect her to get married soon. She had too many things she wanted to do before she included the "M" word in her vocabulary because she was happy with her life as it was. Mom, I want to talk to Lora because I need to give Travis my approval, or disapproval of his fiancé. I am going to call her so we can have lunch because I want to see if she is good enough for my brother now that she wants to marry him. If I am happy with the answers I get from her, then I will be very happy for Travis, but if not, she had better not hurt my brother."

"Tammy, where is this coming from?" Marci asked.

"He is my brother, and if he is making a mistake by marrying the wrong girl, I want to help him get out of it before it is too late."

True to her word, Tammy invited Lora to lunch, and by the time, they finished eating, Tammy congratulated her soon to be sister-in-law on her up-coming wedding. Lora's parents lived ten miles away, and when Marci and Henry went to meet them, Marci was surprised they were so much older than she and Henry. However, by the time they left, it seemed like Lora's mother was a neighbor Marci had not seen for many years.

Now no matter where they happened to meet, the topic of conversation quickly changed to their children's upcoming marriage. There was so much to do, and for the next three months, the two families were busy preparing for their children's wedding. The day came for Lora to shop for the perfect wedding gown, and not only did Lora ask her mother go with her, but she invited Marci and Tammy to help her. Lora tried numerous wedding gowns, and finally found the one she wanted. Everyone agreed she looked gorgeous and that she had selected the perfect wedding dress.

The months passed by extremely fast, and Lora and Travis' big day was here. Before she knew it, and as any new bride would be, Lora was extremely nervous as she walked down the aisle. When Travis saw his blushing bride, he could not take his eyes off her. Even before he saw her in her wedding gown, he knew she was the woman he wanted to spend the rest of his life with as his wife. When Marci saw her son beaming with pride, she knew their son was no longer a child, but a young man very much in love with his bride. Last night their son was dressed in his old jeans and tee shirt, but today, Travis was dressed in his tuxedo, and he looked so handsome. Tammy also looked beautiful as a bridesmaid, and one day she too would be walking down the aisle, but Marci was hoping that day would not come too soon. Travis and Lora's wedding was everything they hoped it would be. Everyone had a wonderful time, and after the reception, the happy couple left to start their lives as husband and wife in Florida.

Weeks after the wedding, Tammy also left, and she did indeed spread her wings. The house was quiet now, and Marci and Henry wondered what they were going to do without their children. Henry and Marci were happy they had their jobs as that helped them pass the time. They knew it was going to be hard on them now that their children were gone. However, they also knew they would survive this episode.

A year passed, and Travis and Lora were doing well as was Tammy. She traveled from state to state, and country to country making sure, she kept in touch with her parents. The last postcard she wrote, she said she was having a great time, but she would be home soon because she had wonderful news she wanted to share with them.

Patient as Marci tried to be, the days seemed to crawl ever so slowly. Marci wondered if her daughter had met a young man she wanted to marry. Was this why she sent that hastily written postcard? Marci was extremely anxious as she waited to hear the good news her daughter had for them. Several weeks later, Tammy surprised her mother by arriving home days before they expected her.

When Tammy saw her mother drive up, she ran outside to greet her. As they waited for Henry to come home, Marci helped Tammy unpack. They talked about everything but the news she had that brought her back home. Tammy had traveled to her heart's content, and all the studying she did abroad was no longer fun, so she wanted to settle down. Marci told Tammy, "You are just like your godmother, Juanita. You always make me wait for your father to get home before you tell me anything".

"Mom I just felt it was time I settled down."

No matter how many times Marci begged her daughter to tell her the news. Tammy said, "Soon as Dad gets home".

"Okay, did you know your brother and Lora are here? They came home so that they would be close to the family when Lora has the baby." Tammy said she knew that. Lora had called her last month, and that she had told Travis her news.

Henry finally came home, and as they were eating dinner, Tammy said, "Mom, do you remember how I wanted to be a catechism teacher like Sister Ruby Suazo? You know, the nun who we thought had eyes all over her head because she always knew what we were up to. I still can't figure how she knew who was misbehaving without her ever turning her head to see who it was. She must have had an angel helping her just as Bishop Sheen did."

"Yes," Marci replied.

"Do you remember how she helped my friend and me break the tradition that only boys could assist the priest, and actually became altar girls," Tammy continued.

Marci did not dare take her eyes off her daughter, as she was not sure where Tammy was going with this. She thought Tammy was going to tell them she joined a convent, and was going to take her vows in a few months. Fearing this is what Tammy was going to tell them, Marci could not hold back anymore and darted a quick glance at her husband.

Unable to contain her fear, Marci asked her daughter, "Honey, are you joining a convent? Is this the reason you came home earlier than we expected? Please don't keep us in suspense, tell us where they are sending you."

Bracing herself for Tammy's answer, Marci's knuckles turned white as she tightened her hand on her coffee cup ready to take a drink to calm her nerves. If this was Tammy's news, and this is what she wanted, Henry and Marci would be very happy for her. Nevertheless, this would mean their little girl would never get married and have children. Marci knew she was being selfish, but she could not see Tammy leading a life as a nun.

Tammy laughed and told her mother, "That was the furthest thing from her mind." Once she said she did not intend on joining a convent, Marci sighed, a sigh of relief.

"No, Mom, I was going to tell you I saw Sister Suazo in Washington, and I was surprised she remembered me. I just wanted to make sure you remembered her. She asked about the two of you, and sent her regards," Tammy said.

Relieved, Marci was then able to enjoy the dinner they prepared. "So, my little angel, what news do you have for us?" Henry asked. "Well," and as Tammy was about to tell her parents her news, the phone rang. Travis was calling to let his family know Lora was in labor and her pains were a minute apart. Now that Henry and Marci's first grandchild was coming, even Tammy's news would have to wait a bit longer.

On their way to the hospital, Marci thought Henry drove at a snail's pace because by the time they got there, their grandson was born. When they saw their grandson, they fell in love with him as they did the day Travis was born. Days after they celebrated the birth of their grandson, Tammy told her parents her news. Seems their little girl accepted the assistant director's position at the Museum of Natural History where her mother worked for thirty years. Her traveling days were over and she would now settle down in the city. What more could Henry and Marci possibly want? Their children were doing well, were happy, and they could visit their parents anytime they wanted. Yet, they were far away, where their parents could not intrude in their lives.

As the years passed, Marci, and Henry' family grew and they now had four grandchildren. Yet, no matter how many grandchildren they had, each one was as special as the first. The children and grandchildren were happy in the lives they were living, and that was all Marci and Henry ever wanted.

Just when Marci thought Tammy was going to remain single, she surprised her parents by introducing them to her fiancé, Toddfrey. Henry's little angel had found someone she would share her life with, and her parents were extremely happy. Toddfrey was a wonderful young man who had a way of making anyone feel as if he had known them all his life. Henry and Marci loved Tammy's fiancé, and when Tammy told her parents they were getting married they celebrated by going out to dinner at the Luna Mansion.

While they were enjoying a good meal, Tammy told her parents 'Toddfrey and she did not want a big church wedding. Instead, they wanted to get married in Las Vegas, and she wanted to know if they would go with them'.

"Honey, what about your friends, don't you think they would want to celebrate your wedding?"

"No. Toddfrey and I have discussed this, and we do not want a fancy and expensive wedding. All we want is to be married and start our lives together. We talked to my Nina, and she said it was a great idea. If we wanted to get married in Las Vegas she would be there."

Marci was stunned that Tammy had told her Nina (godmother) before she told her parents. "Tammy, how long has Juanita known about your plans on getting married?"

To spare his daughter from having to do a lot of explaining, Henry jumped in and said, "Honey, whatever you and Toddfrey want, we will be there for you."

Soon after Toddfrey and Tammy told her parents, they planned their Las Vegas wedding, and decided to get married in a couple of months with her parents, Juanita, Ernest, Toddfrey's parents, Caleb, Travis and Lora.

The following week, Tammy, Juanita, and Marci went to several bridal shops and Tammy selected the wedding gown she wanted. Seeing their little girl model a Sweetheart Strapless Ball wedding gown, Marci, and Juanita started to cry. "Mom, if you don't you like this gown, I can select another one," Tammy said.

"Oh honey, it isn't that we don't like it, we think you look beautiful. The dress is perfect, and Toddfrey will not be able to take his eyes off you. We cannot believe you are getting married. We can't believe you won't be our little girl any more, and in a couple of weeks you will be a married woman," Marci replied as she and Juanita wiped their eyes.

Finding the dress she wanted, she went into the fitting room to change into her regular clothing. Later they went out to eat, and started to prepare for Tammy's big day. Arrangements for Tammy, and Toddfrey's wedding were completed, and it was now a matter of Tammy marrying the man of her dreams, as did Marci.

Wednesday was a beautiful day in Las Vegas, Nevada, and the wedding was a simple one, as that was what the young couple wanted. When the priest pronounced Toddfrey and Tammy man and wife, Marci knew her little girl now belonged to someone else. Soon they would start their marriage as a married couple, as did Travis and Lora. Tammy was no longer theirs, as she now belonged to someone else, but Henry and Marci were blessed in that they now had an addition to their family. Besides, they loved Toddfrey and thought he was a perfect fit to their family. The ceremony was over and everyone went to try their luck at gambling. Whatever lady luck would let them win, it would go to the newlyweds. Gamblers who were at the poker tables congratulated the newlyweds and gave them a bit of their winnings as a wedding gift. After their honeymoon to Cabo San Lucas, Toddfrey and Tammy decided to buy a house in Albuquerque. There, they would be close to the university where Toddfrey was months away from completing his classes in accounting. Tammy was not like her mother where she wanted the country life. She wanted to live in the city where there was more going on than what the country life had to offer.

A year passed, and Marci's birthday was but a day away when Tammy asked her mother to meet her for lunch at the Frontier Restaurant. Not thinking she had anything on her mind other than lunch, Marci agreed to meet her. When Marci arrived at the restaurant Tammy had already placed their order and was waiting for her mother. As Marci sat down, she noticed her daughter was a little nervous. Maybe it was Marci's imagination, but it also looked like her daughter had been out in the sun and gotten a tan. Mother and daughter had a wonderful time, and as they finished their lunch, Tammy reached for her purse. Marci thinking her daughter was paying for their lunch told her lunch was on her.

"Oh thank you Mom," Tammy said, "I already paid for it, besides, I wasn't thinking of the bill. I wanted to give this to you when we went to visit you and Dad last week, but Toddfrey thought I should give it to you for your birthday."

With that, Tammy reached into her purse, and handed her mother a gift-wrapped in brightly shimmering multicolored paper. The wrapping was so pretty, Marci took her time un-wrapping it. Tammy wanting her mother to tear the wrapper and see what she had for her told her, "Mom, don't worry about the wrapping—it's only paper. Just unwrap your gift, and I'll give you the rest of the wrapping if you want it." Marci laughed as she opened her gift. When she did, she didn't know what to say. Tammy and Toddfrey were presenting her with a picture of their future grandchild. Marci's little girl was expecting, and her birthday gift could not be more perfect.

"Mom, that isn't all. Toddfrey and I want you and Daddy to be the godparents to our baby." Marci was so overwhelmed with the gifts her little girl had given her she started to cry. This time Tammy was not in first grade playing house with her dolls pretending she was their mother. Tammy would soon be taking care of her own child, and she was not playing make believe. Again, Henry and Marci were going to be blessed with another grandchild.

Marci did not have her mother there when she gave birth to Travis, or Tammy, but she was going to be there when this child came into the world. This time there would be someone to tell her what to expect, and would have help whenever she needed it. To Marci, this was the most beautiful birthday, and she could not wait to share the news with Henry.

Saint Thérèse

Sunday, December twelfth, after the deacon delivered the sermon, he told the parishioners the relics of Saint Thérèse de Lisieux would be at the Immaculate Conception Church on Central in Albuquerque. Seeing there were quite a few children at Mass he asked them if they knew anything about Saint Thérèse. The children sitting at the front pews replied they did not.

Okay, for the children, and the rest of you who aren't familiar with Saint Thérèse, I will give you a brief summary on her life. I thought there might be some that do not know who she is so I will read from my notes that I have about this saint.

"Saint Thérèse was born October 1, 1873, and entered the Carmelite monastery when she was 15 years old. In 1809, she became a nun at the age of 24, and is known as *"The Little Flower."* Following her death, it was said many miracles were the result of her intercession on behalf of those who prayed to her. Because she loved Jesus' mother, she wrote the following poem in her honor:"

Why I Love You Mary

Oh you who came to smile on me…
At the dawn of life's beginning,
Come once again to smile on me….
Mother! The night is nigh I fear no more your majesty,
So far removed above me
For I have suffered much with you;
Now hear me, Mother mild!

O let me tell you, face to face,
Dear Mary, how I love you;
And say to you forevermore;
I am your little child.

Once the deacon finished reading his notes about Saint Thérèse, he encouraged the parents to take their children with them. When Marci heard Saint Thérèse remains were going to be in Albuquerque she could not wait to get home. Although Marci's children were married, she and Ms. Lucero kept in touch. She wanted to call her children's first grade teacher, and invite her to go with her. Ms. Lucero was excited because she would be near her favorite saint, and told Marci she would love to go. However, in her excitement, Gloria forgot she was going to visit her mother in Española, New Mexico, and told Marci she could not go. Marci told her, "They could take her mother with them."

Gloria told her, "It would be too hard for her mother of eighty-nine-years to travel into Albuquerque as her health had deteriorated. For that reason, Gloria was going to spend the week with her mother, as she had several doctor appointments she had to go too."

The day Saint Thérèse remains were in Albuquerque, Marci was working late. Hoping to get a glimpse of the procession, Marci drove downtown to the Immaculate Conception Church on Central. There, St. Thérèse's relics would be in the church until ten in the evening for anyone who wanted to pay their respects. Marci did not know if it was Saint Thérèse, lady luck or both who wanted her there, but she just so happened to find a parking spot next to the Immaculate Conception Church. As Marci was getting down from her car, she could feel the excitement within the crowd. Looking around, she saw people talking as they sat on the grass while others were standing in line, and yet others were gathering in groups to pray—so she stood and listened.

While Marci waited in line, she looked around, and saw parents with children dressed in their Sunday best. Others had flowers they wanted to leave at Saint Thérèse glass coffin, yet others sang, or prayed their rosary. Waiting for the archbishop to arrive, and escort Saint

Thérèse remains into the church, a male voice made an announcement to those of us who were waiting outside.

For the faithful, and the curious who had gathered, and continued to gather, we were instructed to form two lines to enter the church. When we entered, we were to proceed to the altar, pay their respects to Saint Thérèse, and exit through the side doors. No one was to linger as Saint Thérèse relics would only be there for a couple of hours, and there were many who wanted to view the saint known as, *The Little Flower*.

At exactly six o'clock in the evening, the bells at The Immaculate Conception Church rang, and the people waiting were told a saint was now among them. When Marci heard Saint Thérèse was there, she wanted to kneel, jump up and down, shout, run from one end of the line to the other, but she did not. Instead, Marci remained standing, uncertain as to what her next move was going to be. Like so many others, Marci felt blessed to be in the presence of a saint and she felt so at peace. Then there was a distinct fragrance of roses, and Marci knew it was another sign a saint was indeed in their midst. Marci continued to pray, as she listened to others singing around her.

This once in a lifetime experience was the most amazing gift in her life. Marci was overwhelmed knowing she was in the presence of a saint who was bestowing her blessing upon those who came to pray to her. Shortly after the announcement, the Knights of Columbus, priests from throughout the state, girls and boys dressed in their Holy Communion clothes, and the Archbishop of Santa Fe escorted St. Thérèse de Lisieux into the Immaculate Conception Church. As the procession entered the church, the bells continued to ring joyously until Saint Thérèse glass coffin was placed before the altar. Once the archbishop prayed over St. Thérèse's relics, those in attendance made their way to pay their respects to the saint known as *The Little Flower*.

People continued to gather outside so they too could pray to a saint for requests they wanted granted. Those who were already inside the church started to make their way to the altar. As they left, the multitude of people waiting outside inched their way forward. After Marci waited for three hours, she finally got to the entrance of the church, where a young girl handed her a rose petal and told her to place it on St. Thérèse coffin. While Marci prayed, she felt extremely blessed. Her heart was filled with joy, and she too prayed for favors not only for her family, but also for those she loved, and knew could not be there. When everyone had a chance to pray to Saint Thérèse, she would be escorted to the airport where she would continue her journey throughout the United States.

Days later, Marci called Ms. Lucero, and asked her, if she would like to join her for lunch. She wanted to tell her about St. Thérèse. Gloria accepted the invitation, and on the day they were to meet, Gloria arrived early, because she was anxious to hear everything Marci had to say. Gloria asked Marci to describe what she had seen, and not leave anything out. Marci told Gloria "it was hard to describe how she felt because she had never felt as she did on that special day. I felt a sense of joy, fear, and anxiety, if that makes any sense to you". Knowing there was no way she could do justice to what she saw, and how she felt, Marci tried to think of a way she could explain what happened to her. She then asked Gloria, "Do you remember when you made your first Holy Communion, and how happy you were on that special day?"

"The only thing I remember is that on the day I made my first Holy Communion my parents bought me a beautiful white dress and veil. I was missing two of my front teeth, and when I ate, the mashed potatoes with chili and gravy, some of it went through the hole where my teeth were missing, and fell on my beautiful dress. I know I cried, but it has been such a long time, and that is the only thing I really remember," she said.

"Okay, how about the first time you held your little boy," Marci asked.

Smiling, Gloria said, "Yes, that was the most beautiful feeling, and I will never forget it." "Okay," Marci replied, "Now multiply that feeling a million times because that is how I felt except, it went beyond anything I have ever felt. Can you understand that? It was an extremely exciting time, and I wish you and your mother could have been there."

Marci told Gloria about the people who gathered. How they were told St. Thérèse had arrived. How slowly the people inched forward until she was at the front door where a girl gave her a rose petal to place on St. Thérèse glass coffin. Marci told Gloria she prayed for her, and that she had something to give her.

She asked Gloria to close her eyes, and when she did, Marci placed a small box in her hand. The rose petal, and the Kleenex she touched Saint Thérèse coffin were inside the box. Marci told her friend, "She was giving her something no one else had. Marci knew the rose petal and Kleenex were blessed, and if anyone needed a saint's help, it was her friend, and her children's teacher. "Anytime you feel depressed, remember your favorite saint is here to help you," Marci told her friend."

Gloria was sad because she could not be there, but happy Marci had thought enough of their friendship to bring her such a special gift.

The following Sunday an article was published in the Albuquerque Journal; which Marci clipped, and framed for her friend, and this is an excerpt of the article:

Thousands come to glimpse Thérèse

Downtown drivers exhibited the patience of a saint during the afternoon rush hour Thursday. Possibly because we had a good role model close by. The remains of St. Thérèse of Lisieux were escorted into Downtown Albuquerque on Thursday, minutes before the 5 p.m. commute city's streets by home hits its peak. Employees of Downtown businesses were joined by the thousands of the city's faithful who turned out to view the bones of the saint known as The Little Flower and called the greatest saint of modern times by many Catholics. There were no major traffic accidents involving those who had come to view the ornate jacaranda wood and gilded-silver reliquary, containing the earthly remains of St. Thérèse. No attendance figures were available for the event, but at 4:30 in the afternoon when the doors of the Immaculate

Conception Catholic Church were opened to the viewing public lines of people standing three to five abreast were four blocks long. Some of those waiting in line to enter the church carried roses to leave in tribute. Many held rosaries, and the sound of muttered Lord's Prayer was prevalent, despite the tolling of bells, struck in honor of the occasion. Born in 1873 as Marie-Franchoise Thérèse Martin, Thérèse entered the Carmelite monastery when she was 15. She became a nun in 1809 and, at the age of 24, died of pulmonary tuberculosis. Following her death, many miracles were said to be the result of her intercession on behalf of those who prayed to her. She is most noted for her autobiographical notebooks, kept faithfully throughout her life. Those writings, titled The Story of a Soul, played a significant role when church officials considered her canonization. Spiritual seekers continued to pass through the nave of the Church of the Immaculate Conception until the viewing's closed at 10 p.m."

Caleb

Tuesday after Marci got back from lunch, Bernadette called her into her office. Thinking she was going to be asked to do a presentation at a workshop downtown, she was not prepared for the news she was about to hear.

"Have a seat, Marci; there is something I have to tell you."

"Bernadette, what's wrong, you are scaring me. Tell me what's wrong, is it Emilio, did something happen to him?"

Sitting next to her, Bernadette said, "No, it's not Emilio, its Caleb. He was in a motorcycle accident, and is in the hospital. I don't know the extent of his injuries, but when I spoke to the nurse, she said he was being operated on. I booked a flight for you and Henry to go to Las Vegas. Don't worry about anything here, just go home pack a bag and I'll have Jeremiah take you to the airport". Marci was not able to say anything as she was in a state of shock. Bernadette gave her a glass of water, and made sure she was okay before she let her go home. "Are you able to drive, or do you want me to drive you home?"

"No, I can drive, I, I have to call Henry. Does he know about Caleb?"

"I called him, and he said he was going to go home, and would be waiting for you."

Two hours later, Marci and Henry were in Nevada, and having hailed a taxi, asked him to take them to the Mountain View Hospital.

"Oh that's a nice hospital; best in the state," the taxi driver told Henry.

"Get us there as fast as you can. My brother-in-law was in a motorcycle accident, and is being operated on."

"Sure, I can get you there in fifteen minutes. But don't worry, they have the best doctors there. I'm sure your brother-in-law will be just fine."

As Marci got out of the taxi, she thought of the day she saw her parents in the hospital, and she was afraid of what she was going to see.

"Come on Marci," Henry said. "Henry, my legs won't move. All I can see are Mom and Dad, and I don't think I can see Caleb. What if..." "You can't think that way. You heard the taxi driver. He said this hospital has the best doctors in Las Vegas. Come on honey, you can do it. Your brother is in there and he needs us."

With that, Marci was able to compose herself and they went into the hospital to see how Caleb was doing. Henry asked the volunteer at the Information Desk, "If she could direct them to the emergency room."

"Go down the hall past the elevators, and turn left. When you get to the emergency room, press the button so that the nurse at the desk can let you in."

Henry thanked her, and both he and Marci ran down the hall carrying their luggage.

When they got to the emergency room, Henry asked the nurse, "If she could tell him if Caleb Bennett was still in the operating room."

"I'm not sure, but I can check. Yes, he is still in the recovery room. It will be another hour or so before he gets out, but you can go to the ninth floor and wait for him in the visitor's waiting room."

Hearing he was in the recovery room, Marci and Henry waited. About a half hour later, Marci looked at her watch. She saw more than an hour had passed, so she went to the nurse's desk to ask if her brother was still in recovery. When the nurse checked, she told Marci, "He was in the Intensive Care Unit and only two people were allowed to see him."

"Can you tell me where that is located?" Marci asked.

"Let me have someone take you there. This hospital is so big even I get lost in it if I don't pay attention to which elevator I take." With that, Marci and Henry were taken to Caleb's room, and there, they waited until Caleb woke up.

When Marci saw Caleb, he looked like her father, and she broke down and cried. Henry comforted her, and told her, "Not to worry Caleb was going to be fine because he was a fighter. Caleb has the best doctors, and there is nothing we can do for him. It will probably be another hour, or so before he comes out of the anesthesia, so I think I will try to book us a room we can go to after Caleb knows we are here."

Doctors and nurses came in and out of Caleb's room, and when asked what happened, all the nurse could tell Marci was that Caleb was brought in after he was involved in a motorcycle accident. Marci then asked, "if anyone else was involved."

"No, he tried to avoid hitting a dog, and his motorcycle hit a pothole throwing him onto the sidewalk".

When Marci heard Caleb was the only victim, she was relieved. "What is the extent of his injuries," she asked. The nurse then told Marci, "the doctor would be in to explain what he did," and with that, she left the room. Within minutes, Doctor Augustine came in to check on Caleb. When he saw Marci sitting next to Caleb's bed, he introduced himself, shook her hand and told her "Caleb was in a bad accident, and the only injury he had was to his leg."

"How bad is it?" Marci asked.

"Well, we had to amputate his leg. When he hit the sidewalk, his motorcycle fell on top of him. As it did, the rear wheel was still spinning, and it tore his leg beyond repair. But don't worry, he will be fine. I have seen many of my patients get back on a motorcycle within two years."

"Doctor Augustine, you amputated Caleb's leg, how is he going to get around?"

"Well, he will have to go through physical therapy to learn how to walk. In the meantime, he will be using a wheelchair, and later crutches. But once he accepts the fact that he no longer has two legs, and has to use a prosthetic leg, he will be fine. Do you have any other questions?" "When are you going to tell him?"

"I will tell him tomorrow morning when I make my rounds. He is going to be out for another two hours. If you want to get something to eat, now is the time to do it," Doctor Augustine told Marci.

Once Henry returned, he told Marci, "He rented a car, and got a room not far from the hospital." He then asked Marci, "How Caleb was doing."

Marci told Henry what the doctor told her, and he was as shocked as she was. Henry had more questions than Marci could answer, but she told her husband he could ask the doctor tomorrow when he came in to check on Caleb. Marci and Henry stayed with Caleb until Marci started to fall asleep. Not wanting to leave her brother by himself, Henry had to convince Marci she needed her rest, or she would be of no use to him. With that, Marci and Henry went to the hotel to rest.

After she had spoken to Doctor Augustine, Marci called Bernadette to let her know how Caleb was doing. She asked Bernadette to let everyone know they would be home as soon as they could. Marci also thanked Bernadette for all she had done. Bright, and early the following morning, Henry and Marci went to the hospital. Entering Caleb's hospital room, they saw he was awake and talking to the nurse. "All Caleb could say was that he was sorry for the scare he gave them."

"Hey Caleb," Henry said, "I'm as ready as I can be, but the doctor told me I have to be here for another week or so." "Do you know what happened to you? I mean your operation?"

"Yes, Doctor Augustine came in earlier this morning and told me he had to amputate my leg. I am lucky it wasn't my arms, or my hands. At first, I was angry, and feeling sorry for myself, but thanks to the doctor, and the nurses, I realized how lucky I am."

Turning to Henry, Caleb told him he was going to have to teach him how to walk. "Hey bud, I will do all I can, but you know I can't walk a straight line if I wanted to." And, with that they laughed.

Hearing how well Caleb was taking his loss, Marci was concerned her brother was in denial of what had taken place. "Don't worry sis, I know exactly what happened. I also know that it is going to take me some time before I can play basketball with Travis, but that too will come around." Marci started to cry, and Caleb told her, "If she was going to feel sorry for him, that would just be a loss of energy. Look sis, all three of us are going to need all of our energy when I go live with you, so don't cry."

"Oh hi doc, can you tell my sister not to cry, and that I'm going to be fine."

"Yes, Marci, if your brother continues to believe in that he is going to get well, there is no telling what he can do."

"So doctor, when can I be fitted for my leg?"

"We can't do anything for a while. You need to heal, but you can learn how to use crutches. They aren't as easy to use as some people think, but in your case, I think you will catch on pretty quick. At first,

someone has to be with you in case you fall, so they can help you up."
"So is it okay for me to climb stairs, or do I have to limit my walking to lower levels, elevators, and escalators?"

"No, you can climb whatever you want, but like I said, don't get carried away. I have other patients I have to check on, but I will make my rounds this afternoon. The orderly will bring some crutches in a few minutes, and I want you to walk as far as you can. If you can make it from your bed to the door, that will be just fine. Try to walk as far as you feel you can. I don't want you to overdo it, as that won't be good for you. If you progress as fast as I think you will, I think you can be dismissed by next Wednesday. It's entirely up to you."

"Thank you Doctor Augustine. Oh by the way, do you think I will be able to fly? My sister lives in New Mexico, and that is where I would like to recuperate."

"There won't be a problem with you flying. You will have to be transported in a wheelchair boarding, and when you leave the airplane. I don't want you to over exert yourself. When I do release you, and you get to New Mexico, I want you to call me every week, and any time you feel something is wrong. I need to know how you are doing. You will have to come see me once a month until I see how your leg is healing."

Having answered their questions, Doctor Augustine left to continue his rounds.

"Okay Caleb, I think you are trying to fool us in that you are okay with what happened to you. I still think you are in denial, and you are going to have a breakdown. But for now, I am happy that you are doing well, and anxious to get out of the hospital," Marci told her brother.
"Yes, I also believe that once I fall, I will curse what happened to me, and I will rant and rave, but I also know that I have you, Henry, the kids and our friends to help me. If I need to talk to a doctor, I will talk to Dr. Brewer. He helped you when you were depressed, and I know he will be able to help me."

Caleb learned how to walk with his crutches, and was now walking to the elevators, as far as the front door entrance to the hospital. When Doctor Augustine made his rounds on Wednesday, he told Caleb, "He was going to release him. There was no sense Caleb stay in the hospital when someone else might have use of it."

After Caleb was released, the three went out to eat a real meal. Henry had already purchased three tickets to Albuquerque, and they would leave on Friday after Caleb saw Doctor. Augustine.

The trip back to New Mexico went smoothly, and Caleb had no ill effects to the medication Doctor Augustine gave him before leaving Nevada. When they entered the Albuquerque International Sunport, Emilio was waiting to take them home. Seeing Caleb in a wheelchair made him forget that Henry had asked him not to say anything about Caleb's accident. Emilio forgot what Henry told him, and the first thing he asked Caleb was, "If he could walk on his own." The minute the words were out of his mouth, Emilio apologized.

"That's okay Emilio. I know you were asked not to mention my accident, but how can you not. You won't be the first, or the last."

Rain was forecasted for later in the afternoon, and sure enough, by the time Emilio went to get the van, a light rain started to fall. By the time, Emilio drove to Henry and Marci's house, the rain was really coming down.

"You can use Tammy's room; that way you won't have to climb stairs. You will be closer to the kitchen, and the bathroom is down the hall," Marci told her brother.

The three months spent with his sister and brother-in-law were very good for Caleb. He did talk to Doctor Brewer a couple of times, and every time he went, he felt better about the loss of his leg. While in Los Lunas, Caleb went to visit his friends, and they even played a round of basketball. Caleb was doing so well that he decided he would go back to Nevada and go back to work. Marci and Henry did not want

Caleb to leave, but they knew he would not be happy if he stayed in Los Lunas.

Now the first thing Caleb did when he arrived in Las Vegas was to get him a three-wheeler motorcycle. Because he didn't have to worry about using his feet to steady the motorcycle. All he had to do was to work the gears on the handlebars. Caleb had told Marci he was going to see Doctor Augustine when he got home so he wouldn't be calling her right away. Because of this, Marci did not expect her brother to call her for a couple of hours.

The night of his arrival in Nevada, Caleb called and told "Henry his doctor was extremely happy with the progress he made. The doctor knew Caleb still had a ways to go, and he wanted Caleb to continue his physical therapy." Caleb then told Henry his medical condition, and asked if Marci was nearby.

"Marci went to buy groceries, as there was nothing to eat."

"That's great, because I don't want Marci to see, or hear your reaction to what I'm going to tell you." Caleb replied.

"What is it? Do you have to go through more surgery?"

"No, everything is just fine. After I got home from seeing Doctor Augustine, I went and bought me a three-wheel motorcycle."

"You did what!" exclaimed Henry. "Are you crazy?"

"That was the reaction I thought you were going to have, that is why I'm glad my sister is not home. Now that I have told you, you can tell her. I figured if I didn't get back on a motorcycle now that I had the nerve to do so, I never would do it."

"Caleb you are absolutely crazy, but I will tell Marci. Be ready for a chewing out, but I know in the long run, she will be happy for you."

After Caleb told his brother-in-law all that he had done when he got to Nevada, they stayed talking until Marci got home.

Having put the groceries away, Henry told Marci Caleb called and told her about Caleb's motorcycle. Surprised she didn't throw a fit, and get angry, Henry wasn't sure what to make of Marci's reaction.

"Honey, aren't you angry at your brother?"

"No, not really, when I met Doctor. Augustine, he told me this could happen. I'm surprised Caleb didn't say anything when he was here."

Golden Years

Many good and bad years had come and gone, and Henry and Marci were now in their mid-eighties. Not wanting to burden their children with their medical needs, they did as much as they possibly could. Marci still took her daily walks, but she had to limit her time outdoors. Henry now had to carry an oxygen bottle if he went visiting his friends. Emphysema, had taken a toll on his health, and he was unable to breathe on his own. No longer could he go out into the desert to excavate ruins, as those days were past memories. Yet, he had many memories to share with his grandchildren. Travis and Tammy were doing well and leading productive lives. Their grandchildren and great-grandchildren were growing up so fast they could hardly keep up with them.

Family reunions were fun and Marci and Henry were banned from doing any of the cooking, or housework which neither one objected to. Marci was no longer the ten-year-old girl who loved to stay out in the desert with her father. For her, those days were gone, and they would never return. As much as she loved to stay out in the sun, she knew she could not put herself or her health in jeopardy. Her doctor told her she needed to exercise, but the furthest she could walk was the mile to church and back. For Marci, what better reason to take a walk than to give thanks for all she had in her life. Now it was up to Tammy, Toddfrey, and the greatgrandchildren to watch over Grandpa and Grandma. Whenever Caleb came to visit, Marci and Henry, he always managed to melt the years away, and it seemed as if they were back in the old days.

Friends and family members died some years back, as did Shredder and Cleopatra. The family missed their old friends, and animals but they did leave their offspring behind. Juanita and Ernest moved to Palm Springs where Juanita and her daughter operated a successful boutique shop. Ernest retired, and kept busy working on a number of projects in his shed.

Sunday morning, Marci woke up early enough to go to the eight o'clock Mass. She wanted to tell Henry where she was going, but he was sleeping so soundly. Marci did not have the heart to wake him, just so he would go back to sleep.

As she opened the door to walk outdoors, Marci saw the sun had risen over the Manzano Mountains, and she knew it was going to be a beautiful day. Yet, she remembered the weatherman had predicted rain later in the evening, but sometimes his weather predictions weren't very accurate. She wasn't worried because she would be home before that happened. By the time she walked mid-way, the cool morning air had her putting her scarf over her head and her sweater over her shoulders. While she did this, Marci took time to admire the beautiful flowers still blooming in the neighborhood. For a few minutes, she forgot about the time, and stopped to admire God's work. She thought of her father, and she could hear him say, "Little one, do you know God displays his artwork for all to see, but so few take advantage of it?" In memory of her father, she took a second look at the beauty that surrounded her. Having done that, Marci resumed her walk to church.

By now, some of the neighbors were getting up, and turning their kitchen lights on. She also saw the neighborhood dogs were playing, and heard other dogs barking in the distance. Marci hadn't walked far when she felt a sense of anxiety building in the pit of her stomach. The further away she walked from home, the worse it got. She thought she could shake it off if she walked faster, but that did not help. Not sure what was going on, Marci had a feeling it was not going to go away. The sun was over the Manzano Mountains, but it was still chilly enough that she needed to stay warm.

Glancing at her watch, she saw Mass was about to start, so she hastened her pace to get to church on time. Marci had barely finished her prayers, and was about to sit down when the priest started to walk down the aisle. Removing her sweater, she put it down on the bench, and completely forgot about the feeling she had earlier.

Even though Marci heard most of the sermon, she was having a difficult time keeping her mind focused on it. Maybe it was because her thoughts had drifted off to the sunrise, and the wild flowers blooming all around her. On the other hand, could it be that her father was on her mind. Whatever it was, Marci felt something was going to happen. Mass was over, and as Marci was about to leave, she gathered her scarf and sweater. On her way out, she talked to the deacon for a few minutes and started to walk home.

There were no rain clouds in sight, and the morning was already warming up, as Marci removed her scarf and sweater. Tying the scarf around her neck, and the sweater around her waist, she continued her walk. As she did, the feeling of anxiety returned. Not sure what was going on, Marci simply ignored the feeling.

On her way back, Marci thought about the sermon, and was happy she didn't drive to church. Not paying attention as to where she was walking, Marci tripped over the uneven sidewalk, fell, and hit her head on a rock. As she got up, she felt her head to see if she had any cuts. The only thing she felt was a bump on the side of her forehead. Picking her glasses off the ground, she saw the frame was broken and one of the lens had fallen into the gutter next to the sidewalk. Not hurt, she got up, and with only one lens, Marci thought some vision was better than having none. As she dusted herself off, she continued walking, but was distracted by a car driving by. Marci thought everything around her was distorted, and could not make out what was ahead of her.

Again, she failed to see a section of the sidewalk had been partially removed. Everything was going wrong and Marci felt she was walking further away from home. She knew she had walked away from her familiar surroundings, but did not realize how far she had gone.

Not sure why she needed to rush home, and out of the heat, she knew, she had to get there as fast as she could. To keep from going into a state of panic, Marci started to sing the only hymn she could remember. Unfortunately, at this time Marci could only recall a few of the words. Softly and tenderly, Jesus is calling, calling for you and for me; see, on the portals He's waiting and watching, watching for you and for me. Hard as she tried to remember the rest of the words, these were the only verses Marci could remember, so she sang it over, and over. For a while this was comforting, but the more she sang, the dryer her mouth got. Then she stopped singing and thought about the pleasant things; like her children, grandchildren, and great-grandchildren. Thinking about her family, she now wished she had driven to church because she had not told anyone where she was going.

Having left the car at home no one would think of going to look for her. Henry would assume she went to have a cup of coffee with one of the neighbors, and he would wait for her to come home. Yet, he would be a bit concerned, as his beloved wife was not well. She was starting to forget things, at times, she would lose her way, and he would have to go look for her. Marci knew she had walked more than a mile, and tried to concentrate on finding her way back. In her state of confusion, she heard someone calling her, and looked around but could not see anyone. Hoping someone was nearby, she yelled, "Please if you can hear me, I need your help. I have lost my way, and I need to get back home to feed my cats and dogs." Again, she heard someone calling her, but no one was there.

Yet, a voice continued to fade in and out, but no one came to help her. Then Marci heard a dog barking, but could barely see him. She thought it was a dog, but what if it is a hungry coyote or worse. The residents were warned about the mountain lions that were coming down from the mountain in search of food. So what if it was a mountain lion, that had come down from El Cerro de Los Lunas, then what was she to do? Without her glasses, she could barely see the animal running toward her, and chills ran up, and down her spine. Marci closed her eyes as she got on her knees and started to pray.

Before she had a chance to get up, the dog was a few feet from her snarling, and growling, and Marci was not sure how to react. Not knowing if she should run or stay where she was, she decided not to move. When the dog stopped growling, and barked. Marci thought he might be a friendly dog, and she had walked into his territory. But what if he wasn't, what if he was waiting for her to run so he could attack her? Slowly, Marci extended her hand, and the dog stopped barking. Marci did not move, as she was not sure what this dog was going to do. Guess the dog was as scared as she was because he too was just as cautious. As Marci extended her hand in friendship, the dog sniffed it, moved forward, and started to lick it.

With a sigh of relief, Marci talked to him, and he allowed her to hold on to his fur. As she was hugging the dog, she heard children laughing. Running ahead of her, the dog looked back as if he wanted her to follow him. It was as if to tell her he needed her help and everything was going to be all right. When he got close to the children, he went back to where Marci was, and again licked her hand.

With the sun shining directly in her eyes, Marci could not see the children she heard laughing. However, when her eyes focused on what was ahead of her, she got scared because she could see children were in danger of falling into a ditch.

Suddenly Marci thought of the *Llorona,* and she did not want her to claim these children as her own. She now knew why this dog brought her here. He knew the danger they were in, and he needed her help. Even though she could barely see the children, she heard the water, and knew it was moving swiftly. Her mouth was dry, and she could not warn them of the danger they were in. Even though Marci was tired, thirsty and hungry, she ran toward the children in time to catch a child from falling into the ditch as she played with puppies that belonged to the dog that rescued her. When she was able to talk to the children, she asked, "Where are your parents and why they weren't with you?"

As she was talking to the kids, a middle-aged man with long hair, and a scraggly beard came riding on a motorcycle toward the children. This must have been someone the children recognized because they ran to greet him. Relieved the children now had someone that was going to supervise them, Marci turned her attention to the dog. It was obvious he did not like the man as he growled and tried to bite him. The man paid little or no attention to either the dog, or Marci, other than to kick the dog a couple of times.

When the man got tired of hearing the dog bark, and talked to the children, he decided to leave. Marci watched as the man rode off on his motorcycle, and that is when she saw his house. The scraggly bearded man disappeared into his house, and women came running to get their children. Marci tried talking to the women, but they left without saying a word; it was as if she did not exist. When the women took their children with them, she saw the adobe houses, and could not believe she had not seen them earlier. As she shaded her eyes to look at the houses—they disappeared. Had she hurt her head when she fell, and was now feeling the effects from the fall? Did she have a concussion, and was this why she was seeing and hearing things?

If so, how was it that Marci could hear the dog whimpering? Kneeling next to him, she saw he was hurt. The dirty looking man kicked the dog hard enough that his boot broke the dog's skin causing him to bleed. Removing the scarf from her neck, Marci got down on her stomach, and was about to dip it into the water so she could wash his wound. Not sure how deep the ditch was Marci got a stick to measure its depth. The water was about two feet deep, and even though it was moving swiftly, Marci did not feel threatened by it. Lying on her stomach, Marci soaked her scarf and realized she was thirsty.

Lifting her cupped hands filled with water Marci saw the dog staring at her. Instead of drinking the water, she offered it to the dog until he had enough. Although the water was muddy brown, Marci scooped some into her hand and forced herself to drink it. Never had she enjoyed a drink of water as much as she did at that very moment. The water was extremely cold, so she imagined herself drinking a glass of iced tea.

Marci did not know how long it would be before she found her way back home, so she made sure she drank something even if it was water from the ditch. Having drunk the dirty water, she then took care of the dog's injury. Grateful she helped him; the dog licked her hand and ran away. However, she too must have sensed Marci was lost and looking for something or someone, and returned to help her. Afraid the dog would disappear; Marci tried to pick her up, but realized she could not carry the dog for it was too heavy. Tired, and trying to save her energy, Marci thought of the women who came for their children. So where did the women come from that she had not seen them? Marci knew she was seeing things when the homes disappeared, but reappeared as she walked towards them. Marci saw women doing their household chores; others were supervising the children who earlier were playing near the ditch.

When she opened the gate, several women saw Marci and asked her what took her so long in getting there. "Marci asked the woman to tell her where she was because she was lost." The woman thought Marci was joking, but the look on her face told her otherwise. When Marci was told she was in Dixon, she could not believe it because that was not where she lived. Marci knew Dixon for their delicious apples, but how did she get there? The woman then had Marci sit down and tell her what happened.

By this time, other women had gathered around Marci, and she told them her story. When Marci finished, everyone started to disappear until she was alone in a garden full of red chili as far as the eye could see. Again, Marci heard someone call her name. It was so clear, comforting, and close by, but she was afraid to turn around to see who was calling her. Instead, Marci started to cry, and she heard a man say, "Come here my silly little girl." She could not believe it was her father's voice, and that he had come to help her. Marci knew everything was going to be all right and she had nothing more to fear.

Again, she heard someone calling her. The voice was not her father's, but it was a male voice, and this one was louder than before. This time Marci did not fight her instinct to follow the voice. Instead, Marci let the dog run ahead of her because it seemed as if she knew enough to lead Marci home. Marci wondered if the dog had also heard the voice that was calling her, but that did not matter, for she would be home soon. The further Marci walked, the louder the voice got. Ahead of her, she saw her family waiting for her with open arms. Marci's entire family was there with her grandchildren and her parents. But, if her parents were there, did that mean she was dying, and they were there to take her with them? Was this why her family was with her, and why she could hear her father?

Whenever she heard her name, she saw Laleena's face. The last time Laleena called Marci's name, she saw her great-granddaughter's hand coming closer as if she was going to touch her face. Feeling a hand on her shoulder, Marci was afraid of what she would see. She knew she had to see what was going on, and Marci opened her eyes. As soon as she did, she saw the familiar surroundings of her bedroom. When she was able to focus as to where she was, she heard her six-year-old great granddaughter, say, "Wake up Grammy, I am hungry, and so is Shred."

Another dream ended, and Marci was about to spend another beautiful day with her great-granddaughter. Getting up and ready to prepare breakfast for Henry, and their youngest great-grandchild, Laleena asked, "Grammy, why were you crying, and laughing when you were sleeping?"

Marci did not know how she could explain her dream to a child because it was so vivid. Instead, Marci told her, "She was laughing because her puppy was licking her ear, and it tickled her." As for the crying part, Marci told Laleena, "I was crying because I did not want to wake up," and Laleena was happy with Grammy's explanation. Henry was not happy with what Marci told Laleena.

"Okay Marci, give me the real scoop. I know you haven't been feeling well so spill," he told his wife.

"Well Henry, this morning as I was going to church, I thought of my father, and remembered how much he loved looking out the backyard to admire what God created. As I walked to church, I thought how scared I was when we moved to New Mexico, and how much I now love the acre of land my father built our house on. Today several children who were being baptized were immersed in the baptismal fount, and I thought it was a bit cold for those poor babies. Guess I was also thinking how nice it was to see so many children in church so early in the morning. Then as I was coming home, I was concentrating on today's sermon. Before I knew it, a man on a motorcycle raced passed me and nicked a dog that was crossing the street with his motorcycle. The dog came out of nowhere, and ran in front of me, causing me to fall. When I tripped and fell, the lens of my glasses fell, and the other one cracked. When I put them on everything was so out of focus, and because I could not see, I fell one more time. As I was entering our front yard, Sal had come over, and asked me if I wanted some apples. He said he had gone to Dixon and bought a bushel, which was too much for him. Not realizing how hot it would be by the time I got out of church, I got tired and thought I would take a short nap. Once you came home from church, I was going to prepare breakfast. I didn't think I would sleep so long, and that you would bring Laleena home with you. Sweetheart, you know I would tell you if I am not feeling well. Anyway, now that you know what happened, and I am okay, what do you say I get my other pair of glasses, and we take our precious Laleena out to breakfast?" Henry wasn't convinced this was the whole truth, but after they got married, he had learned to go along with what Marci told him, and if there was something really wrong, he knew he would be the first to know.

One day, Marci and Henry will join their parents, and someone else will live in Marci's house. Then they too, will make their own memories as Marci and Caleb did and will enjoy Marci's Acre of Land.

ABOUT THE AUTHOR

When the author speaks about her family and friends, Angie says, it's like trying to put a jigsaw puzzle together. I get to know their personality, and day by day, I know more about them. Like a puzzle, I start putting the pieces together until I put the final piece in place. Having completed the puzzle of characters, the author has come up with characters most families can relate to. Retired, Angie continues to write and enjoys spending time teaching her great-grandchildren how to make tortillas, and to help her with her daily chores.

ACKNOWLEDGEMENT

To my mother, Rosita Gabaldon, and my father, Rafael Gabaldon, my family and friends a most heartfelt thanks for allowing me to introduce you to my readers. You make a terrific group of characters.

www.ingramcontent.com/pod-product-compliance
Ingram Content Group UK Ltd.
Pitfield, Milton Keynes, MK11 3LW, UK
UKHW062259290726
14090UKWH00017B/785

9 798901 244401